UNDER PRESSURE

Gareth Lock MSc

DIVING DEEPER WITH HUMAN FACTORS

Copyright © Gareth Lock 2019

ISBN 978-1-9995849-7-9

First Published March 2019

Imprint - Gareth Lock

Designed, Printed & Published by Vision Maker Press

Printed in Great Britain by www.visionmakerpress.com

Material within this book, including text and images, are protected by copyright. It may not be copied, reproduced, republished, downloaded, posted, broadcast or transmitted in any way except for your own personal, non-commercial use. Prior written consent of the copyright holder must be obtained for any other use of material. Copyright in all materials and/or works comprising or contained within this book remains with Author and other copyright owner(s) as specified. No part of this book may be distributed or copied for any commercial purpose.

Photograph credit:
Front cover Becky Kagan Schott. Rear photo (Main) Tom St George (Small) Gareth Lock

CONTENTS

Dedications	01
Foreword	03
Book Outline	07
Chapter 1:	15
Human Factors and Non-Technical Skills	
Chapter 2:	33
Diving Safety and Systems Thinking: The need to consider interactions and goals within the system	
Chapter 3:	53
Human Error: A terrible term to apply if we want to learn from what happened!	
Chapter 4:	75
Risk and Uncertainty: Why numbers don't mean much when it comes to your risk perception and appetite	
Chapter 5:	97
Psychological Safety and a Just Culture: the route to improving learning	
Chapter 6:	123
Decision-making in Diving: 'Choices' are not what many perceive them to be	

Chapter 7 : 151
  Situational awareness: Just because it's there,
  it doesn't mean you've recognised its significance

Chapter 8: 173
  Communications: If only people could
  communicate clearly!

Chapter 9: 203
  Teamwork and Teaming: Doing more with less

Chapter 10: 233
  Leadership and Followership in Diving:
  The need for it is far more common than you'd think!

Chapter 11: 265
  Performance Shaping Factors

Chapter 12: 289
  Learning from Failure:
  Improving performance through feedback
  and reporting

Chapter 13: 307
  Bringing it all together

Chapter 14: 321
  Conclusions

Contributors 325

DEDICATIONS

There have been so many people who have helped me on my journey in human factors, diving and writing this book. However, a few stand out.

Catherine Lock, my loving wife, who has put up with my absences as I travel around the world delivering training programmes and when I am home, working on the business of the 'The Human Diver' and this book. Thank you for believing in my dreams and supporting me in getting me to where I am now. I couldn't have done it without you.

Gene Hobbs and Dr. Dawn Kernagis, who both got me fired up with the research I was doing back in 2011 and who have been there to bounce ideas off, especially when it comes to the struggles with the Establishment.

Steven Shorrock, who has acted as an inspiration over the years. The way that he effortlessly takes complex human factors and ergonomics topics and converts them into lay-people speak is something I aspire to achieve.

Richard Lundgren, Richard Walker, Guy Shockey and Mark Powell for shaping my technical diving and actively supporting the work I do in getting human factors into technical and rebreather diving.

Professor Simon Mitchell, for encouraging me to get back into the academic domain and supporting the work I do since I first wrote my white paper on the topic in 2011. One of his most supportive comments was made at TekDiveUSA 2018, the bi-annual technical diving conference held in the USA, when he said that *"Human factors is currently the most important topic in sport diving."*

FOREWORD

"The heat of the July sun was oppressive, and our team members who were geared up just wanted to get in the water as soon as possible. As we rocked on the open water, the individuals who had already completed their dive were assisting the crew getting ready to enter the water.

Communication just felt off that day. For a team that had gelled together quickly and had worked daily in relative happiness and harmony, the interpersonal vibes were off that day. I could feel it, but I hesitated to say anything as the dive preparation proceeded. I was absolutely one of the most junior people on the boat. Other team members and even the dive boat crew had exceptional expertise in this type of diving; plus, I couldn't quite put my finger on what it was that felt 'off'. We were going through our checklist and communicating with each other, but there was a feeling of tension that continued to grow as the second team prepared for entry.

As I moved towards the back of the boat to help move the divers to the water, I heard some rumbling from one of the outbound divers as he stepped towards the platform. He had decided to change the team plan and add a photo session as their team was descending from the boat. Describing his new plan in detail as he prepared to enter the water, his dive partners, along with the rest of us, were taken by surprise at this last-minute goal added to an already-busy dive plan. From my original training in cave and tech diving, the first thing that came to mind was, 'Plan your dive, dive your plan.' I even said this to the team lead from my earlier dive and she nodded in agreement. However, no one said it out loud.

The other team members, visibly stressed, started to prepare for their entry. Long story short, this growing symphony of strain and frustration *culminated when one of the divers entered the water and had a heavy piece of gear become partially detached – enough to tip him over in the water and leave him somewhat out of control. Thankfully, the team was well-trained enough to make sure his life support system was secure and the problem was fixed. Their dive was aborted, and the silence as they returned to the boat was just as loud as the growing strain we all felt at the start of the dive.*

The debrief commenced after everyone had removed their kit and stepped into a dry space on the boat as a downpour moved over us. There was an awkward silence for the first few minutes, because we all knew inside that each and every one of us saw a situation brewing, but didn't or couldn't say anything. We each had good reasons for not stepping in, or at least what seemed to be good reasons at the time. However, we all understood the potential consequences could have been much worse if the training and timing of others in the water wasn't as good as it was. We also knew that any one of us just saying something along the lines of, 'Can we step down for a few minutes and reassess?' or 'Something doesn't feel right about this dive' or 'I am not comfortable with this last-minute change in plans' would have likely changed the outcome of that dive.

The debrief session was intense, honest, and probably one of the strongest growth points of our team over the course of that mission."

In every opportunity I have had the privilege to work, from diving projects to undertaking research with individuals who conduct missions in extreme environments, human and team performance has always been about so much more than being stronger, harder and faster. From a performance perspective, we emphasise harnessing the three 'R's' for becoming the best individual or best team member possible: Readiness, Resilience, and Recovery. These three phases, which overlap and are in a continuous cycle with each other, often involve optimising the body through approaches that involve nutrition, the muscular, nervous and immune systems and sleep.

The repeated point of emphasis from every operational group we work with, however, comes back to the mind. Not only how do we maximise cognitive abilities and keep those abilities sustained, but how do we train and sustain the proper attitude and mindset to deal with the technical, cultural and operational environments? At the end of the day, learning how to establish a culture of open communication that allows everyone to understand and embrace the fact we are all fallible and focusing on what needs to be done to maximize safety is probably the most important piece of the complex human performance puzzle to put together. However, this piece of the puzzle is very often left out because, from the outside, it seems like the hardest one to fit into the puzzle, or – unfortunately - individuals and organisations do not even realize that the piece is missing in the first place.

The most effective leaders I have been exposed to throughout my career all place a strong emphasis on the concept of what Gareth details in this book as 'Just Culture'. These leaders promote and reinforce the idea that no operation is conducted with 100% perfection. Furthermore, they are not there to ensure that individuals or teams are perfect; but to evaluate the ability of individuals to adapt and react to the inevitable mistakes that take place during a mission on a continuous basis – an evaluation which crucially also includes themselves. They emphasise the point that all individuals and all teams make mistakes irrespective of experience. It is part of being human, and we have to learn how to embrace our fallibility, our openness to discuss our mistakes (and what we have done right), with the idea of always learning and, in return, becoming a better individual, a better teammate and a better team. Unfortunately, from experience and conversations over my years in the diving community, this mentality is often absent from divers and dive teams. Largely, and like so many other communities, many of the divers or dive instructors are not ignoring that piece of the puzzle; they are simply unaware that the piece is missing.

'Under Pressure' makes this puzzle piece not only clear to see, but also tangible for any individual or organisation to grasp and incorporate into their performance puzzle. Through Gareth's personal experience with the British Royal Air Force (RAF) and as an experienced technical diver, to his extensive research and global expertise on the topic of human factors, *'Under Pressure'* takes us step-by-step through the concepts and lessons that are critical to incorporating a Just Culture into any environment. The diving community, along with any group of individuals working in a mission-oriented environment, now have a textbook for building a thorough understanding of what a culture of safety looks like. Additionally, how to build that mindset from the individual through the team with the application of non-technical skills to deliver performance and not just safety.

Dawn Kernagis, PhD
Research Scientist, Human Performance and Resilience in Extreme Environments
Institute for Human and Machine Cognition

Book Outline

This book provides a brief introduction to the topic of non-technical skills and human factors in diving and a greater insight into decision-making in diving. The case studies provided show how it is quite easy to miss critical information when stresses are high, or when goals are clouding our judgements. However, this is easy to see in hindsight and we must remember this whenever we read an account written after an incident or adverse event. Divers, in the main, don't get up in the morning and decide today is a good day to make a monumental cock-up that could cost me, my buddy or my student's life. Whatever they have done makes sense and if we are to improve diving safety, we need to understand that local rationality.

The application of non-technical skills and human factors to diving will improve the performance of divers so they can achieve more, have more fun, and as a by-product of improved performance, be safer. However, the biggest hurdle to including human factors and non-technical skills in your own practices is the need to really recognise that we are all fallible, not just other divers. As Dr Atul Gawande, the surgeon behind, 'The Checklist Manifesto' and who led the World Health Organisation Safe Surgical Checklist project highlighted, more than 90% of surgeons, if they were going to be patients in a surgical theatre, would want their surgical team to use a checklist, but only 20% of them actually used one themselves![1] Is that because they think other surgeons aren't as good as they are?!

The book is based around the globally-unique programmes I have put together which take the knowledge, skills and attitudes regarding human factors, non-technical skills and 'Just Culture' from high-risk

---
[1] https://www.bbc.co.uk/programmes/b00729d9/episodes/player. Reith Lectures. December 2014.

industries such as aviation, oil & gas and healthcare and framing them in the context of recreational, technical, cave and rebreather diving. The materials are also suitable for those involved in public safety, scientific diving, commercial and military diving.

It has been written in a format which allows the readers to dip in and out of each section to gain essential knowledge, but the greatest effect will be to read the book from start to finish. There is a good reason for this: these skills are interdependent and for maximum effect need to be executed in a psychologically-safe environment in which a Just Culture is prevalent. For example, developing your leadership skills without understanding the effect of the biases which impact your own and your followers' decision-making, will reduce your effectiveness as a leader. As you progress through the book and learn more about the skills, you will realise the true interdependence of non-technical skills and their relationship with technical skills.

Each chapter follows the same format:
- A relatively detailed case study highlighting a success or failure;
- human factors and non-technical skills theory interspersed with examples from diving;
- another case study to highlight the contribution of non-technical skills to success;
- each chapter will close with a summary;
- references are also provided at the end of each chapter for those who want to dig deeper.

Chapter 13 has been written to provide a brief summary of each topic from each chapter and how you can build this into your diving and/or instruction.

In the same way that art schools cannot provide you with a 'proven method to create stunning art', this book will not provide you with a 'proven method to improve your diving'. Rather it will give you the self-awareness and adaptability to apply the skills in an interdependent manner, understanding the strengths and weaknesses of human performance in an ambiguous and uncertain world.

There is no one right answer about how to solve problems, other than maybe learning from yours and others' failures along the way. Unfortunately, while there is no shortcut to life, we can accelerate the learning process by learning from those who have made mistakes; who have identified the lessons they learned; and then abstracting them to our own domains and applying them; and finally ensuring that our own feedback systems are in place, so we can learn from our mistakes when they happen.

Chapter Synopses

Chapter 1: The Role of Human Factors and Non-Technical Skills in High-Performing Teams

Safety is boring! That's why this book doesn't focus on safety; it focusses on the skills and mindset required to be a high-performing diving team, individual diver or instructor/instructor-trainer. This chapter identifies what non-technical skills mean in the context of diving and why they are so important - using a number of examples of dives where things didn't go to plan, but also how the application of the skills can create exciting and memorable dives, for the right reasons and not the wrong ones!

Chapter 2: Systems Thinking: The whole is greater than the sum of the parts

Systems thinking has been shown to be the most effective way of improving performance and safety. This is because while it is possible to improve specific components or people within a system, unless you look at their interactions with other people, equipment and the environment, you cannot make an improvement in the performance of the system.

In diving, there are numerous systems in place: a rebreather, diver, instructor, social and physical environment all make up a system. You can manufacture a rebreather which passes the required standards, but that doesn't mean that it will be safe to use as a system (or part of a system), unless you take into account the components of the system.

This chapter will give you an overview of systems thinking and why it is essential to consider it if you want to improve your performance, your safety and the safety of others.

Chapter 3: 'Human Error' and why it isn't that simple

Human error is a term often used as a 'catch-all', but has limited value when it comes to learning to improve. In the '70s & '80s, multiple research papers and presentations stated that 80% of aviation accidents were caused by 'human error'. Since the 1990s it has been recognised this attribution is flawed because 'human error' is normal and a 'general' term does not help learning from specifics.

This chapter will provide you with a summary of human error, error-producing conditions and why we need to search for the 'rich-context' stories if we want to improve.

Chapter 4: Risk Management or Gambling your life away

Much of diving is about risk management, but divers don't realise this because of the way in which the sport is portrayed; the suppression of diving incidents and accidents' information; and the often adversarial and confrontational nature of near-miss discussions within the diving community when 'stupid' mistakes are made.

This chapter will focus on risk; what it is; how we can manage it; and the biases we face when it comes to making 'risk-based decisions' in a dynamic environment. The aim isn't to scare divers, but rather to give them an indication as to how far we can drift and still think we are being safe.

Chapter 5: Just Culture and Psychological Safety
This chapter will highlight that without a Just Culture in place, learning is limited; and the same accidents/incidents will continue to occur with the individual divers often being blamed for the failure, rather than systemic factors. A Just Culture facilitates reporting and learning from adverse events leading to improved safety; whereas blame is the enemy of safety with incomplete stories being told, leading to poor incident analyses and sub-optimal behaviours when it comes to hiding near-misses.

Chapter 6: Decision-making
Decision-making has been defined as the process of reaching a judgement or choosing an option to meet the needs of a given situation. It can be broken down into the following main areas: understanding the situation at hand/defining the problem; determining a potential course of action or the option(s) available based on the information immediately at hand; selecting and executing that option; and then undertaking some form of review process to determine if the decision was effective in terms of the goals set.

This chapter will describe the different decision-making models and processes we use; their strengths and weaknesses; and how to overcome some of the cognitive limitations we have.

Chapter 7: Situational Awareness
Situational awareness is often talked about in diver training, but there isn't much detail about how it is developed and, more importantly, what can cause it to be 'lost'. Situational awareness is the concept by which we perceive data through our senses; process it so that we understand the here and now; and then using mental models of reality based on previous experiences, create a future model of what might happen. This is often simplified as What? So What? Now What?

This chapter will describe how the body/brain perceives information, the working memory and its associated strengths/

weaknesses, before moving on to how your individual and team situational awareness can be improved in the context of diving.

Chapter 8: Communication
If only we could solve communication problems, then we wouldn't have any confusion or conflict! Communication sits in the middle of the model of non-technical skills and is crucial to high performance. Understanding the barriers and enablers to effective communication is essential if we are to improve performance and reduce error.

This chapter will focus on the different models of communication, how to decide which one to use and how to increase the likelihood of effective communication taking place through the use of different questioning techniques, briefs and debriefs.

Chapter 9: Teamwork and Teaming
A team is not a group of people who work together; rather, a team is a group who trust each other, and creating trust is a challenge in a peer-to-peer social environment and even harder without a clear leadership role being present. Teamwork is the core to high performance, because teams can achieve far more than just looking at the sum of its individual parts. However, teams don't just happen: they take time to develop and they all go through the same development process with conflict and frustration eventually leading to things 'just happening' when there is role clarity, effective communication and the need and want to hold each other accountable.

This chapter will focus on how to develop effective and high-performance dive teams using knowledge and understanding from the military, aviation and healthcare domains. It will also look at why teams fail and what can be done to address that. Fundamentally, effective teams understand the difference between teamwork and taskwork and develop their skills to meet both requirements.

Chapter 10: Leadership and Followership

Most groups have some form of leadership present, be that formal or informal. Leaders can easily set the tone, positively or negatively, within the group and effective followers will provide support. However, destructive goal pursuit, where the goal is more important than the safety and well-being of the team-members, combined with poor leadership, can easily lead to accidents or incidents. This is especially true with beginners who do not necessarily have the assertion skills and don't recognise the authority gradient which is present.

This chapter will focus on leadership and leadership styles in the context of diving and how knowledge of these can improve diving enjoyment, goal attainment and instructional abilities. The chapter will also cover the topic of followership and why it is so important in a recreational activity where decisions need to be made considering a team and not just individuals.

Chapter 11: Performance Shaping Factors

You can have the best technical skills in the world and be able to apply a high level of technical and non-technical skills, but if you don't understand the impact of stress and fatigue on your own and others' performance, then you are destined to failure.

This chapter will provide divers, especially supervisors, an overview of how stress and fatigue shape human performance and what can be done to manage these factors thereby improving diving safety. Furthermore, linking with the chapter on human error (chapter three), error-producing conditions will be covered in more detail here.

Chapter 12: Living with Failure

Failure is everywhere. However, we cannot innovate or improve if we don't fail. Despite this, failure has been given an incredibly negative attribution by most parts of modern society, normally because something has been lost or didn't reach fruition, be that a goal, money or a tangible product. What if we turned it around so that learning from failure was seen as the key to improvement? What if we looked at the failed processes and unsuccessful outcomes as lessons and opportunities to learn and not just identify where the failures happened?

This chapter will focus on learning from experience and will give you specific tools whereby you can apply 20:20 hindsight before a major trip or expedition, or use learning reviews to understand what really happened - rather than what should have happened. Telling stories about things which didn't happen doesn't help learning.

Chapter 13: Bringing it all Together
This chapter will summarise the learning points from each of the chapters and provide readers with quick wins on how to apply the contents of this book into their own diving, instruction and leadership.

Chapter 1

Human Factors and Non-Technical Skills

"Accidents are complex processes involving the entire socio-technical system. Traditional event-chain models cannot describe this process adequately."

Professor Nancy Leveson, *Engineering A Safer World*

On 15 January 2009, an Airbus A320 took off from New York's La Guardia airport laden with 150 passengers and 5 crew, enroute to Charlotte Douglas. 135 seconds after the wheels left the tarmac and at an altitude of height of 2818 feet, it flew through a flock of Canadian geese. A loud bang was heard, and both engines suffered an immediate loss of power. Alarms started to sound in the cockpit with flashing warning lights signalling to the crew that there was a problem which needed their immediate attention. The noise from the alarms, the vibration from the airframe, and the visual stimuli from the captions and displays, all required processing to ensure that important and relevant information was not lost.

The Airbus, as with all modern passenger jets, had been designed to operate with one engine failing at the most critical stage of flight without a loss of altitude. However, the crew were now faced with potentially two failed engines, as they did not have a clear indication as to what was happening, although they knew that they had lost power. They had to deal with ambiguous information and make the best decision they could, given the limited information they had.

At the most basic level, while there is a procedure for a double-engine failure in a two-engine aircraft, it is only applicable when the aircraft is at high altitude. Altitude was not a luxury the crew had, and time was of the essence. The crew started to work through the checklists. Twenty-two seconds after the bird strike, Captain Sullenberger, the captain of the aircraft, transmitted on the radio, "Mayday, Mayday, Mayday, this is Cactus 1539[2], hit birds. We've lost thrust on both engines. We're turning back towards LaGuardia..." to ensure that Air Traffic Control (ATC) was aware of the situation and that they could start their own emergency procedures, which would include clearing airspace.

This transmission would have also been heard by other aircraft crew who would now know not to transmit unless there was anything equally urgent. The training previously undertaken by aircrew and Air Traffic Control (ATC) meant that each of this diverse 'team' knew what would likely happen next - they shared a common situation awareness model.

The problem with checklists is that, sometimes, they don't align with the situations being encountered by the crew and so the operators have to adapt. In some environments, deviation from procedures is met with negative criticism, because there is an assumption that they must be followed at all costs, even if this leads to a wrong outcome. For the crew of Cactus 1549, there was no checklist for double engine failure at low altitude, so they were in adaptation territory, a point picked up in the [American] National Transport and Safety Board (NTSB) accident investigation. However, the Captain knew that they would need some form of electrical power generation to power the aircraft systems and so turned on the Auxiliary Power Unit: a small 'engine' which would generate enough electrical power to power the radios, flight control systems and other emergency equipment. This was a deviation from the standard operating procedure (SOP), because the emergency checklist had this action as step number 11 in the 15-item list of actions. This was a deviation that was needed, because the situation dictated it; and they understood the rationale behind the checklist design.

Thirty-five seconds after the massive bird strike which had reduced the thrust from the engines to almost zero, and after they had

---

2 The correct call sign was in fact Cactus 1549.

mentally run simulations with potential outcomes, they turned back towards La Guardia airfield which was 8.5 miles away. All the time the clock was ticking, the aircraft was descending, and the ground was getting closer. Shortly afterwards, Captain Sullenberger informed his crew and Air Traffic Control that he was going to be ditching into the Hudson River, the only place he could see which was long enough and clear enough to put the aircraft down in this densely populated area and have any chance of survival. However, I am sure that he was aware that the survival in such circumstances was slim, despite it being a regular scenario covered in training simulations, but this was the best possible hand to play in a terrible game. Once that decision was made, the execution of the ditching drills took place with professionalism and calm.

At 3:11 p.m., 360 seconds after take-off, 229 seconds after the bird strike, and 90 seconds after the Mayday call, Flight 1549 touched down onto the surface of the icy, cold Hudson River in a level trajectory at 140 mph (230 km/h). The aircraft came to a rest and remained floating on the surface with no fatalities and only a few minor injuries caused by the massive deceleration which caused legs and arms to flail. The aircraft remained relatively intact and upright.

The crew executed the emergency evacuation drill using the over-wing doors. The evacuation slides were deployed and became life-rafts, as they were designed to do. One passenger panicked and opened the rear door which was unable to be resealed and led to the cabin filling with water from the rear. In addition, water was coming through the cargo doors and the fuselage. The Captain was the last to leave the aircraft having walked through the cabin twice, through the 5C water, to ensure there was no-one left behind. Fortunately, due to where they had landed, there were already a number of boats and passenger ferries already congregating on the scene to help people from the life-rafts to safety. The last person was recovered from the aircraft 44 minutes after the touchdown.

There is no doubt that this event was only possible through the high level of technical skill i.e. the piloting of Captain Sullenberger, his First Officer and cabin crew. However, having technical skills is not enough to be a high-performing team. They needed non-technical skills, crew resource management skills - or 'soft skills'. These include:

- situational awareness - to determine what was most relevant at the time and focus on that, excluding 'irrelevant' information;
- effective decision-making skills - to sift through the masses of data being received through their eyes, ears and tactile feedback systems and then to determine the best possible decision with all the information they had gathered;
- effective communication skills - to share their knowledge and decision-making processes so that a shared mental model was available to others within the team;
- strong and stable leadership - which imparted role clarity and confidence to ensure the actions which needed to be executed in a timely manner were clearly understood;
- strong followers - who listened, challenged when needed and trusted their Captain to make the right decision, and who worked towards a common goal, which is a clear sign of effective teamwork; and
- the recognition that stress would limit their cognitive skills - and so remained as calm as possible despite the dire situation they were in. The calm was a result of the realistic training in simulators and the detailed debriefs which crews undertake to learn from the continual failures and errors made.

However, these non-technical skills did not just pertain to the execution of their technical skills using the team inside the aircraft; they also applied to those supporting organisations and wider 'team' members outside the aircraft. These included Air Traffic Control (ATC), the emergency services and other aircrafts in the vicinity of the emergency.

Aviation is considered one of the pinnacles of excellence when it comes to human factors and non-technical skills training and application. The consequences of errors and violations are massive which is why organisations spend so much time, money and effort in reducing the likelihood of accidents and incidents by focusing on the human within the system. The behaviours, traits and actions of divers are no different than pilots, air traffic controllers and maintenance teams when it comes to human performance. Some of you could argue that civil and military aviation operations have a regulator which states they have to have such training systems in place; however, in the supposed absence of such a regulator, most organisations would keep human factors and non-technical skills programmes, because it makes sense to do so as they lead to improved performance - and safety comes as a by-product of that high performance.

What is Human Factors?
Human Factors is the scientific discipline which looks at the performance, interactions, health and well-being of humans as part of a wider system - a system which can include other people and organisations as well as hardware.

Its formal roots go all the way back to the Second World War where 'pilot error' was examined, for the first time, in great detail. Firstly, by the psychologist Alphonse Chapanis, who looked at why pilots on the B-17 Flying Fortress were raising the landing gear instead of the flaps when taxiing in after a high-workload wartime mission - a problem that wasn't occurring with other aircrafts of the time. The issue? The landing gear and flaps switches were almost identical and were being confused, no matter how experienced the pilots were. The solution? Put a small wheel on the landing gear lever and a small wedge on the flap lever, so that tactile feedback was possible. The result? No more issues like this happened. Ever.

Secondly, shortly after the war, two psychologists Paul Fitts and Richard Jones examined 460 errors made in operating aircraft controls by reading reports and interviewing pilots. At the time, the basic premise was that, *"It has been customary to assume that prevention of accidents due to materiel failure or poor maintenance is the responsibility of engineering personnel and that accidents due to errors of pilots or supervisory personnel are the responsibility of those in charge of selection, training, and operations."* However, Fitts and Jones took a different view as part of their research hypothesis and showed that, while there were cognitive and human performance limitations which contributed to these errors, cockpit design and layout was the real cause of many 'pilot errors'. In their report, they concluded, *"Practically all pilots of present day AAF [Army Air Forces] aircraft, regardless of experience or skill, report that they sometimes make errors in using cockpit controls. The frequency of these errors and therefore the incidence of aircraft accidents can be reduced substantially by designing and locating controls in accordance with human requirements"*[1].

Non-Technical Skills, Crew Resource Management and Team Resource Management are all a sub-set of 'human factors'. A little further on you'll see why the term 'human factors' has been used in my programmes even though it is not technically correct.

Technical Skills versus Non-Technical Skills

What are non-technical skills? To understand non-technical skills, let's look at what technical skills are. In the context of a pilot, their technical skills are related to flying the aircraft, moving the flying controls and throttles to keep the aircraft on its planned trajectory. In a surgical environment, a surgeon can incise and suture. On a drilling platform, the driller will control the speed and pressure of the drill to progress down the hole in line with the plan. These are all technical skills to achieve their requisite goal.

Their non-technical skills relate to being able to perceive, process and apply the relevant information; make effective decisions based on that information; to communicate to the rest of the team ensuring they have a shared mental model as well as execute commands as needed; to recognise the effects of stress and fatigue on their team; and to maintain and manage stressors for optimal performance. These don't directly relate to the goal at hand, but without non-technical skills, you can't get very far.

In high-risk domains, without effective non-technical skills, accidents happen like the collision of two Boeing 747 aircraft in

Tenerife on 27 March 1977 which lead to the loss of 583 people when a 'loss' of situational awareness and miscommunication occurred[2]. Or the loss of the Deep Water Horizon platform in the Gulf of Mexico on 20 April 2010, when the drilling crew had made assumptions about what was going on in the hole[3]. Or the surgeon who removed the wrong kidney while being watched by a student nurse who recognised the problem but was unable to speak up and counter the surgeon[4].

In diving, things are a little more complicated because we have the terms 'recreational diving' and 'technical diving' which are used regularly. However, there isn't a clear definition of what the latter means, as each agency applies different metrics.

Do non-technical skills mean recreational skills? No. In the context of human factors and human performance in diving, which is what this book is all about, technical skills relate to the use of buoyancy control devices; putting up a deployed surface marker buoy (dSMB); laying a line in a cave or wreck; and using video/photography equipment to create lasting memories, or similar activities. Non-technical skills relate to communicating the plan for a photo shoot; the awareness when laying the line so that it doesn't get caught in a trap which would prevent a blind-exit; or the decision to end a dive as the current has picked up and staying to the planned bottom time would mean that gas reserves would be insufficient.

In normal operations, non-technical skills have significant benefits, because they help everyone 'sing from the same song sheet'; but in situations where irregularities are present e.g. when the plan deviates or there is an emergency, then non-technical skills really come to the fore. If there are no surprises, there won't be any accidents; and non-technical skills help reduce the number of surprises we have.

The reason why my programmes have 'human factors' in their titles is because when I ran the first pilot class in January 2016, the students (Phil Short, Tim Clements, Michael Thomas and John Kendall), asked me what the term 'non-technical skills in diving' meant as it didn't make sense given the points made above concerning technical and recreational diving. At that point, I decided to use the term 'human factors skills in diving'. I knew it was wrong, but a large education piece was needed to get over the knowledge barrier at the time; and that I hoped, over time, it would be possible to get the term 'non-technical skills' back into the vocabulary. This attribution of the term 'human factors' to Crew Resource Management (CRM)-type programmes in healthcare has caused all sorts of issues when it comes to developing performance and safety in healthcare, because the decision-makers often think that just because they have a CRM programme in place, they have addressed the human factors issues which are present. CRM is only a sub-set of Human Factors and therefore many opportunities to improve performance and safety are lost.

The Application of Non-Technical Skills in Diving

These non-technical skills just sound like common sense, so how do they apply to diving? The following brief case studies highlight where the application of non-technical skills was insufficient.

Open Circuit Recreational

An Advanced Open Water (AOW) diver with around 50 dives was acting as an 'assistant' to the instructor and dive-centre owner on a guided dive with five Open Water (OW) divers and recent graduates from the school they themselves had learned at. The AOW diver felt a social obligation to help the Open Water Scuba Instructor (OWSI) who was leading the dive, because the OWSI had done so much to help her conquer her fear of mask-clearing during her own training. However, she was also wary that, over time, her role had moved from being a diver on the trip to being almost the divemaster, by helping other divers out which she wasn't trained to do. In addition, the instructor regularly asked her, at the last minute, to help out and change teams to ensure the 'experience' dives happened.

On this particular occasion, the AOW diver was buddied with a low-skilled OW diver who was arrogant and did not communicate well. In fact, she didn't believe that 3 of the 5 on this trip should have received their OW certificates, given their poor in-water skills. As they approached the dive site, the visibility could be seen to be poor from the boat and the surface conditions weren't great. The instructor said to the AOW diver, "Don't lose the divers. I want you at the back shepherding them."

They entered the water and descended to 24m and made their way in the poor visibility. On two occasions, the OW buddy had to be brought back down by the AOW diver as they ascended out of control. At one point, the OW diver turned around really quickly and knocked the AOW diver into the reef. Unfortunately, the AOW diver became entangled in some line there and the OW diver swam off oblivious to the entanglement. When the 5 divers and instructor reached the shot-line ready to ascend, the instructor realised the AOW diver was missing. They couldn't trust the five divers to ascend on their own and didn't have enough time to wait at the bottom and conduct a search so the six ascended. On the surface, the buddied OW diver said that the AOW diver had swum off looking at fish in a certain area.

In the meantime, the AOW diver had managed to free themselves; but in their panic, while stuck on the bottom, they breathed their gas down to almost zero and had to do a rapid ascent. They surfaced, feeling very scared and sick with panic, just as the instructor was speaking to the other six on the surface. On seeing the AOW diver break the surface, the instructor swam over and shouted at them for abandoning their buddy on the bottom. The AOW diver felt very alone and wanted to give up diving as she was not given the opportunity to tell her side of the story.

Contributory factors
- Violation for personal gain on the part of the instructor/dive-centre owner taking OW divers to 24m.
- Authority gradient between the instructor and AOW diver meant that the AOW diver felt they couldn't end the dive before they even got in the water or once in the water.
- Inferred peer pressure to help out when they weren't qualified or experienced enough to act in a supervisory role.

- Poor technical skills on the part of the OW divers and the AOW limited their capacity to be aware of hazards and risks.
- Limited awareness on the part of the instructor regarding the location of all the divers during the dive.
- Positive note - good decision on the part of the instructor to ascend with the five OW divers in poor conditions and not keep them on the bottom or get them to ascend on their own.

Open Circuit (OC) Technical

Two divers descended a shot-line in very poor visibility to a depth of 45m while breathing weak Nitrox. As they descended, one of the primary torches failed and the team swapped position, so the diver with the brightest torch was in front. On reaching the bottom, they started to move around the huge wreck with the hull on their right. Shortly afterwards, the hull 'disappeared' and they both thought they had swum off the wreck. They turned right to find the wreck and after a little while they realised they were inside the wreck at a dead-end with no line laid to get back out.

Both divers panicked, one of them losing their mask in the process. The diver, who lost his mask, took out his spare and managed to find his way back out, but did not see his buddy while doing this. While still stressed and breathing heavily, he used a spool to go back into the section of the wreck he had just come from to look for his buddy. After a few minutes, he realised he wasn't there as he reached the same dead-end they had previously reached. With the fear of telling his buddy's wife of her husband's death playing on his mind, he ascended and completed his 30 minutes of decompression.

On surfacing, he found that his buddy had made his way out and had made a straight ascent to the surface as he had almost no 'deco' (decompression) to complete. Both divers had a precautionary recompression chamber run that evening.

Contributory factors
- No contingency plan - failure wasn't expected. Neither had dived

in visibility so poor before and neither had a reel for lining off.
- Time/money/social pressures to complete the dive. Both divers had travelled two days to get to the dive site and to be able to dive this wreck as part of a week long live-aboard trip - and didn't want to lose out on a dive.
- Equipment reliability and test. The torch had only just been serviced after a fault and had not been tested to make sure the fault had been fixed. The divers on losing a primary light in poor visibility decided to carry on despite the poor (1-2m) visibility.
- Nitrogen and carbon dioxide narcosis clouded the divers' decision-making abilities.
- Expectation bias that the hull disappearing meant that they had swum off the wreck and not that a massive hole in the hull was present.
- Reduced awareness due to [nitrogen and carbon dioxide] narcosis and visibility such that they did not notice they were swimming into the wreck - until they reached the end of the section and hit metal, above and to the sides.
- Excessive levels of distress caused by uncertainty and narcosis.

Closed Circuit Rebreathers

Two experienced OC Trimix divers, one of whom was an Open Water Scuba Instructor (OWSI), were undertaking an Air Diluent Closed Circuit Rebreather (CCR) class at an inland dive site. After the first dive of the last day had been completed and lunch finished, the class returned to the dive entry point to start their final dive of the day. However, on checking gas pressures, one of the students realised that their diluent cylinder only had 70 bar (approx. 1000psi) in it. This was not enough to complete the dive, so they took the cylinder off and rushed up to the gas station to get an air top. They paid for it, not noticing a higher price than normal (as they had been out of diving for some time) and returned to the entry point, now realising that time was getting on to complete the dive before the centre closed. After putting the diluent cylinder back on, they got ready to dive.

All three entered the water and started their descent down the shot-line. As they descended, the subject started to get a high pO2 alarm on their Head Up Display (HUD). They added diluent to their loop, but the alarm remained. As they reached the bottom of the shot at 18m, the student signalled to the instructor that something wasn't right, but the instructor swam off not acknowledging the communication. The student bailed out and the noise of the open circuit regulator brought the instructor back. The student again signalled that something wasn't right. The instructor flushed diluent through the loop and the pO2 was still high. At 18m, the pO2 should have been 0.6, but it was reading 2.0. The instructor signalled for everyone to ascend.

On surfacing and analysing the gas, the diluent cylinder was found to contain 72% O2. The 'air top' had in fact been an 'O2 top' on top of 70 bar of air. The gas hadn't been analysed by the diver or the fill station prior to it being connected to the rebreather.

Contributory factors
- Despite the course standards saying so, the instructor and students never analysed their gas all week. This violation was set in motion by the instructor role-modelling poor behaviours on day 1.
- Time pressures - given the last dive of the day & course and that the refilling station was close enough to get a fill and still complete the class, but far enough away which required rushing to complete the pre-dive sequence.
- Incomplete pre-dive sequence and pre-breathing process carried out prior to the dive. A full diluent flush was not required as part of the checklist; only operation of the Manual Add Valves, but a full flush and test of the controller would have picked up that the diluent gas was not air.
- Poor confirmation on the communication at the bottom of the shot-line when the instructor swam off.
- Not noticing at the end of the first dive that 70 bar would be inadequate for the second dive and getting the fill done over

the lunchtime period, thereby reducing the time pressures and subsequent stress.
- Social pressure to conform and get in the water as quickly as possible.

Each one of these diving case studies has multiple non-technical skills deficiencies and yet the topic of non-technical skills is not covered in much detail in diver and instructor training. This book and the training programmes which are produced and supplied by The Human Diver aim to address that shortfall.

The Application of Non-Technical Skills Increases Fun and Improves Safety

The following shows what happens when effective non-technical skills do come to the fore.

Six divers had decided to undertake a 30m dive from a Rigid Hull Inflatable Boat (RHIB). John and Dave were diving as a team with their local university dive club and had over 2000 dives between them. Graham was relatively newly trained as a marshal (surface manager) and had not worked with Brian, the cox, before. On the dive boat, there were two new divers to the club: Gail and Mark. Both Gail and Mark had successfully completed a check-out dive & dry suit familiarisation course with another instructor in the club, and they were already certified for 40m diving. Graham was keen to do a drift dive in 32m of water. The Cox was somewhat worried about the conditions as there seemed to be waves forming. However, as long as all divers were certified to 30m diving and effective at getting into the water and back onto the RHIB, he was happy that the risk was acceptable. To allow the Cox and Marshal to dive, John and Dave would take over in the coxswain and marshal roles after the first dive.

At the dive site, there was a small swell, no white horses, but it was not possible to prevent an uncomfortable rolling of the dive boat. As John was starting to prepare his equipment, he observed Gail and Mark who appeared to be very apprehensive and struggled to perform simple tasks as part of their buddy check. Low Pressure

(LP) hoses were not connected, Submersible Pressure Gauges (SPGs) were not clipped off and there seemed to be a lot of effort used on simple tasks like putting drysuit and gloves on. Furthermore, both appeared to be physically shaking and very pale. John asked the dive marshal if he had noticed the apparent stress building with Gail and Mark. He had not because he was focused on getting his own dive kit ready for his dive. John suggested to the dive marshal to ask them if they would prefer to dive the sheltered bay with a maximum depth of 10m, quietly reminding him that it was their duty of care to stop diving operations if he believed that the conditions or behaviour of the divers were not safe.

At this point, the Marshal picked up on the cues and, in a calm and professional manner, sat with the anxious divers to discuss the diving plan. It was then established that Gail and Mark would very much like to do the shallower dive, because apart from the club drysuit course, it came to light that they had never dived in drysuits before, from a dive boat, in high flow, or in water deeper than 20m before. While they were certified for the depths and drysuit, they had become extremely stressed as they had thought the dive would be a maximum of 20m on a wall, rather than 32m flat seabed in extreme spring tides in much faster and colder water than they were used too. They had not wanted to "make a fuss" by telling the more experienced divers on the boat that they were concerned.

The dive plan was changed, and the boat was moved to a very sheltered bay with perfect conditions and no tidal movement. After they arrived at the new location, Gail and Mark relaxed and on restarting their briefing and checks, they quickly and calmly fixed the small issues observed during their first aborted dive. They used the dive both to enjoy the kelp forest at 10m, but also to practice their ascents and using a dSMB in cold water.

In their de-brief they concluded that they needed to do lots more shallow dives to get used to the new cold water conditions, and that they would prefer, in the future, to be paired with club members with more experience, until they felt more comfortable in the water.

Proactively, they set their own depth limit to 15m until they felt more comfortable with drysuit ascents.

Contributory factors
- There were a number of factors which worked against Gail and Mark and these will be covered in more detail during the book. However, the reason for detailing this story is to show how non-technical skills can be used to improve performance and prevent incidents from happening.
- Situational awareness to notice that Gail and Mark were apprehensive and that their behaviour was not normal.
- Assertion skills to reinforce to the dive marshal that events were not likely to go to plan given the mental state of Gail and Mark. Despite the marshal Graham) being present and observing the same scene as John, they did not have the same mental model which John did because of his previous experience.
- Leadership skills on the part of the dive marshal in communicating with Gail and Mark to ascertain their issues with a view to resolving them.
- Debrief leading to effective decision-making for the future by Gail and Mark to limit their diving exposure until more experienced.

The Interdependence of Non-Technical Skills
Over the years, diver training organisations and clubs have developed in water 'technical skills' for their divers, instructors and instructor trainers to maximise safety and enjoyment. In addition, equipment manufacturers have developed and adopted standards which increase the reliability and performance of equipment making diving safer. However, very few, if any, of the training sessions provided by training agencies focus on the 'soft skills' or non-technical skills required to make effective decisions in dynamic and uncertain environments, especially when operating in a team environment.

Model of Non-Technical Skills and their Interdependence

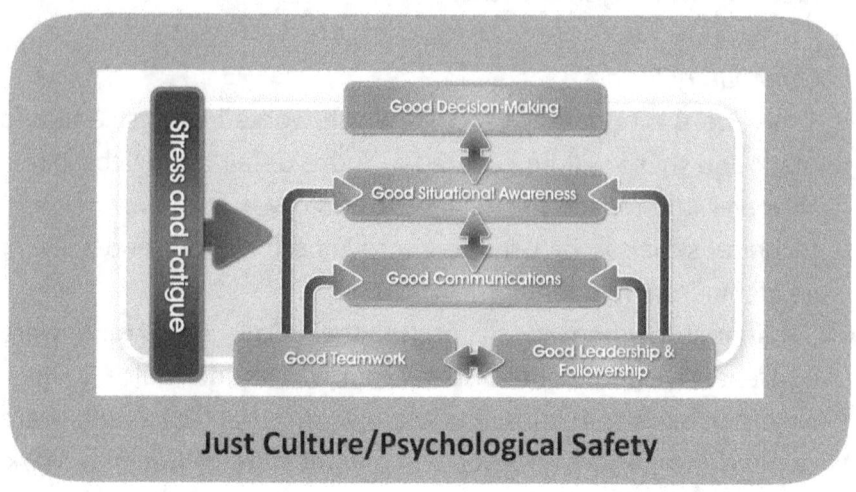

Figure 1: Model of Non-Technical Skills, Psychological Safety and Just Culture

The model at Figure 1 is a simple framework I have created for my own teaching to explain the linkages and interdependence of the non-technical skills. It has decision-making at the very top, as ultimately this is what we want to achieve as part of any process. Feeding into decision-making is situational awareness where we: perceive, process and project this information into a future state. To gain relevant situational awareness, we need effective communications between our team members and any technical systems we use such as dive computers or rebreather controllers. To support this, we need effective teamwork, robust leadership and trusting followers. However, all of these skills can be negatively impacted by stress and fatigue degrading any positive benefits gained. We also need to have a psychologically-safe environment and a Just Culture present, so that failure does not have a stigma associated with it. This safe environment is essential because it allows learning from failure to occur, recognised as the most effective way of creating improvement which will have long-lasting value.

Understanding 'the System'

If we are to improve performance of people and organisation, we must understand the concept of a system and how to improve the system and not just the components. We can certainly improve decision-making with applications, software, flow-diagrams to gather more data and crunch the numbers, or communications by having team training sessions and profiles undertaken; but without understanding the interactions within the system, we might only make minor improvements or worse still, we crash the system and nothing works. Chapter 2 will provide an overview of systems thinking and how it contributes to a changed view on human performance and safety; without such a revised view, improvements will have limited impact on safety.

References
(1) Fitts, P.M. and Jones, R.E. (1947). Analysis of factors contributing to 460 "pilot error" experiences in operating aircraft controls. Dayton, OH: Aero Medical Laboratory, Air Material Command, Wright-Patterson Air Force Base, 1947
(2) http://aviation-safety.net/database/record.php?id=19770327-0&lang=en
(3) 'Deepwater Horizon Accident Report' available from https://www.bp.com/content/dam/bp/pdf/ sustainability/issue-reports/Deepwater_Horizon_Accident_Investigation_Report.pdf
(4) Doctor suspended for removing wrong kidney. BMJ 2004;328:246

Additional Reading
Leveson, N. (2012) Engineering a Safe World.
https://mitpress.mit.edu/books/engineering-safer-world

Chapter 2

Diving Safety and Systems Thinking: The need to consider interactions and goals within the system

"Safety is an emergent property of systems; it does not reside in a person, device or department of an organisation or system. Safety cannot be purchased or manufactured; it is not a feature that is separate from the other components of the system. The state of safety in any system is always dynamic; continuous systemic change insures that hazard and its management are constantly changing."

Richard Cook MD[1]

The following narrative from Cameron Russo, a technical and cave diver, about his exploration of a cave system with his diving and living partner, Alison shows how systems thinking considers not just the technical equipment which people think are the 'system', but also the environment and their own physical, physiological and cognitive interactions. Sometimes we miss the interactions and the changes that are created as a consequence. Those interactions can have potentially fatal consequences if we are not careful.

Case Study: That hole is big enough to get through...
My dive team, Alison Perkins and I, were approximately 6 weeks into a trip in Quintana Roo, Mexico. Cave diving every day, fun diving, exploring, surveying, mapping, taking photos and assisting scientists. This particular day was our seventh day exploring a cave we had been working in. Progressively getting further and further in, verifying a 20-year-old stick

map we had been given from the original explorers as well as finding and exploring new leads.

The dive plan was to travel approximately 100 minutes on the Diver Propulsion Vehicle (DPV) or scooter, navigating 8 intersections (jumps/T's) to an agreed point in the cave, and start exploring from there. A planned total run time of somewhere between 4 to 6 hours (depending on how successful the exploration was) using RB80 rebreathers, 1x drive bottle, 1x safety bottle, 1x O2 bottle, 1x XK1 DPV each, full cave equipment including exploration reels, and an XJoy37 DPV tow behind safety scooter shared for the team.

All equipment was checked on the surface before leaving the shop for the drive to the site using a personal checklist we had, and again in the water using our GUE EDGE (pre-dive check) procedures. It was my turn to be in the number one position, so I led the dive and Ali had the tow behind DPV.

This cave has an average depth of 18m, so we expected some O2 decompression before exit. We dropped our O2 bottles on the line on a big boulder at 6m depth near the entrance. We then started the travel portion of the dive.

Being part of the Ox Bel Ha cave system, this cave is a dark cave and has a strong halocline at 15m depth. Scootering in a dark cave with all that equipment requires constant intense concentration while on the trigger. Your profile in the water is quite big, and bottles or reels or the RB itself can crash into the cave if you're not careful. Despite feeling like we knew the cave well, we tried not to rush, and were intentional with stopping to place cookies at all intersections.

We were about 20 minutes before our agreed start of exploration point, following an existing line, travelling through a section of cave we had not yet been through. In the lead, I turned down the speed on my DPV to quite a slow speed. Thinking ahead to the map and exploration ahead of us, I remembered that the stick map we were verifying showed this section as a short series of sharp bends, which can indicate small passage size. To my surprise the cave started to shallow up and widen. I noticed the water change from crystal clear to a light tea colour with some tannic water – we had hit a super shallow dome. The way forward was now narrow ceiling to floor, but still wide. Thinking this was the short section we had seen on the map, I decided to continue on with all our equipment (DPV, RB80, 2 tanks on our sides, reels on our hip, and Ali with a tow behind DPV). Ali was immediately behind me, so I came off the DPV and we started to swim through this section. The line then did two 90-degree right-hand turns in quick succession taking us around the edge of this huge circular tannic dome. Stalagmites and stalactites covered the middle of the dome, and there was no space to easily turn around. Continuing to swim awkwardly in the slightly smaller space, I hit a hard-left bend in the cave where the line, and our way forward, went down through a narrow slot with a series of stalactites pointing down ready to catch everything!

Wanting to get through this short annoying section and get on with the exploration, I misjudged the shape and size of the slot. More importantly, I forgot that Ali had a DPV attached to her behind, as I worked my way through the slot. Getting stuck for 30 seconds, grunting and shoving my way through with some physical force, I was through with a few scratches on my rebreather. I did not signal to Ali to stop. I turned around to see Ali trying to work her way through the slot. Like me she also had some trouble with the RB, but worse, the tow behind DPV was caught on one of the stalactites. The DPV was stopping her from moving forward, and her RB was stopping her from moving backward.

Being able to talk (a bit) while on the RB was helpful. Ali told me how she was stuck. Despite her not being able to see me, I was able to reassure her that I was right there, and to wait one minute.

I took off my safety bottle and DPV, clipping both to the line. Now being of somewhat smaller profile I was able to work my way back to Ali and with some difficulty reaching, unhook the DPV from her butt D-Ring - thus allowing her to move forward. With some brute force Ali was then able to push herself and her RB through the slot to be on the same side as me.

We took a few deep breaths and thumbed the dive.

Ali turned to move back through the slot. This time, without the tow DPV, she was able to navigate it with only a couple scrapes. I put back on my safety bottle, picked up my DPV, and decided to push the tow DPV and my personal DPV ahead of me through the slot. This was awkward, required some time, but I managed it without incident.

We swam back around the tannic dome; Ali clipped the tow DPV back on; and we headed for home.

The long scooter home was mentally draining for me. I had to concentrate hard to focus on where I was going and not on the incident that we had just had. We decided to do the full planned 20 minutes decompression on O2, despite the shorter dive.

We exited the water safe and sound after 245 minutes.

If we look at Cameron's incident and the entrapment, we can see that there are numerous components or elements to this particular system: Cameron and Alison's experience, technical skills, attitudes, behaviours and cognitive skills; the configuration, design and quantity of their dive equipment; the physical cave structure and linked aquatic environment; and their personal goals and motivations. Therefore, it is interesting to examine the notes which Cameron sent over with his narrative to show, in hindsight, what he would have done differently next time and they all relate to interactions within the system.

- "I should have dropped more equipment earlier",
- "I probably should have not even gone through the slot at all" and
- "I definitely should have somehow signalled Ali to stop her trying to go through!"

Unfortunately, we are often plagued by hindsight bias when we look at incidents, near misses or accidents which means we can easily identify interactions much more easily than when we are 'in the moment'. Our situational awareness and decision-making processes are clouded by what is important there and then, what risks we perceive to be relevant at that time and what we expect to see coming up (Chapter 7 on situational awareness will expand on this in much more detail).

Our limited mental capacity means we often miss the cues or clues which could identify unwanted interactions within the system, especially if we have never encountered them before. In the case of

Cameron and Alison, the goal was to explore a new section of cave, a section where no-one else had ever been before. This narrowed the focus to 'exploring' rather than what interactions might happen. As you will see 'Exploration fever' appears in a couple more of the narratives and goal-orientated operations will be discussed in the leadership chapter (see Chapter 10).

Notwithstanding the limited capacity to recognise the seriousness of the interaction, the feedback was immediate when he got stuck and then Alison got stuck. Cameron realised that the plan would need to change and adapted accordingly. This adaptability comes through experience as it allows previous situations to be exploited in the 'here and now'. Gary Klein, following his work with fire chiefs and others operating in dynamic and uncertain environments, developed the concept of naturalistic decision-making whereby 'intuitive' decisions 'happened' based on experiences recalled from the subconscious. This will be discussed in more detail in Chapter 6 on decision-making.

Building experiences and knowing what to do when unexpected interactions within the system happen reminds me of a discussion I had with Becky Kagan Schott, an award-winning underwater photographer and CCR instructor, about the 'Go Pro' culture and the need to push the limits - without understanding the backstory and experience required to undertake these activities in a safe manner. To explain this in more detail, the metaphor of an iceberg is useful.

Modern society and communities see successes in high definition video and surround sound. What the consumers of such media do not see are the hours of dedication and the associated investment of money and time, blood, sweat and tears, failures, close-calls, aborted dives and scary learning moments. All they see is 'AWESOME!' and sometimes they think they can do the same - and instead get themselves into a whole world of hurt in the process. In 'normal operations', novices are likely to be able to undertake the task at hand without too much going wrong because the situation is linear – i.e. 'do this, that happens'; this is especially the case with automated systems like rebreathers where the automation is managing the life support and we can't see what is happening inside the box.

However, as soon as the system behaviour changes and unexpected interactions occur, then a massive cascade effect happens and quickly the 'rules of the game' which have been learned are no longer valid and experience is needed to think 'around the problem' – think of Sully's problem-solving from Chapter 1. Unfortunately, when it comes to knowledge-based decision-making (which is what happened in the case of Cameron and Alison's story), the error rate is in the order of 1 in 2 - in effect a 50:50 chance you'll make the right decision. These aren't great odds when the outcome associated with risk involves death. Furthermore, these aren't simple 1:1 interactions that are being managed: there are multiple competing goals which need to be prioritised and if you're a novice, it isn't easy to identify where to start.

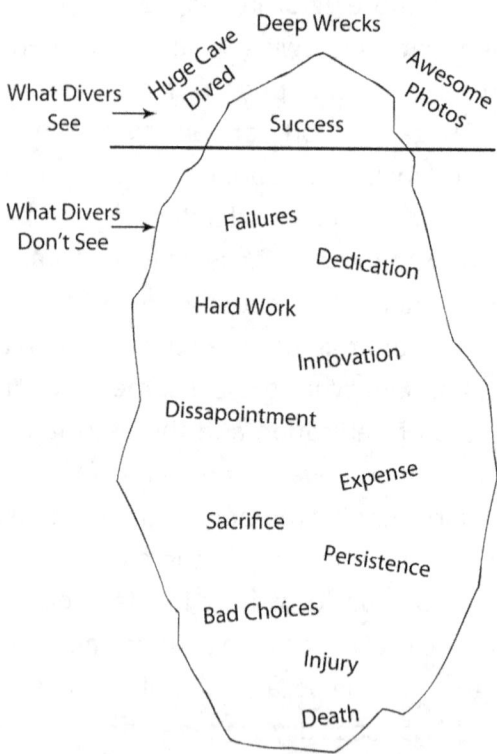

Figure 2: The Iceberg Effect: Success is seen above the surface, but below are all the things required to get to success.

System interactions don't just happen at the individual level where a diver is using a piece of equipment on a dive, but also at much higher levels. David Manheim, a researcher, wrote an interesting blog[2] which looks at this very issue and has many parallels with the diving community and how training (and equipment) standards have developed. He and Steve Shorrock, a human factors researcher, propose that once limits are set, they become the target e.g. the minimum number of hours for a pilot to fly per month to remain current is X hours. This minimum standard then becomes the norm, because airlines want to reduce their training budget to the minimum amount possible to save money.

Now imagine that the minimum number of dives for an entry level diving class is 4 and each dive must be at least 20 mins in length. Guess what happens if the local environment drives quantity and not quality and there is no feedback post-class to determine whether the learning was sufficient to dive safely in an autonomous manner? The caveat is that the skills must be 'mastered'. However, there is no metric of mastery and it is the instructor who is carrying the risk if a diver has an issue in the future. If their paperwork is compliant, they are likely 'safe'. This same process applies as we move up the training system with an expectation that previous training courses have provided the necessary skills, knowledge and attitude for the student to progress to the class about to be taken.

For good evolutionary reasons, humans are conditioned to look at what has gone wrong and focus on this so that future adverse events are prevented. However, this often means that we miss the good or excellent 'stuff' that happens and this doesn't get highlighted to those involved in the system. If you think about it, there is far more stuff that happens right than wrong in a system, but we only discuss the bad stuff (if it is reported at all). However, improving systems also means looking at the good stuff; how and why it happened; and what we can do to replicate that ourselves.

Systems are not just mechanical, electronic or electrical in nature, they are anything which involves multiple elements creating something greater than the sum of the individual parts. A diver training system involves divers, instructors, training materials, a dive centre or operation, diving equipment, a training organisation with its instructor trainers and Quality Assurance/Quality Control process, as well as the physical and social environments in which the training takes place. To understand how to improve diving safety, there is a need to take a systems view, otherwise we can improve one aspect which has a knock-on effect causing unintended consequences in another part of the system. Russell Ackoff, a pioneer in the field of operations research, systems thinking and management science, wrote much about systems improvement and the challenges in developing the manufacturing industry to become more lean and efficient in the 1960s and 1970s. He defined a system as[3]:

"A system is a whole defined by one or more functions, that consists of two or more essential parts that satisfy the following conditions: (1) each of these parts can affect the behaviour or properties of the whole; (2) none of these parts has an independent effect on the whole; the way an essential part affects the whole depends on what other parts are doing; and (3) every possible subset of the essential parts can affect the behaviour or properties of the whole but none can do so independently of the others."

Simple, Complicated or Complex?

Systems can be described using three terms: simple, complicated and complex.

- **Simple Systems**. A simple system is something which is linear in nature and can be explained using cause and effect. For example, X does Y and causes Z. The Buoyancy Compensation Device (BCD) inflator assembly is a simple system because when the button is pressed, the valve opens, the gas travels through the hole and inflates the BCD. When pressure is released by the diver, the valve closes, and the gas flow stops and so does the inflation process. The button or valve on their own does not constitute a system because a system achieves or creates something. In the case of the valve, it only provides a means by which gas can be passed from a low-pressure hose into the BCD bladder when commanded by a diver.

- **Complicated Systems**. A complicated system is where there are multiple components, each of which has moving parts to it. We can disassemble the system and the sub-systems to the component level, examine them, put them back together in the same way we took them apart and the system still works. A good example would be a rebreather. The manufacturer has written a manual which allows a diver to assemble, disassemble and carry out basic servicing on the unit. The diver (or servicing technician) will go through each of the steps, executing the checklist until they have all of the parts lying on the table in front of them (at a level commensurate with their expertise). They replace or repair one component and then start the assembly process, following the repeatable steps. Once assembled, the unit can be tested, and it will perform to the specification. The diver (technician) can visit any rebreather (as long as it hasn't been modified), read the manual and follow the steps and achieve the outcome expected.
- **Complex Systems**. We often think we understand the components of a complex system, but if we try to disassemble it and put it back together, it fails to perform the same way. Ackoff highlighted this interdependence and complexity in a number of lectures he delivered in Systems Thinking by using the analogy of a high-performance motor car. Imagine we purchase one each of 150 cars which are available to buy right now, and we place them in a massive hangar awaiting the arrival of 100 of the most highly skilled automotive engineers in the world to examine the cars, determine the best parts and then build the best car possible. The engineers arrive, examine all the cars and their performance and start their deliberations as to what the best parts from each car would be used to build the final car. From their discussions and technical arguments, they pick the engine from a Ferrari, the suspension from a Jeep, the brakes from a Porsche, the chassis

from a Tesla, the wheels from a BMW and so on until they have all the components needed to make a car, placed in a neat pile. Then they try to assemble the pieces to make the perfect car! Obviously, they fail, and even worse, we don't have anything we can use, because they have not taken into account the interactions which are key to the efficiency and effectiveness of the system.

You might argue that that is just engineering and has little relevance to divers and diving. However, as soon as you add humans into a system, the system becomes complex. We are all different, our group behaviours are different to our individual behaviours and all our behaviours are influenced by previous experiences, current knowledge and the environment in which we are operating. This means we can't accurately predict behaviours or interactions, nor can we reduce the system to its component parts to understand it.

To demonstrate this, rather than give an example which relates to a diver as this would be problematic due to the various definitions of 'a diver', I am going to use a child and explain how they are both a system and part of a system. The reason for choosing a child is that everyone has the experience of being a child and many people have the experience of raising a child.

Referring to the above definitions of simple, complicated and complex, we know that some actions can be simple (child gets hurt, child cries). However, as we can't disassemble a child, we are not able to examine in great detail how they are socially and technically/physically interacting with the world; and we are not able to accurately and reliably predict what will happen if we do something to them like remove a favourite toy or praise them for their work. And yet, despite the numerous books on the subject of raising a child, often with conflicting advice, we manage to successfully raise them without having a manual - because we apply non-technical skills and 'learning from experience' to develop them. We recognise that one size doesn't fit all and that some children will take much longer to learn than others. Paradoxically, often it is the adult who does the most learning during the child's developmental process as we are also part of the system which is constantly adapting and evolving around them.

If we now apply this to diving and diver training, dealing with complexity is why effective training cannot be delivered in a rote manner because each student is different and their interactions with the other class members and instructor will be unique too. Furthermore, their post-class actions will also be unique and will likely not be accurately repeatable. Linking this to training research, it has been shown that the most effective way for most people to learn is to have a mixture of formal training, mentoring and 'learning on the job'. Researchers Lombardo and Eichinger[4] described this as 70:20:10 with 10% delivered in a formal classroom setting, 20% through a mentoring/leadership framework post-class and then 70% through 'learning on the job' whereby perfect practice, success and informed failure lead to high performance.

We need to recognise that any system involving people is complex because people are unpredictable: they can be ambiguous in their communication and behaviour; and at the same time, they can be adaptable and resilient and consequently, learned behaviours will change future responses. We can use concepts and frameworks to generalise what we should do in a given circumstance, but each person, each team, each organisation is different, because the interactions taking place are different.

Given the above, if we want to make improvements to reduce the stresses associated with uncertainty and improve our fun or safety, there is a need to understand and develop the skills that deal with interactions (non-technical skills, learning from experience and resilience) and not just the technical skills of each individual or the team. However, for that to happen, there must be some form of feedback within the system. As has been shown in nature and engineering, the quality of feedback within the system has a direct impact on the speed of adaptation and the system's resilience. If the feedback is late or vague, then improvements are difficult or worse, and could be counterproductive.

As such, it is worth considering the following well-used phrase from Todd Conklin, a well-known and respected safety advisor in the US: *"Safety is not the absence of events; safety is the presence of defenses."*[5]

Looking at safety from a systems or non-systems perspective leads to different sets of considerations and attributes. For example, if we take a view of the world which doesn't take into account Systems Thinking, we might look at components, single causes, symptoms and failures and respond with reactive investigations and take a 'silo' view e.g. diver's decision-making, equipment manufacturer or the training agency. Whereas if we take a counter-view, one look at an operation or event using a systems-view, we get component interactions, multiple causal and contributory factors and hazards, and from this comes the realisation that we need to design safety into the system by looking at the interactions and context and not just follow standards which are based on the minimum requirements in ideal circumstances. As Steven Shorrock wrote in a blog titled *Never/Zero Thinking*[6], *"Never events require that always conditions are always present."*

You might be thinking how does all this theory translate to diving? The following narrative from Jamie Obern, a technical diving and cave instructor operating from Tutukaka, New Zealand, highlights the need to consider the system as a whole and ensure that those in the system can fail safely - even if that means that you are at the furthest point possible into a cave system.

Case Study: When you think it can't get worse...
We are eight days into the expedition and finally, I've reached the area of the cave I've been dreaming about for months. We are down at 68m in the catacombs, with good visibility, no video camera to distract us and enough gas to look around for at least 20 minutes. Mel hasn't been to this area before so is simply taking everything in, but I have been here before and I'm on a mission. I'm looking for the way forward, a tunnel leading on; something the few divers who have been here before might have missed. There are two leads on the left, but a short investigation proves they are connected and make a simple U-shape. Next, I reel out to where we had

ended our line on the last trip, to have another look into a crack which I knew led into a small hole – but just as I had noted before, it is still too tight to pass through. A part of me had hoped the recent heavy rains might have opened it up a bit, but with enough time to really study the hole, it is clear there is only a tiny amount of gravel and the rest is solid rock. Dammit, we're running out of time again and still there is no way forward.

As I back out of the crack, I finally become aware of Mel's increasingly agitated attempts to get my attention. I've been fully-focussed on examining the hole and now she's not looking happy, pointing up into the dead-end tunnel behind me. Oh shit – the recent rains have changed the cave and our bubbles have dislodged a huge wall of silt - which is now advancing rapidly towards us. I look around for somewhere to tie off the reel, quickly trying to identify a good spot by sight before the silt blinds us. I see a suitable rock but cannot complete the tie-off before we lose visibility.

And at this point I make a mistake and do exactly what I preach to my students not to do. Instead of just leaving my reel, I decide to cut it off. It's a beginner's mistake – I should know better – but at this stage I know I have plenty of time, so I calmly tie a loop into the end of the line and tidy away my reel. But what happens next is a slap in the face for my complacency. I'm wearing dry-gloves, but my hands are still a little cold and the thick fingers make me clumsier than normal. As I hurry to put my knife away, I somehow manage to nick my left hand, not enough to draw blood, but enough to flood the glove with 6 degree water. Suddenly the gremlins start to appear in my head.

By now, of course, Mel is exuding, 'WTF are you doing vibes', wondering why I'm not simply moving out of the silted area and exiting the cave. Even without sight, I know what she's thinking, and I finally get my act together and we move along the line. After 50m or so the visibility starts to clear up, just as we reach the tightest restriction in the cave. Going first, Mel misjudges the way through: she stays too far to the right and jams herself. She backs out and tries again, still unaware of my flooded glove and the fact that my hand is going numb. Finally, she's through, but now the silt has caught me again and I'm forced to negotiate the restriction in reduced vis. – which means more time and more gas. My mind is whirring – how can one simple error have led to this?

At last, I'm through and into a bigger passage again. We ascend up the deep gravel slope, pausing partway to keep our ascent rates to the profile we'd agreed. I indicate the flooded glove to Mel, and she nods her understanding – with a numb hand she will have to help me through the gas switches. We pass through the next tight area of cave and reach our first deco bottles at 36m. The switch isn't slick, but we get onto our richer mix and start tidying up in preparation for the final tricky area of cave. With five bottles and a scooter each, we have to pass the 'gravel restriction': the area of cave where many would be explorers give up. We also have to complete several minutes of decompression stops whilst uncomfortably wedged on this slope, but everything is fine and we reach our next deco bottles at 21m.

By now the water has started to seep past the wrist-dam in my glove and up my arm. I'm starting to chill and I can feel my body giving an involuntary shake every minute or so. My breathing rate is also starting to climb and I force myself to think happy thoughts and relax. With help from Mel to speed things up, we complete the switch and ditch the scooters and empty bottom stages for the support divers to collect. Now that we are past the gravel restriction, the buoyant empty stages slide slowly up the line towards the shallows – at last the cave is starting to help us. We complete our stops at 21m, 18m, 15m, and 12m and move to 9m. My breathing is still too heavy, so I'm thankful I was conservative with my reserve gas calculations. The world feels like a nicer place at last – I just need to manage 10 minutes at 9m and then we can climb into the habitat and get warm.

But the cave hasn't given up trying to kill us yet – it has one final blow to hand out. Just as I start to relax my deco reg free flows. In my bulky undergarments, I can't reach across to the valve with my right hand and the fingers on my left hand are nearly useless. In the confined space Mel and I do an impression of Disney's ballet dancing hippos as she tries to get to my valve. We finally turn the tank off, but now I definitely don't have enough gas to complete the stop and all the movement has forced even more cold water up my arm and across my chest. I'm now shaking almost constantly, and we decide to cut the 9m stop short and climb into the habitat at 6m.

As we reach 6m Rob's friendly face appears. Today is his first time doing support and he's expecting to simply collect our empty bottles, get the OK from us and make sure we're comfortable in the habitat. Based on the team's past form, he's also expecting the possibility of a practical joke and his first thoughts when he sees the look on our faces is 'yeah right' only to realise we're not joking. Suddenly his relaxed support dive isn't so relaxed!

I get into the habitat first, followed by Mel who gives Rob a note explaining the situation. She also checks that the extra O2 bottles we placed in the cave 'just-in-case' are still there hanging beneath the habitat. Finally, my world really does become a nicer place. The temperature in the habitat rises to a balmy 13 degrees; we can chat and with plenty of spare O2, we have time to recalculate the extra deco we need to do. After 10 minutes or so my shaking has subsided and I can reflect on the dive.

For the last hour it has felt like a hyper-active three-year-old has suddenly got hold of the remote controller for my life and has been randomly pushing buttons just for fun – with time standing still at one moment and then rushing past on fast-forward the next. I think back to the 'one' simple error I made and realise it was actually a series of errors. In my rush to start exploring, I hadn't focussed on laying the line properly: I should have tied it off before heading into the crack and I should definitely have laid it better through the deep restriction. I was also too wrapped up in looking for the way forward and forgot about my buddy, who was trying to warn me about the silt long before it became a problem. As for not leaving my reel – how many times have I berated students about that?

But it's not all doom and gloom. The time and effort spent setting up a habitat has proved completely worthwhile, our reserve gas calculations and safety bottles were good, our support team were great and the extra money spent getting dry-gloves with wrist-dams seems like the best *decision ever. Sitting in the habitat, the only thing I wanted to check was the free-flowing reg, which we later discovered had been compromised by gravel from the slope. Finally, 50 minutes after entering the habitat, we re-entered the water and ascended the last few metres to the surface pool – not exactly comfortable, but alive and without any complications such as hypothermia or Decompression Sickness (DCS).*

In cave diving, things do go wrong and far more often than we might care to acknowledge, but that's why we train and why we plan. If we had expected all the dives on this trip to go perfectly, then we wouldn't have spent weeks sorting out the habitat, days carrying in extra safety bottles or hours running different deco schedules to understand our various bailout options. We also wouldn't have spent years building our experience and getting a team together – but we did – and this is the reason why.

Jamie's team had expected to fail at some point. The interaction which caused it (cutting of the glove), to a certain extent, is irrelevant, and therefore they planned for a number of different eventualities. You might think that this would be the norm for such a dive and you'd probably be right to have a support team and maybe a habitat to rest in. However, if you look back at the introduction where the AOW diver got entangled, the same hazard is present - drowning - and therefore recognising that unwanted interactions are present in any dive is essential. This illustrates why we should look at each dive with genuine curiosity as to what might happen rather than dismiss them as unlikely because we haven't encountered them before. This might take the fun out of "let's jump in and see what happens", as this quickly loses its appeal when the unexpected happens and you are left stuck somewhere, out of gas or wondering how you are going to get out of this alive. Chapter 4 will delve into risk and uncertainty in more detail, especially the biases involved, as it takes a conscious effort to look beyond the "we've always done it this way" mindset.

Jamie provided some additional reflective comments when he submitted his narrative. If we look at those now, we can see that a number of interactions were either not considered as not being relevant or ignored because the goal was overriding what would appear to be logical decision-making.

I was considerably more experienced as a cave diver than my buddy (or anyone else on the team) and had the attitude that Mel was simply coming along for the ride and I was doing all the "heavy-lifting". I wasn't interested in Mel's concerns and not paying any attention to her underwater as I expected her to be nervous and possibly call the dive. There were also additional tensions between us as a result of non-related dive issues and so our communications and planning prior to the dive was less than open/candid.

This was my 7th trip to this cave and it felt like I had made no progress since my 3rd trip when I had briefly reached the same area of the cave, following someone else's line. As NZ's only cave diving instructor, I felt I needed to 'leave my mark' and wasn't sure how many more chances I would get before someone else explored this cave.

The support divers for this dive were the three students from my very first GUE Fundamentals class and I wanted to impress them. Furthermore, given their experience, they weren't experienced enough and/or confident enough to challenge any of my decisions/actions. Reflecting on this more, even if they had the confidence to speak up, it's doubtful whether I would have listened to them, given the very large difference in cave diving experience at the time.

We had experienced no silt on any previous trips, so I raced through the deep restriction making no effort to avoid the line trap I knew was there – assuming the visibility would be perfect during the exit.

Jamie's account highlights numerous personal and team failures covering cognitive and interpersonal skills, but at the same time, the team had planned for possible technical system failures by having a habitat, reserve cylinders and a support team. They also reviewed the failure in detail, post-event and changed their processes so that future events would be safer. One of the greatest changes wasn't technical or about a process; it was Jamie's attitude towards the team and their ability to support the lead divers. Teams are built on trust and trust is a two-way street.

Divers are part of a socio-technical system. Diving is a social activity with all of the inherent problems that this can bring when it comes to peer-pressure, social conformance and personal/professional relationships. Diving also requires a level of technical hardware to provide life-support, and the greater the risks involved in diving, the more that interactions across the system need to be addressed. To maximise safety, at the same time as managing trade-offs between cost, time, quality, fun and effort we need to examine successes and failures in the context of a system. Don't just look at outcomes, rather look at the people, the equipment, the social environment, the physical environment and their interactions. Chapters 12 and 13 will provide more guidance on what to look at when things didn't go to plan and will also provide you with topics to look at when reinforcing successes.

Summary of Key Points
- Diving is a system and divers are part of that system. A system which includes instructors, training agencies, insurance companies, equipment manufacturers, dive centres and societal expectations/pressures. In fact, anyone or anything that is involved in getting under the water and exploring our awesome oceans, lakes and rivers is part of the system.
- Focusing on a component in the system e.g. the diver and their performance and improving it, is unlikely to make an overall improvement in system safety. At the personal level, improving buoyancy, trim and technical skills like sending a dSMB up without improving non-technical skills like teamwork, communication and situational awareness will not improve your overall safety. At the organisational level, rewarding instructors for huge numbers of certifications without checking standards compliance WILL have an impact on system behaviour at the local level which consequently will impact diver safety.
- Examining and improving interactions within the system will have the greatest impact on diving safety. Incident investigations need to look not just at the diver and what they did, but also how it

made sense and that means looking further back in time to include social conformance, goals and expectations, their training/development and the 'components of the system' involved. 'Air gaps' between organisations and instructors/clients/students do nothing to improve diving safety, but they do protect a component of it from litigation. Ironically, an unintended consequence of this transference to the instructor/diver means that insurance premiums are at an all-time high, which means it will soon be uneconomically-viable to continue to teach, especially on rebreathers.

- When successes or failures happen to you or others, don't just look at the person closest to the 'sharp end': their behaviour is a product of the system they are in. Learn to have effective debriefs which focus not just on technical skills, but non-technical skills, the environment and the interactions, so that you understand how you and the team arrived at this mental model and identify how to close the gaps prior to or during future dives.
- Safety is a system property. You cannot punish safety into a system, but you can punish compliance and that isn't the same as safety. If you are an instructor, just because the paperwork is in place, it doesn't mean you are safe. It means you can transfer the risk to the insurance company and therefore be safe from litigation. Operational safety is a different matter and that is what really counts.
- Safety is not the absence of accidents and incidents. It is the presence of barriers and defences, and the ability of the system to fail safely. Look at what failures can happen by looking at your own performance and that of others, recognising that you and they are both human and therefore likely to fail the same way. Now consider what you will do to ensure you fail safely.

Questions to consider
- Think back to your last diving trip. What interactions between part of the system (people, equipment, environment) worked and why? What didn't work and why?
- Do you consider potential unintended consequences on bigger dives? How do you identify them as part of your risk management process?
- When was the last time you bought something and realised it didn't work with how you currently do something, so you had to change your technical skills, or does that piece of equipment just lie in the garage gathering dust?

References
(1) Cook, R. (1998) How Complex Systems Fail. http://web.mit.edu/2.75/resources/random/How%20Complex%20Systems%20Fail.pdf

(2) Manheim, D. (2018) Shorrock's Law of Limits. Retrieved from https://medium.com/@davidmanheim/shorrocks-law-of-limits-9d1b2880b13

(3) Ackoff, R. (1998) A Systemic View of Transformational Leadership. https://pdfs.semanticscholar.org/dd7e/f924e44861877b76d65a865754d741d07b0f.pdf

(4) Lombardo, M; Eichinger, R. (1996). The Career Architect Development Planner (1st ed.). Minneapolis: Lominger. p. iv. ISBN 0-9655712-1-1.

(5) Conklin, Todd. (2012) Pre-Accident Investigations: An Introduction to Organizational Safety (p. 8). Ashgate Publishing Ltd. Kindle Edition.

(6) Shorrock, S. (2016) Never/Zero Thinking. https://humanisticsystems.com/2016/02/27/neverzero-thinking/

Additional Reading
Leveson, N. (2017). Engineering a safer world: systems thinking applied to safety. https://mitpress.mit.edu/books/engineering-safer-world

Conklin, T. (2016). Pre-Accident Investigations: Better Questions - An Applied Approach to Operational Learning. CRC Press.

Chapter 3

Human Error. A terrible term to apply if we want to learn from what happened!

"'Human error' after all, is no more than a label. It is a judgment. It is an attribution that we make, after the fact, about the behaviour of other people, or about our own."

Sidney Dekker[1]

Tim Clements, a CCR IT and cave diver, describes a task where he and his partner had to retrieve twelve hydrophones from twelve different shot-line locations in an array with depths varying from 3 to 24m and due to some cognitive failures, things didn't go quite to plan! The pressure was on because the scientific data was part of his wife's research project.

Case Study: Losing the plot!

The total path to be travelled was 1.3km and the dive team chose to use both CCR and DPV to optimise breathing gas and travel time. The dive was a repeat of previous dives to recover the hydrophones, download the recorded data and then redeploy them - the task was familiar and had been previously completed without incident or complication.

During the dive my mask leaked. A small, but niggly thing, distracting me and requiring frequent clearing. This makes CCR buoyancy control more difficult, especially in shallow water, as gas used to clear the mask must be replaced from the diluent bottle, which in turn requires addition of O2 to make the desired nitrox in the loop. Any extra gas and the diver rises, the pO2 drops and the CCR injects again.

On the deeper transits, this wasn't too much of an issue. The navigation suffered a little from distraction, requiring an adjustment, but the deep hydrophones were retrieved and stored in a mesh bag towed on the right-hand side, balancing the bailout bottle on the left-hand side.

In the shallows, the distraction and frustration increased. I was becoming increasingly aware of buoyancy changes from gas injection while in the shallow water and could not get settled into a stable DPV towing position. The towed bag on the right was lying over my backup display and torch clips and this was causing issues with dive performance and comfort levels. With three hydrophones remaining, at positions #3, #2 and #1, I decided to stop and reset. Clipping the bag and DPV to shot #3, I untangled the torch and backup display cables, got everything how I like it again and felt much better. That is, apart from the mask, which still leaked. Hydrophone #3 was cut free, put in the bag and the shears stored in their belt pouch. We scootered to shot #2. Leaving shot 2, I knew we only had one to go, about 10m away around a corner. Hydrophone #1 was retrieved and we scootered along to investigate a nearby site for another project on our route back. A short survey, a little video and we were done. I surfaced to mark the position on a rock and decided to scooter back on the surface, leaving mask issues happily behind and feeling distinctly underwhelmed by the dive.

Arriving home and handing over the bag, we realised that hydrophone #2 was missing. After some frustrated searching of the car and the shore site the next day, it was time to admit it was lost. I played back the dive, felt sure that it had been retrieved, confirmed by the memory of the second diver, but that it had fallen from the bag on the way back.

The next step was a search on open circuit of the lake bed under my route back to the exit point, the survey shelf and the boulder scree from there to shot #1. Searching the boulder scree was complicated by the 1.5m high plant growth. 85 minutes of fingertip searching later and all we had was an empty can of Thatchers gold cider. This confirmed that our technique could find an object of the correct size.

My mind began to suggest that the bag had not been as 'full' as usual at shot #1. Also, the fact that hydrophone #2 had fallen out past hydrophone #1 which was put in after #2 didn't make sense.

Two divers searched from shot #2 to shot #1. Over this short distance, they searched slowly from 2m down to 18m through the plants. No hydrophone was found.

It was a few more days before the next search could be made. In that time, I revisualised the dive several times. The hydrophone was not only valuable in itself, but contained a year's worth of PhD data for my wife. The stakes felt elevated, but the fact that this was a lake of finite dimensions remained as the only reassurance. I was convinced that I had removed the hydrophone, and had a distinct strong memory, both mental and physical of steering the DPV away from shot #2 to shot #1. The second diver had been to my right at this point and always had a clear view of the hydrophone removal, but this time, had nothing helpful to add.

We finally got back in the water for another search about 10 days later. The plan was simple. Go to shot #2, descend and search to shot #1, then retrace the exit route again. My buddy dropped down the shot to the boulder scree and plants at about 4m, while I descended the shot to a clump of vegetation at approximately 2m. Passing this, I found the hydrophone, attached by all three cable ties. I had never removed it. We turned the dive, elated but with some serious post dive / mission analysis to complete.

Running back over the dives to review why such a simple mistake had gone undetected was humbling. I had always prided myself that I had never lost an item of scientific gear and had strived to improve my technique over a quarter century of working underwater. I had begun scientific diving as a single-tank diver looking like a Christmas tree covered in quadrats, current metres, slates and sometimes video, graduating to an organised CCR and DPV platform with gear placements reviewed, visualised and worked into a dive plan that allowed normal function and good emergency reaction. We had dived as a team, with signals and confirmation of tasks complete - no 'same ocean' buddy system here. It had worked fine over a sequence of dives. How had I simply not removed hydrophone #2, and more importantly, why had the post-dive visualisation not provided more information?

In Tim's case, there were a number of factors at play which led to a series of 'errors' being made; and one error which then had pretty large consequences, given the efforts required to recover the 'lost' piece of equipment. These factors included having done the job numerous times before so both physical and mental 'muscle memory' play a part in what 'will' happen (expectation - see the Situational Awareness chapter for more on this), the mask leaking which provided a little distraction and minor workload on top of an emotionally important task - the research data was for his wife! What is interesting is that the buddy should not have been subject to the same stressors as Tim, but there are likely other reasons why the buddy missed the hydrophone - they were taking their lead from a very experienced diver (Tim) and also the fact that the buddy was employed by Tim as a dive instructor. The presence of authority gradient has shown to be causal or contributory in nature in aviation, maritime and healthcare accidents such as the Tenerife crash in 1977 or the Costa Concordia grounding and capsizing in January 2012. So, while a simple 'human error' occurred which led to the dive ending with the perception that the hydrophone had been lost, the reasons for this are pretty complex. This chapter will look at what human error really means and why it is important to be able to distinguish between the different types of errors and violations or 'at risk behaviours'.

Human Error
Human error can be viewed through one of two lenses. We can see human error as a cause of failure, or we can see human error as a symptom of failure[2]. Unfortunately, the first is the most prevalent. However, as we will see, if we don't consider the second view, we won't improve safety too much because we won't go beyond blaming the individual.

In 1990, Professor James Reason wrote, *Human Error* and in it he clearly articulated that such a simplistic term adds little value to learning by attributing it as a single cause to an accident. In the 1970s and 1980s, numerous accident reports and research papers stated that 80-90% of aviation accidents were caused by 'human error'. The same attribution has been applied in medicine and other high-risk domains. However, since the 1990s the aviation operational and research communities have recognised that this attribution is flawed because 'human error' is normal and using a simplistic term does not help learning when specific details are needed to understand the context. The same goes for 'violations' as a cause for accidents - without understanding the reason for the violation, the system will likely create the circumstances in which the diver (human) has to make a similar decision or subconscious 'choice'.

Slips, Lapses, Mistakes and Violations/Non-Compliance

It is sometimes hard to discern the difference between the different types of human error and violations/non-compliance in diving and there are very good reasons for this. Firstly, we lack details in incident reports and so we can only focus on the outcome; secondly, the observer's position biases the perspective i.e. who are they and what is their position and/or experience; and finally, there are so many 'standards' in the diving industry that what is right for one person or organisation is wrong for another.

The following example of driving above the speed limit will highlight the different factors to consider. As speeding is such a common occurrence, we do not always see it as a human failure. Being clear about the reasons why it might occur can help create a better understanding of errors and violations.

Some reasons why people speed include:

- Driving someone to hospital - under normal circumstances we might not speed, but because we are driving someone to hospital, we consciously decide to break a known rule - this is an exceptional non-compliance.
- We always drive above the speed limit - we believe that it is okay to speed and do so habitually - this is a routine non-compliance.
- We drive with the speed of surrounding traffic - the speed of the traffic around us, tailgating drivers and aggressive overtaking encourage us to speed when we would normally stick to the speed limit - this is a situational non-compliance.

- We misread the speedometer - this is a slip or lapse.
- We do not realise we are in a 30mph speed zone - this is a rule-based mistake.
- We forget we are in a 30mph speed zone - this is a slip or lapse.
- We are distracted by the passenger - this is a slip or lapse.
- We are in an unfamiliar car - we are not used to the car driving so smoothly and we are not aware we are speeding - this is a knowledge-based mistake.

Therefore, it cannot be assumed that an observed failure, such as speeding, is always a non-compliance occurrence. Speeding may be an error or a non-compliance occurrence - the reason for the non-compliance may also change depending on circumstance. In diving, we don't often capture the rationality, and so we often jump to the conclusion that it is always a violation or non-compliance and should be punished in some form or another. The Just Culture chapter (Chapter 5) will cover this topic in more detail.

If all events are treated in the same way, the problem is unlikely to be rectified. The root cause(s) of the problem should be understood - for example, if people are speeding because they do not realise they are in a 30mph zone, then a good solution might be to make speed limit signs much clearer, or introduce vehicle activated signs that flash when there is a speeding car. This is likely to be more effective than training people about the rule (which they may already know and understand).

Digging into the Detail

High-risk domains such as aviation and nuclear energy have heavily contributed to the research into safety, human factors and human performance because failures or adverse events can have such massive effects in terms of the loss of life, as well as social and environmental impacts. Over time, tools, models and frameworks have been developed which provide additional levels of granularity or detail into why and how the unwanted event occurred at the individual level. Examples of this are: Generic Error-Modelling System (GEMS) (slips, lapses, mistakes and violations) or to look further back in time or up the organisational 'tree' with tools such as the Human Factors Analysis Classification System (HFACS) and Root Cause Analysis (RCA). However, even with all of these tools, it is very difficult to adequately explain the unexpected and unwanted interactions within a system which lead to an accident because of the emergent nature of failures. More powerful and resource intensive tools like Systems-Theoretic Accident Model (STAMP) and Functional Resonance Analysis Model (FRAM) have been developed which look at interactions within a system.

Despite the availability of the simple tools, there has been no published application of the use of such formal tools to investigate a diving incident or accident and only simple outcome models or categorisations are used. The problem with simple models is that they often hide the reality. e.g. in a British Sub Aqua Club incident report a diver who runs out of gas due to distraction or high workload who then has a rapid ascent which leads to decompression sickness (DCS) would have their incident categorised in the annual report as a DCS incident and yet these are *just* outcomes. Another example would be the research by Divers Alert Network (DAN) which showed that 41% of the fatalities which they could attribute to triggers were caused by insufficient gas[3]. However, without understanding why the gas ran out doesn't really help you prevent future incidents, because we all know that being underwater without a breathing gas supply is likely to end up as a fatality or serious injury. Context is vitally important if safety and performance are to be improved.

Paradoxically, an article written by human factors Olsen and Shorrock focusing on Air Traffic Controller performance showed that as more granularity or detail is added to a framework, schema or taxonomy to help define the causal and contributory factors, the less reliability there is in terms of a consensus of opinion from those doing the assessments[4]. This is because each observer of the system will have their own experiences and expectations about how something should be done and it takes considerable training and a diverse investigation team to isolate personal biases from the investigative and analysis process. In simple, linear problems, it is easy to define a standard, but when problems are encountered with conflicting goals of time, resource and outcomes, then it isn't so easy to define 'what is right'. As a global diving community, operational standards are few and far between and even when looking at diver training, the lack of active quality assurance and quality control means that operational drift is more likely to occur, even if the initial certification/qualification process was intense and of a high quality.

The research also shows that depending on the perspective of the reviewer, a certain topic of interest will be the focal point for where errors are 'discovered' e.g. during research which looked at the errors made by air traffic controllers, observers consisted of a mixture of psychologists and specially-trained air traffic controllers. The observers who were air traffic controllers noticed problems related to the equipment, the messages being relayed and the radar plots, etc; whereas the psychologists were focussing on cognitive issues and how decisions were made. Ironically, when operators who were looking at the 'events' with a view to improving performance were questioned about what they saw, they recounted that the operational controllers were finding ways to adapt to the dynamic situation they were facing, even if that meant they were having to 'break rules' or -'cut corners' to achieve their goals - goals which are often in conflict with each other. As such, understanding the perspective of both the reviewer(s) and the person(s) involved is essential if we are to improve safety and performance.

A simple, reductionist approach does very little to achieve an improved level of safety, especially when observers have the benefit of hindsight and know the outcome. They can easily join the dots which weren't apparent to the diver at the time. If they were apparent and noted as relevant, then they would have been acted upon. Therefore, in the context of this book, 'human error' when used as an attribution for causality is placed inside inverted commas to identify that it is a generic term and not a specific one.

Global Underwater Explorers lead for CCR training, Richard

Lundgren, provides an account of a near-miss in which a diver could have easily died due to breathing a gas which wasn't compatible with life. In it we can see that it isn't just the 'error' which the diver made that we need to look at, but the context and the divers involved which led to the situation developing in the manner it did. The WITH model[3] of error- producing conditions will be explained more in chapter 11 of this book as this provides a good guide for those in supervisory or leadership positions to be pro-active in their risk management.

Case Study: Searching for the Admiral's Fleet

In the mid-nineties, I was part of a major project to search for the Swedish admiral's lost fleet, a project which has been going for three years and would go on for many more. The next trip was about to kick off and we had perfect weather for it. Dead calm seas and bright skies. All those present had a positive feeling caused by the previous day's successful wreck hunt, where a new promising target was found. This day we had the chance to make history and we were all eager to claim it!

Little did we know that it all could have been so easily put to an abrupt and unexpected end because of what happened in the next 60 minutes.

One diver was arriving late having been delayed due to a long and complicated trip down to the island we were operating from. Initially, the unwelcome delay caused some amusement among the waiting divers, but the sensation soon turned to frustration and anxiety.

When he finally arrived, we were now seriously delayed. The diver excused himself and started to pack his gear into the boat, eagerly assisted by the other divers who were all now well-motivated and ready to leave the dock. Drysuit, fins, wings were all quickly moved from the truck assisted by many helping hands. Also, doubles and decompression bottles...

"Hey, what are you doing! Stop that!" I said.

I was the surface manager that day with the task of ensuring that

---

3 The WITH model has been derived from the nuclear industry and looks at conditions which are likely to lead to errors being made. The letters stand for Work (the physical work environment including social pressures), Individual (the individual worker's traits/behaviours/limitations), Task (the complexity of the task and processes/rules associated with it) and Human (normal human fallibility and cognitive biases).

everything loaded on the boat was as it was supposed to be. My language was direct and my mood grumpy due to the delay, and there was a building fear that we would miss the opportunity waiting for us.

"Why should we stop? We need to get going!" one of the other team members called out, feeling equally frustrated and eager to get going as I was.

"The tanks need to get out of the boat, now! They are not marked!" I said.

"Chill out will you? They are all good to go! Don't be such a bureaucrat!" the delayed diver angrily replied, siding with the crew in an attempt to deflect some of the criticism for being late.

"We are going nowhere until the tanks are all off the boat, pressure checked, analysed and marked up! Stop messing around wasting time - do it!" I roared.

There were no helping hands this time as the now furious delayed diver had to unload his cylinders and start the verification process. There was lots of mumbling and swearing. All tanks checked out fine; they were properly marked and loaded back into the boat. All bar one that is.

"Dammit, I have forgot to fill the oxygen - the cylinder is empty!" said the delayed diver referring to his oxygen decompression cylinder.

The team's massive frustrations were made very clear to the delayed diver.

"Go get it filled then. Take your time," I said now more under control, trying to be calm as I realised that the situation was quite stressful, and that stress promotes mistakes.

As the diver walked away with the cylinder in order to use the fill station situated in one of the harbour facilities, the other divers were obviously complaining due to the further delay. It was easy to understand their feelings, but at the same time we needed to be better than this. The situation was stressful for all of us: me, the divers and mostly for the delayed diver.

"Hey, get your own stuff together, double-check your gear and be ready to depart rather than complaining!" I said conversationally, trying to reduce some of the tension.

"We almost lost the day because of this!" one diver shouted.

"We will lose more than that if we continue making mistakes like this due to stress," I replied.

The delayed diver came running back carrying his refilled decompression bottle and started to board the boat.

"Hey, not again! Get that tank marked properly!" I said with a stern voice.

"Come on! I just filled the cylinder with oxygen myself! It is analysed - I've just not had the time to mark it! It's OXYGEN, get it?" he shouted furiously.

"XxXxxxxXXXX!" shouted the waiting divers in despair.

"Seriously! Either you do what is expected of you or we are departing without you! Final chance!" I made this statement calmly to prevent the others overhearing what I had just said.

"I don't have the darn analyser, I forgot it at the fill station!" said the delayed diver.

"Here you are, use mine!" I said and handed over my analyser.

The diver calibrated the analyser and started to analyse his oxygen decompression bottle.

"Ha, your analyser does not work!" The delayed diver shouted in a high-pitched stressed voice.

"Well, how come?" I queried, mystified.

"It's reading zero! You should really take care of your equipment better!" the delayed diver said, now challenging me.

"And your pressure?" I asked.

"185 bar! Your analyser is not working! Let's be done with this and just go! I know its OXYGEN!" stated the delayed diver.

"Nope!" I said casually.

The delayed diver deployed the regulator attached to the oxygen decompression cylinder in rage, pressurised and started to breathe forcefully from the second stage.

"You see, nothing wrong with the gaaaaas....!" screamed the delayed diver in a high-pitched helium voice, before he lost his balance and sat down hard on his butt.

In aviation, it is recognised that 'human error' happens all the time. It has been reported that between 3 and 6 errors per hour occur on the flight deck, but they are all (or nearly all) trapped before they become an issue. Given that errors are normal, the aviation community has built on the concept of Crew Resource Management (CRM) and developed the Threat and Error Model (TEM) which looks at when errors are more likely to happen and how to modify their behaviours accordingly, especially when it comes to communications and teamwork. The nuclear industry developed the WITH model to address this issue too.

In the case of the incorrect filling of the cylinder with 100% helium instead of 100% oxygen above, we can see that having procedures in place, procedures which are non-discretionary in nature, can save people's lives because they trap errors before they can propagate to an end state of a fatality. Unfortunately, as will be described in Chapter 10 (Leadership), the absence of such robust procedures cost Carl Spencer his life. Carl was the expedition leader of the 2012 Britannic expedition and because he was so busy running the expedition, he made a number of critical errors and there was no ability to fail safely. He died of oxygen toxicity after he breathed 50% at 40m – the bottle was not marked as a 50% bottle.

Such procedures and concepts are useful, but they need to be tempered with what happens in the real world. As such, there is an essential need for a feedback loop to ensure that instances of 'errors' and 'at-risk' behaviours can be considered as part of the system design.

The Sharp End and the Blunt End

Within any system involving people, there is a 'sharp end' and a 'blunt end'. The 'sharp end' consists of those people who execute the plan against the 'rules' of the game which have been written. The sharp end could be:
- pilots who have to operate their aircraft in line with the safety procedures and protocols published, cognisant of the time

pressures to maintain a schedule and financial pressures to minimise fuel burned; or
- surgeons who have the patient's safety at heart, but also need to balance the pressures to reduce waiting lists and use equipment which may not have been designed with the operating theatre team in mind; or
- in the case of diving, instructors and dive centre owners who have to balance training procedures with real world pressures to maintain commercial viability in a cut-throat environment; or
- divers who have to balance their spare time available with the disposable income for a discretionary leisure activity which might mean that they don't service their equipment when they should or undertake continuation training to ensure that their skills are at the level they should be.

The 'blunt end' consists of those in the organisations who write the international, local, organisational and company standards policies and 'rules' which the 'sharp end' must use to execute their role. Often those in these positions have very little contact with those at the sharp end, which means their view of the world is different.

To explain this apparent disconnect, a concept exists called 'Work as Imagined/Work as Done' in which there is a difference between what system and equipment designers and managers imagine should happen or should get done at the 'sharp end' and what actually happens, given the conflicting goals which have to be balanced in real time. As long as nothing goes wrong, the 'Work As Imagined' appears to be correct, although adaptations and modifications are happening all the time. However, if something does go wrong, there is an immediate comparison between 'Work As Done' and 'Work As Imagined' and it is normally the user/operator who is blamed for not doing something correctly, even if doing the right thing is not possible, because of the system's constraints.

There is always a conflict between the 'sharp end' and the 'blunt end', mainly because of the goals which need to be managed and the resources allocated to achieve them. When things go wrong, it is easy to think it is the fault of those at the 'sharp end' who have 'caused' it and yet those at the 'sharp end' are normally the ones who have inherited the flawed rules, procedures, hardware and equipment from those at the 'blunt end'. Furthermore, it is normally those at the 'blunt end' who undertake the investigation to determine where fault lies within the system and human nature means that often we aren't introspective and, so again, the fault lies with those at the 'sharp end'! Closing the gap between 'Work As Done' and 'Work As Imagined' is essential if safety and performance are to be improved. However, that doesn't always mean moving 'Work As Done' closer to 'Work As Imagined'; first, there is a need to understand why the deviation is in place to start with.

As such, it is very easy to think that by attributing 'human error' to accidents, that we have solved the problem. In fact, if the term 'human error' ends up in an accident report, it means one of a number of things: The authors (or those who commissioned the report) are happy with a 'catch all' term that doesn't permit detailed learning to occur, or that they stopped investigating; either because they didn't want to find the answer, or they didn't have the resources (time, money or data) to find out how something happened. Often, it is much simpler to blame the fallible human, because the more we blame those at the 'sharp end', the less we have to do to examine the 'blunt end' and find the systemic failures which are present. If 'human error' is consistently attributed, it probably says more about the organisation or culture than it does about the individual.

The components of 'Human Error' Notwithstanding the above, there is a need to have some means of helping to categorise broad 'buckets of information' so that we can identify trends or systemic failures, even if the categories are not experienced in a linear manner. Indeed, on closer examination, often it is the convergence of many, apparently, unrelated factors which create an accident. This categorisation process is where taxonomies or frameworks can help. James Reason in his book, *Human Error*[5] provides an insight as to how 'human error' could be defined with his *Generic Error-Modelling System* (GEMS) to look at the basic human error types (slips, lapses, mistakes and violations). This system is based on looking at how failures occur against the basic human performance model by Jens Rasmussen, who was one of the original researchers looking at human error and human performance, identified. His human performance model looked at skills-based, rules-based and knowledge-based decision-making. Figure 3 shows the different error types.

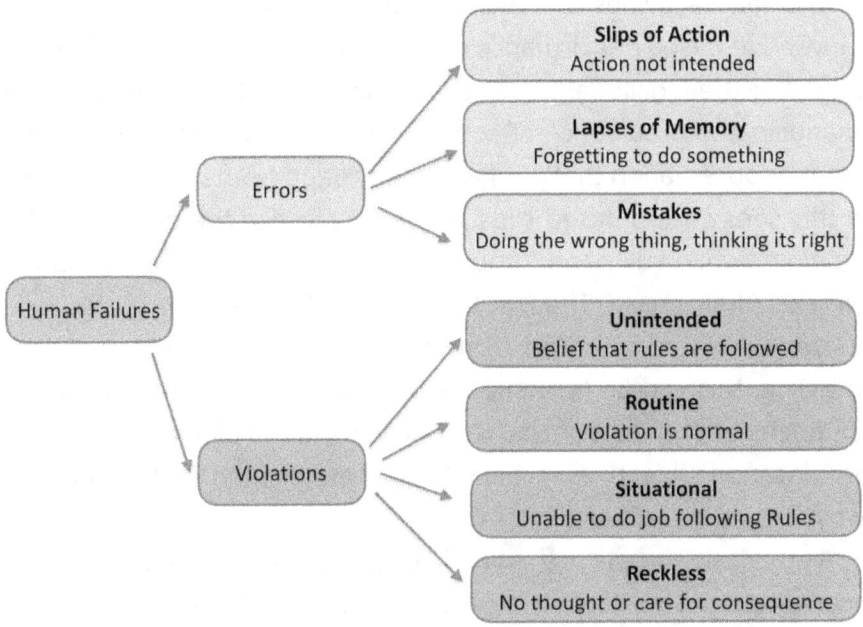

Figure 3: Different types of error and violation and how they are manifested

Slips, Mistakes, Lapses & Violations Diagram

Reason describes how these three error types were matched against three different performance levels by Rasmussen - Skills-based for slips and lapses; rules-based for rule-based mistakes; and knowledge-based for knowledge-based mistakes. Reason explains that to understand which performance level was being used (Skills, Rules or Knowledge) the question should be asked as to whether or not the individual was engaged in problem solving at the time an error occurred.

In his model, Rasmussen states that behaviour at the skills-based level, *"represents sensorimotor performance during acts or activities that, after a statement of an intention, take place without conscious control as smooth, automated, and highly integrated patterns of behaviour*[6]. Reason goes on to describe that although skills-based performance can also be invoked during problem-solving to achieve local goals, such behaviour is primarily a way of dealing with routine and non-problematic activities in familiar situations. Both rules-based and knowledge-based performance on the other hand are only called into play after the individual has become conscious of a problem i.e. the unanticipated occurrence of some externally or internally produced event or observation that demands a deviation from the current plan. In this sense, skills-based slips generally precede the detection of a problem, while rules- and knowledge-based mistakes arise during the execution phase. Thus, a defining condition for both rules- and knowledge-based mistakes is an awareness that a problem exists. In diving, this can be an issue because a fair amount of training is conducted in the 'learn, observe, practice' (akin to Bloom's Taxonomy of Education Objectives – levels 1 to 3) rather than understand the 'why' behind the action (levels 4-6)[4].

A practical example of this would be a second stage free-flow which necessitates a shutdown while diving a twinset. The diver recognises from the noise and bubbles in their face that their back-up regulator second stage is free-flowing (skills-based); they reach back to the right post to shutdown (rules-based); and start shutting the valve down by turning the valve clockwise (skills-based). However, the free-flowing doesn't stop (rules-based) and so they go to shut down the left post without opening the right post (rules-based mistake). The diver shuts down the left post and subsequently runs out of gas. They now have to work out what has happened and what to do about it (knowledge-based) and then execute the action (skills-based).

---

[4] Blooms Levels: 1 - Knowledge is defined as remembering of previously learned material. 2 - Comprehension is defined as the ability to grasp the meaning of material. 3 - Application refers to the ability to use learned material in new and concrete situations. 4 - Analysis refers to the ability to break down material into its component parts so that it's organisational structure may be understood. 5 - Synthesis refers to the ability to put parts together to form a new whole. 6 - Evaluation is concerned with the ability to judge the value of material (statement, novel, poem, research report) for a given purpose.

As we can see, moving from one type of behaviour or performance level to another happens dynamically and therefore categorising issues (Skills, Rules or Knowledge) in real time is difficult. However, what Reason shows is that the error rates associated with the different decision-making processes are different and, as such, this demonstrates the need for training which provides divers with the ability to work at the different performance levels.

- Skills-based. This is determined to have an error rate of approximately 1:10 000, where errors are normally associated with distractions and the cognitive flow for the 'automatic' behaviour is interrupted. e.g. the button on the inflator hose to deflate the wing is pressed instead of the inflate. Skills-based performance is improved through deliberate practice, repeating the same skills with feedback to ensure that not just 'practice makes perfect' but 'perfect practice makes perfect'.
- Rules-based. An error rate of approximately 1:100 is present and this is normally caused by applying the wrong rule to the current situation. Rules could be considered to be technical or social in nature. Using the above example regarding the shutdown drill, the diver did not follow the correct rule (open right post before shutting down left post). Rules-based performance is improved by exposing divers to different scenarios with subtle differences, so that the different rules can be identified and then applied. As greater experience is developed, these activities move into more skills-based performance.
- Knowledge-based. Error rates of between 1:2 and 1:10 are experienced. This is predominately because the operator does not have the experience or knowledge about how to solve the problem. At worst, it could be a 50:50 guess as to the solution. The challenge is how to improve decision-making in this domain, because there is a finite amount of time/money to learn everything and be exposed to every failure mode during a diver training class. However, what can be done is to develop an understanding of why certain things are done a certain way which allows the operator to

think around the problem, rather than have a direct answer. For this to be effective, the instructor needs to have a high-level of knowledge to teach not just rote responses (rules-based).

Human Error can have Multiple Meanings

Professor Erik Hollnagel, in his book, *Human Reliability Analysis: Context and Control*[7] he described 'human error' as having one of three meanings: the cause of failure, the failure itself and as a process.

Error as the cause of failure: 'This event was due to human error.' The assumption is that error is some basic category or type of human behaviour that precedes and generates a failure. It leads to variations on the myth that safety is protecting the system and stakeholders from erratic, unreliable people. An often-heard term relating to this is, *"You can't fix stupid"*.

- Error as the failure itself, i.e. the consequences that flow from an event: *"The choice of dive location was an error"* In this sense the term 'error' simply asserts that the outcome was bad, producing negative consequences (e.g. caused injuries to the diver).
- Error as a process, or more precisely, departures from the 'good' process. Here, the sense of error is of deviation from a standard, that is a model of what is good practice, but the difficulty is there are different models of what is the process that should be followed. In diving, given the vast variance in standards and skills, what standard is applicable, how standards should be described, and most importantly, what does it mean when deviations from the standards do not result in bad outcomes.

Each of these meanings introduces problems when it comes to learning from adverse events. The first two because they are about 'blaming the individual' rather than looking at the system, and the last one because there are few things in diving which are defined by community-wide standards and then followed as sacrosanct by the community. If drift is normal and teams or individuals operate without standards, then it is hard to call out drift and consequently new baselines are set.

Summary of Key Points

- Human error is around us all the time. We are all fallible. Even the most experienced amongst us. The difference between 'experts' and 'novices' is that the experts will pick up, anticipate, detect and correct small errors before they are anywhere close to a critical failure.
- Different performance levels (Skills-based, Rules-based and Knowledge-based) have different error rates, as well as different reasons why the errors happen.
- In skills-based decisions/performance, it is normally distraction that causes an error to propagate. Therefore, something which keeps the focus in the right place and slows us down when in a critical environment is needed e.g. written checklists which are followed, or team accountability for when verbal checks are used.
- In rules-based decisions/performance, we need to understand why the rule is in place and not just look for confirmatory evidence to prove we are doing the right thing, but to look wider and understand the context.
- During knowledge-based situations, don't be surprised if errors occur. If someone has never been exposed to such a situation before, why would they know what to do? They can resort to a rule-based decision e.g. end the dive, but the circumstances might not allow that e.g. their buddy/guide/instructor won't end the dive and so they have to consciously work out what to do, balancing the competing goals they have.
- If you want to improve system safety, don't just focus on the 'errant human' as that is easy. Rather look at the wider system and 'work as done' and compare it to what 'work as imagined' is. If the rules are being consistently broken, then there is a fair chance that the 'rules' are not fit for purpose. Look at the gaps between work as imagined, work as prescribed, work as disclosed and work as done. If work as disclosed is very close to the work as prescribed, you might not have a Just Culture in place.
- Consider that the term 'human error' can have one of three meanings: error as the 'cause'; error as the failure itself; or error

as a departure from the 'good' process, none of which really help learning!
- If you write 'human error' or 'diver error' in an accident report, the reporting process likely stopped too early or the data wasn't available to conduct any more investigations. In either case, learning is likely to be limited and we will continue to focus on the prevention of outcomes - without understanding the precursors or antecedents to an accident or incident.

Questions to Consider
- Where have you seen 'human error' attributed to a diving incident or accident? Given what you have read above, do you think that term is still valid?
- If you are in an organisation such as a training agency or a dive centre, do you now look at your errant operations with a slightly different view now?
- How are you going to change your personal, dive team or organisational learning, considering these new views?
- In your diving, what is the difference between deviation, drift and innovation?

References
(1) Dekker, S. (2017). *The Field Guide to Understanding 'Human Error'*. 3rd ed. Boca Raton: CRC Press.
(2) Woods, D. D., Johannesen, L. J., Cook, R. I., & Sarter, N. B. (1994). *Behind human error: Cognitive systems, computers and hindsight*. Dayton, OH: CSERIAC.
(3) Denoble, PJ, Caruso, JL, de Dear, GL, Pieper, CF, and Vann, RD, (2008). *Common causes of open-circuit recreational diving fatalities*. Undersea Hyperb Med, 35 (6), 393–406
(4) Olsen, N.S., (2012). *Reliability studies of incident coding systems in high hazard industries: A narrative review of study methodology*. Applied Ergonomics.
(5) Reason, J.T., (1990). *Human Error*. England: Cambridge University Press.
(6) Rasmussen, (1983). *Skills, Rules, and Knowledge; signals, signs, and symbols, and other distinctions in human performance models*.
(7) Hollnagel, E. (1993). *Human Reliability Analysis: Context and Control*. Academic Press.

Additional Reading

CAA (2014) *Flight-crew human factors handbook. CAP 737*. Gatwick: Civil Aviation Authority. www.caa.org

Dekker, S. (2014). *The field guide to understanding "Human Error"*. Boca Raton, FL: CRC Press.

Dörner, D. (1996). *The logic of failure: Recognizing and avoiding error in complex situations*. New York, NY: Metropolitan Books.

Reason, J.T. (1990). *Human Error*. England: Cambridge University Press.

Strauch, B. (2018). *Investigating Human Error: Incidents, accidents and complex systems*. Taylor & Francis.

Chapter 4

Risk and Uncertainty. Why numbers don't mean much when it comes to your risk perception and appetite

"All accidents could be prevented, but only if we had the ability to predict with 100% certainty what the immediate future would hold. We can't do that, so we have to take a gamble on the few probable futures against all the billions of possible futures."

Duncan MacKillop

Case Study: Letting go of the line, or running out of gas?

The following narrative from cave-diving explorer, Steve Boegarts, describes an event where he was exiting from an exploration dive which involved laying line and surveying in a cave system. On his return, he found that the line to the surface wasn't where he expected it and he was faced with a number of uncertainties which had major consequences. As will be clear during this chapter, risk and uncertainty are not the same thing. Risk is measurable; uncertainties are not. What are the probabilities of finding the exit if you let go of the line when you are in zero visibility?

During my exit after a very successful cave exploration dive during which I had emptied all my reels and gathered lots of survey data, I ran into an area of zero visibility.

Puzzled, I moved to touch contact on the line, pushing my scooter in front of me. It quickly became apparent why the visibility was so bad, as the line disappeared into the silt indicating that a tie-off point had broken while I had been diving and buried itself and the line attached to it deep in the silt.

As I moved forward, the line ran at a steep angle down into the silt and within a few meters, my left arm was fully extended holding the line and I was buried up to my left shoulder in the silt, with my head turned all the way to the right to keep my face and the second stage I was breathing from, out of it. I could go no further and pulling on the line I could feel the weight of the stalactite it was attached to, but it was too heavy to pull up and I was also concerned about it breaking.

I decided to backup, deploy my safety spool and find the exit side of the guideline. I marked the line with an arrow just before the point at which it was buried and then reached back to my reels to retrieve my safety spool. I checked all my reels several times, but it was gone.

At this point, I realised Murphy had decided to mess with me for a decision I made more than 3 hours ago, while kitting up at the start of the dive. I knew I was probably going to lay a lot of line and would need to do a lot of survey so decided to take three survey slates with me, all of which I put in my pouch. So, I took my safety spool out to make room for them and clipped it off to my butt D ring with the rest of my reels. At some point during the dive, my safety spool had detached itself and I had not noticed.

I was in zero viz on a guideline, I could not follow without a reel with which to do a lost line search! Swimming away from a guideline in zero viz in the hope of finding the other end of it is not something to be undertaken lightly, but at that point I did not see an alternative course of action and I was confident of my ability to swim in a straight line even with no visual references as I have practiced that skill extensively.

I clipped my scooters off either side of the line arrow I had just placed to act like giant personal markers and also because I didn't want to be swimming blind in zero viz, looking for a line - while pushing one scooter and towing another behind me.

I moved forward slowly sweeping my hand back and forth over the surface of the silt, trying not to disturb it even more while searching for the line.

My first attempt was unsuccessful, and I ran into a wall without finding the exit side. Now I had to turn 180 degrees and very carefully backtrack to my starting point, so that I could try again.

After a little while I ran into another wall which was unexpected and indicated that I was going the wrong way!

At this point my adrenaline spiked, so I took a deep calming breath and tracked to my right slightly. Just at the point where I was starting to think I had gone too far and would not be able to find my way back to the line I had swum away from, I bumped into one of my scooters... hallelujah!

Now that I was back at my starting point, I was able to reorient myself and adjust my search angle to try again. After a tense, slow, blind swim, I found the other end of the guideline where it reappeared from the silt and marked it with a line arrow...fan-bloody-tantastic!

I sat there for a minute checking how much gas I had, and happily, I had plenty of reserves left - so swimming out from that point was no issue.

The obvious lesson from this dive was one that I already knew and had ignored at my peril...keep your safety spool in a pouch or pocket where you are less likely to lose it.

During deco, I realised that I had overlooked another potential solution to my problem. I had several empty exploration reels with me. I could have swum back into the cave a little distance past several tie-offs, then cut the guideline and reeled a section of line back up, as I headed back out to the exit and the buried line, so that I could perform my missing guideline search properly. That would have been far safer than swimming away from the guideline in zero viz, with no line and the possibility of not being able to find my way back to my original starting point - if unsuccessful in my search.

Having found the exit side of the guideline, I would then have had a continuous guideline back to my scooters, so I could have retrieved them easily too, which may have been critical if this incident had happened further back in the cave - where I may not have had sufficient reserve gas to swim out. In hindsight this solution seemed obvious, but in a stressful situation, especially one that has not been considered previously, possible solutions are not always obvious.

Another take home lesson for me was to spend a bit more time considering other potential solutions to problems, rather than just trusting in my abilities and going straight into "action mode".

The stalactite is still buried in the silt with line attached, but the lesson from this day continues to hover over me like the fabled Sword of legend; and it is not a mistake I will repeat again - although I am sure I will make other new ones.

Risk and safety could be considered to be opposite sides of the same coin. More risk has the potential to reduce safety - if the risks are materialised. But they don't mean risky means unsafe!

Steve Bogaert's account highlights the multiple risks or uncertainties faced in diving and sometimes the need to choose between the best of two terrible situations: stay where you are and run out of gas; or choose another option which has the potential to end up in a similarly fatal situation, such as leaving a line in zero vis and hope that you can find a way out. Interestingly, whenever I have recounted Steve's story to others, their immediate reaction is. "Oh no, how could he do that. That's suicide!" I then ask them, "So what would you do?" and their responses are normally the same: "I don't know." They certainly don't think about the option which Steve came up with on his swim home about going back into the cave to cut already laid line.

The ability to deal with uncertainty is a key skill, because it is the fear of the unknown which often creates panic and then a total loss of control. To that end, this chapter will look at risk; risk management and uncertainty; and identifying why the diving community needs to recognise that it is uncertainty we are managing when we go diving, not risk. Risk is measurable, uncertainty is not and the latter is mainly informed by emotion, heuristics and biases; whereas the former can be managed through logic and analysis, if you have data which can be relied upon.

Diving has an irreducible level of risk or uncertainty because, ultimately, we cannot remove the probability of death due to drowning. That is: unless we don't go diving. So, what is the numerical risk of dying while diving? The answer is, unfortunately, 'we don't know'. Organisations such as Divers Alert Network might tell you it is 0.48:100 000[1] dives based on their figures; the figures from the

British Sub Aqua Club are between 0.54 and 1.03:100 000 dives[1]; and the marketing people from agencies might tell you something else. The problem is that risk means different things to different people, especially when we aren't talking about fatalities e.g. a colleague of mine learned to dive in the Caribbean on a cruise liner. Her first open water dive was to 30m/100ft with the aim of seeing sharks. Most people were more worried about the risk of being eaten by a shark, compared to the fact they were over a 100m drop to the bottom and they were beginner divers. She nearly ran out of gas as she was so in awe of the situation she was in.

Risk also means different things when it is presented in a different frame of reference, be that as a relative or an absolute risk. For example, in 1995, there was a scare concerning risks associated with taking 3rd generation contraceptive pills compared to 2nd generation pills. As presented to the General Practitioners and the media, the risk of venous thromboembolism (VT) was doubled. However, the absolute risk had increased from approximately 1 in 7000 to 2 and only 2% of those who suffered from VT died[3]. The unintended consequences meant that the abortion rate rose by 8% (more than 13000 additional abortions); a similar amount of unwanted pregnancies occurred and the cost to the healthcare service was more than £60m[4]. Ironically, the risk of VT is higher in pregnancy than either the 2nd or 3rd generation pill. As risk researcher Gerd Gigerenzer highlights in his book *Risk Savvy*, the community at large doesn't understand the difference between risk and uncertainty and how this impacts our decision-making processes. This can have severe consequences when it comes to high risk sports like diving and how the risks are presented. It also has an impact on instructors who may assume that insurance will cover the underwritten risks materialising during a class, but may not comprehend that there isn't a bottomless pot of money to cover the multitude of claims taking place across the industry. Shared risk, at some point, runs out of money and so premiums must rise.

Language is so important when we look at risk and uncertainty, because they shape attitudes and cultures. Risk aversion, even in the context of safety, is not necessarily a good thing. Individuals and companies that are risk averse tend to limit opportunities for learning and growth. If we consider those that are risk averse in diving: they don't get to see new stuff, even if that is a wreck or cave which has been explored by others, and so they will remain in their comfort zone. Where high levels of risk aversion exist, there will be a limited appetite to learn, progress and innovate, and a tendency to get stuck on "what we know". Risk awareness, however, is a worthy goal and drives an approach that allows us to manage our risks, and make informed and conscious decisions, permitting growth, innovation and forward momentum.

Another point to consider is the language of risk and uncertainty itself and what specific words like 'certainly', 'possibility', 'always', 'frequently', etc. mean. If you visit the Probability Survey website (http://www.probabilitysurvey.com/), you will see what I mean. When I last checked, "Always" doesn't mean 100% certainty to some people; and "Often" had a range of meaning covering 45% to 80% probability; and "Might happen" ranged from 10% to 60%. Not great when you are trying to describe the likelihood of something happening to someone else as part of a brief.

Uncertainty and Risk

The world is not a certain place and as such we cannot guarantee that everything will happen as expected. To manage risks like 'safety of life', reputation and/or finances, domains like aviation and nuclear use probabilistic modelling to determine the likelihood of a failure of a component e.g. Failure Modes Effects Analysis (FMEA) or human decision- making e.g. Human Error Analysis Reporting Tool (HEART). They even undertake 'human-in-the-system' interaction simulations and modelling to understand what the combined 'human-machine' failure rates are likely to be. However, nothing like this exists in diving, and therefore, much of the risk-based decisions made by divers are no more than educated guesses and unfortunately in many cases, these are poorly-educated ones too.

Risk or uncertainty can be a good thing. If we were able to predict what would happen 100% of the time, the diving world would be a pretty boring place and the sport wouldn't likely have same appeal. For a start, cave exploration wouldn't be a challenge as we'd know what was around the corner; wreck identification would be simple; recovering the bell would be easy; consistently knowing where the shoals of fish or sharks were would make it easy for guides to drop you in the right place (but it would also mean the fishermen would remove them from the sea!) However, such certainty would remove much of the fun and excitement of diving. Notwithstanding this, 'HMS Seabed' can be a bit disappointing when it happens too often! As Cameron Russo said when he submitted his narrative to me, *"Exploration is a powerful drug!"*

Risk is often used in a negative context, because we associate it with losses; but risk covers both positive and negative outcomes. At its highest level, risk is defined as the likelihood of an event multiplied by the consequence of the event happening. The consequences can either be positive (gain or success) or negative (loss or failure). The problem in diving is that quality data does not exist which allows us to define likelihood accurately and the spectrum of outcomes can be pretty massive so even if a risk does materialise e.g. uncontrolled rapid ascent, it doesn't mean that DCS or death is a certainty.

As will be shown in the decision-making chapter, many poor decisions are made because of poor perception of the problem, rather than poor execution of an action against a well-perceived problem. Unfortunately for risk management to be done well, we need to look at 2nd and 3rd order interactions i.e. what happens after this immediate decision and the decision after that. This process is not easy and takes effort and time, something not normally applied in a recreational activity.

'Rolling the dice': a false metaphor

In everyday language, there is a distinction made between "certainty" and "risk"; however, the terms "risk" and "uncertainty" are mostly used interchangeably. Unfortunately, they are not equal.

In a world of known risks, everything, including the probabilities, is known for certain e.g. the risk of rolling a six on a fair dice is 1:6, because there are only six possible outcomes. However, due to the variable nature of the rolling, the sides shown on top are not likely to be 1, 2, 3, 4, 5 or 6 on each of six subsequent rolls. It takes a significant number of rolls to get an even distribution and that is only one variable influenced by the environment. The following images show the outcomes of rolls of two dice over 10, 100 and 10,000 rolls. Here we can see that even when we get to 10, 000 rolls of the dice, we don't get an even distribution of the numbers 2-12. Now imagine how many variables go into the risk factors for a dive.

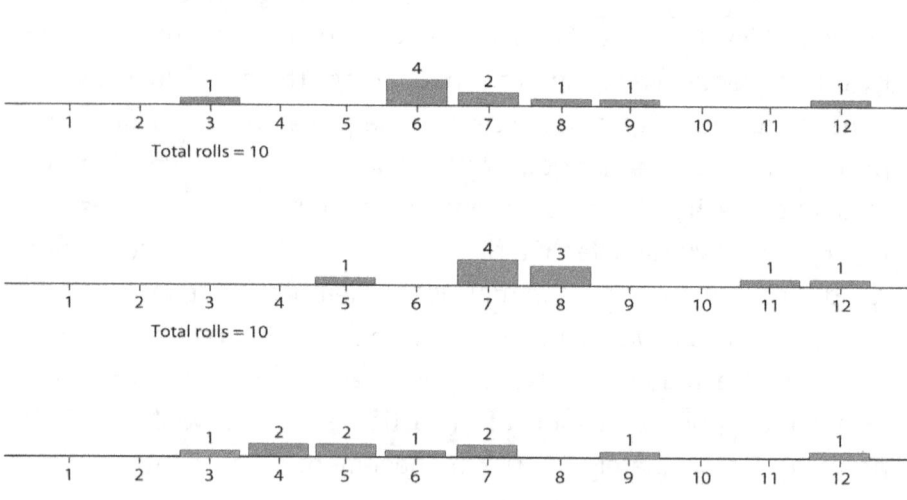

UNDER PRESSURE   Chapter 4

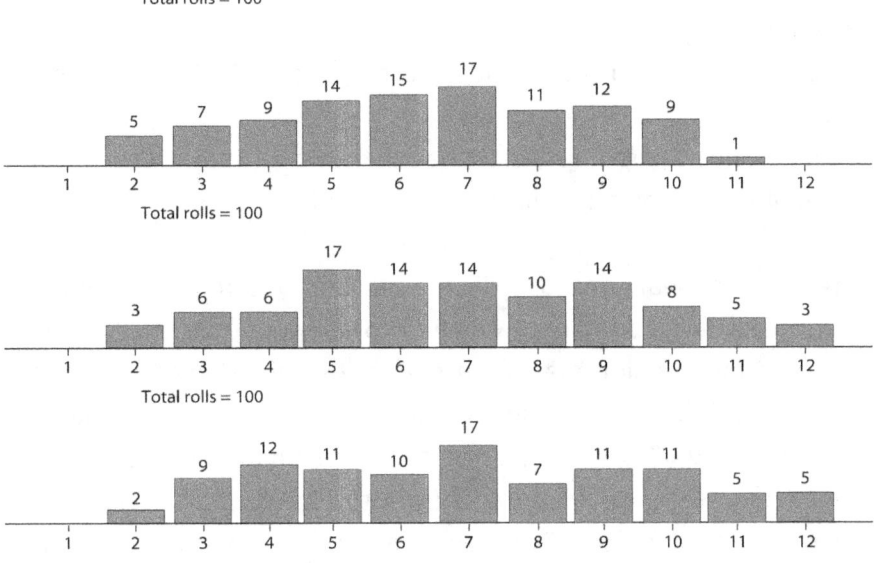

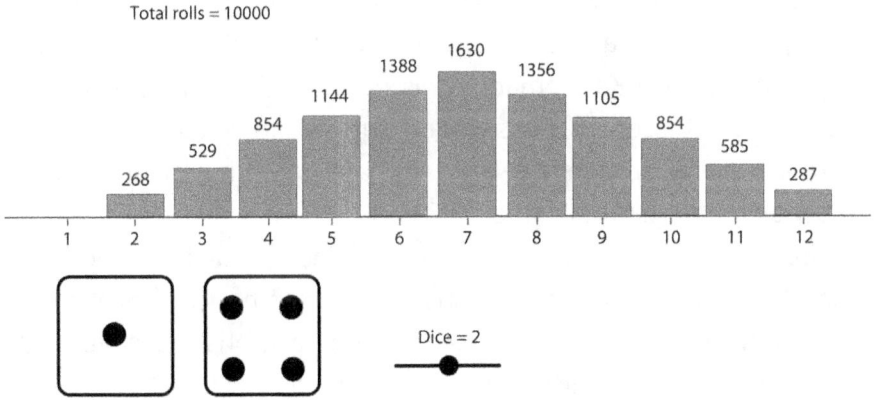

Figure 4: Screenshots from a two-dice simulator showing different distributions based on the number of rolls of the dice

To consider the magnitude of the problem, just looking at decompression factors, Dr Neal Pollock lists 25 in his paper[5] on 'Factors in Decompression Stress'.

In an uncertain world, not everything is known, and one cannot

calculate the best option. As such, when making decisions, Gigerenzer describes two concepts that are required if we are to manage risk and uncertainty effectively:
- Risk: If risks are known, good decisions require logic and statistical thinking.
- Uncertainty: If some risks are unknown, good decisions also require intuition and smart rules of thumb.

One thing is clear, because diving has both 'normal' and dynamic & uncertain environments, we need to use a combination of both concepts for decision-making in diving. As you will see in Chapter 6 (Decision-Making), intuition or subconscious decision-making is used for a significant number of the decisions we make, because we are efficient creatures, minimising the amount of energy spent when making decisions. The good thing is that in many cases, this quick process works out ok and we have a successful outcome. 'Close enough' is often 'Good enough'. However, this intuitive decision-making process is subject to being tricked by cognitive failures and biases, which can lead us to the wrong decision. Nobel prize-winner and author Daniel Kahneman, in his book, *'Thinking. Fast and Slow'*, describes the three situations when intuition can be correct:
- There is regularity in the world you are operating - which means behaviours are predictable.
- You undertake lots of practice - so you know what 'good' looks like and are relying on direct experience and not 'hunches' and finally,
- Immediate feedback is provided for the decisions you have made - so you can learn and adjust for the next time.

Building on both Kahneman and Gigerenzer's comments, 'rules of thumb' come from experience or personal development. For example, in my own diving, I know that when I am diving twin 12-litre cylinders and average breathing rates, for every 10m of depth, the minimum gas required to ascend to the next gas source is 15 bar. So, for a 30m dive, the minimum gas I need is 45 bar (rounded to 50 bar). This is something that I have learned from diving the same configuration in similar depths and similar workloads. The same figures do not apply when operating outside this defined set of parameters.

Hindsight is not too Helpful
Due to hindsight, our previous experiences can cloud judgments of others when recalling an event, forgetting that the diver involved in the unexpected event may not have the same experience(s) as we do. Hindsight bias often shows up with comments like, *"I knew that was going to happen because of X"* or, *"I would have done it this way because..."* This false narrative happens for a couple of reasons. Firstly, the outcome is known, so it is easy to join the dots backwards and apply confirmation bias - finding the answer you were looking for. Secondly, the commentators likely have a different set of experiences and 'rules of thumb' to the person involved in the event, and therefore, have a different set of mental models to compare reality against.

Therefore, we need to consider this following fundamental point when it comes to uncertainty. All actions are in fact gambles on the future state of the system. We do not have a crystal ball to see what the outcome will be. While some of the gambles we take have pretty even odds, and therefore, we are quite certain in their outcomes, they are not 100% certain and consequently don't pay off. Hopefully, as we are in a fit mental and physical state after the event, we can personally learn from those unsuccessful gambles and share the decision-making processes with others, thereby improving their library of mental models to reduce uncertainty.

I will use a driving example to demonstrate managing uncertainty. Imagine being at a junction and turning across the flow of traffic. In the majority of occasions, we don't make a calculated decision about when to pull out into traffic i.e. we don't measure the distance or time between cars. However, when we are learning to drive, we are making a conscious effort to follow 'rules' which we have been taught during our driver training, using other information based, predominately, around the concept of time. However, this conscious effort takes time and effort, which means we are often lagging behind reality and not 'in the flow'. Consequently, we look for 'rules of thumb' to minimise the efforts based on previous experiences. This process is all linked with situational awareness, System 1 and recognition-primed decision-making which will be covered in the chapters six and seven.

Why do divers take risks?

It seems so silly to some that divers would go deep underwater, or a long way back in a cave, or use equipment which isn't perfectly serviceable or with known flaws and faults, and yet they do. What we need to realise is that a risk always comes with rewards and we are trading one for the other. In hindsight, with an adverse outcome, we can see that the risk was potentially not worth the reward, but we don't have crystal balls to forecast the situation.

Some of those risks might appear to be part of the activity e.g. for those playing rugby, impact injuries like a broken collarbone are considered an acceptable risk, or when skiing, there is a risk of a limb or head injury. In both of these cases, the observers are not normally critical of the activity and those who are injured will often talk about what happened. However, in diving, one of the hazards faced is often associated with a stigma and the presence of denial is very real.

That hazard is, of course, DCS. The stigma associated with it was covered in a very well-written article in a 1993 edition of aquaCORPS by researcher Jennifer C. Hunt[6] in which she describes the multiple levels at which DCS can impact us e.g. physical, mental and social and this means, that often, divers don't want to talk about their event. As such, the evidence which divers use to make such risk-based decisions is not necessarily available. However, as we will see, most decisions relating to risk and uncertainty are not made logically.

For example, let's examine a diving scenario - one which will likely be familiar to many of you. You have been blown-out for four weekends in a row and you now have an opportunity to dive this weekend as the weather is fabulous and the visibility has been reported as 10m+. However, you aren't due to dive for another four weeks for a variety of reasons and you can't reschedule. Just as you are getting your gear ready to put on, you notice that you have a malfunction with your gear, something manageable but will cause you additional workload and reduce your margin of safety on the dive, e.g. a leaking 2nd stage on your primary regulator. This is a failure you wouldn't normally accept, because you get to dive lots. If you don't dive, your buddy will have to sit out too, as there isn't anybody else to dive with at such short notice and the tides don't allow sequential solo dives.

At this point, you are managing uncertainty, not risk, because the numbers are not calculable. You decide to dive and nothing adverse happens and you have an awesome dive. Your management of uncertainty was 'good'. But what if two or three other minor issues had happened on the dive and because of your reduced capacity, an out-of-gas situation and rapid ascent occurred. How well do you think your uncertainty management was then? Certainty is only 100% after the event, but we have an illusion of certainty beforehand.

Gigerenzer describes two such kinds of illusion or cognitive failure when it comes to certainty. The first is where we confuse a world of risk with one of certainty; this is known as the 'zero-risk illusion'. In this situation, we believe that when numbers are provided to us about the risks involved, we sometimes believe them as being certain e.g. approximately 1:200,000 dives ends up as a fatality in diving. However, we don't know the time, exposure, experience, depth and the multitude of other variables involved - so how relevant is that risk figure to my diving exposure? We can also have the thought that, *"200,000 is a huge number of dives, way more than I'm ever going to do, so it doesn't apply to me"*.

Another example would be of rebreather controller (and rebreather system) reliability. Many make the assumption that electronics and computers only fail rarely; therefore, rebreathers are really reliable and we can trust them. We don't hear about all of the issues which divers are loath to talk about, having invested thousands of pounds/dollars on something which isn't reliable, especially if it is only intermittent.

In both cases, either because of availability bias (we haven't heard about it, therefore it doesn't happen) or because statistically the numbers are small, we can be lulled into a false sense of security of safety, especially as the diving community isn't great at sharing stories of near-misses and the reasons why they happened.

The second is confusing a world of uncertainty with one of known risk. This has been described as the 'turkey illusion' or calculable-risk illusion. This illusion is based on the rule of succession, developed by the mathematician Pierre-Simon Laplace, and follows that the probability of something happening again is linked to whether it happened n times before. This is written as $P = (n+1)/(n+2)$.

The name 'turkey illusion' is because of the following scenario. Imagine you are the turkey and 'n' is the number of days the farmer feeds you. After the first day, the probability that the farmer will feed you the next day is 2/3, after the second day it increases to 3/4, and so on. As such, you are becoming more and more certain every day that this will continue. At the same time, the alternative, that he might kill you, becomes less and less likely. On day one hundred, it is almost certain the farmer will come to feed you. But unknown to you, that day is the day before Christmas or Thanksgiving. Just when the probability of being fed is higher than ever before, you're are killed.

Think about how this applies to your diving. Success on a previous dive doesn't necessarily guarantee success on subsequent dives; and at the same time, we are doing this for fun and therefore accepting that uncertainty can create some of the thrill (the reward!).

The following narrative from Roger Williams, a Full Cave instructor based in Tulum, Mexico, highlights how the perception of risk, goal-driven behaviours and previous experiences turning out ok, can end up with a very dangerous situation. Note that this isn't a chain of events because they are not linked, but rather multiple factors which combine at the wrong time.

Case Study: Looking before you leap isn't enough
The volcanic rock shore of the south coast of Oahu takes a hell of a beating by the sea, which makes for a dramatic shoreline. As the waves pound the relatively soft rock, they carve sea caves and blowholes that

send spray 50 feet in the air. There are sheer cliffs hundreds of feet tall that plunge 50 feet underwater, littered about with colossal rubble that has been crumbling off the island for a million years. Even the gentlest of waves which come from 7,000 miles of uninterrupted expanse of ocean breaking against this coast, are a demonstration of an unstoppable force meeting an immovable object. So occasionally, driving past the enormous natural jetty on a flat day, one needs to make the snap decision, "We're diving here TODAY!"

On one such day, a few friends and I made that decision. We rushed to the dive shop where we worked to collect our gear, and back to the Lookout to start the long hike down to the water.

The parking lot is about 200 feet above the entry point in terms of elevation. One must gear up completely; walk along the shoulder of the highway that cuts around the south side of the island for about a 1/4 mile; then cross the road from ocean-side to mountain-side. There you 'leg over' a jersey rail, so that you can shuffle down a 30 foot ravine, at the bottom of which is a low, narrow foot tunnel that crosses back under the highway. The tunnel opens to some rock-faces that require a bit of careful foot placement as you scale down to a wide flat, dappled with shallow tide pools filled with juvenile reef fish and cowries.

When you are finished picking your way across the algae-slick rocks and getting buffeted with sea-spray, you find yourself on a small spit of rock looking down about 10 feet to the water. Here you stand, fins in hand (for there is nowhere to safely put your fins on without falling on the sharp, slippery rock), check that your wing is empty, and wait...

... watching the waves...

... timing a set...

... watching for juuuuuust before the third wave of a large set is about to crash into the jagged precipice below you...

... and jump!

The wave should crash as you are in midair, then pull you safely away from the cliff as it recedes, and you immediately start sinking with your negative entry.

Thirty feet below the surface, there is a wide, placid, sandy patch where you can don fins, establish buoyancy, await your buddies, and begin to *enjoy the dive to which you have committed.*

Yes: committed. There is no exit near the entry, much less an emergency extraction point. Even if one swims hell-for-leather for the exit, you are underwater for a solid 1/2 hour from entry to where you can safely surface and climb to dry land again.

The entire hike takes about 1/2 hour and is quite tiring. Which is why, when we finally made it to the water's edge on this day and the seas had picked up a bit, we decided to jump. Despite the fact that neither of my companions had been there before, the waves were only just barely on the wrong side of diveable, and the long trek back up seemed more daunting then just a short moment's short drop to the sea. They were both excellent, long-experienced dive professionals and it's just a single jump. We talked about it for a few minutes and in the end, they deferred to me to make the call; in my laziness I said, "Let's go for it."

I was to go first. So, there I stood, fins in my right hand, holding my mask and reg to my face with my left, watching the waves. As a good one came, I jumped.

Sinking. Sinking. Sinking. I started to don my left fin on the way down. 10 feet underwater I made my first inhale... against nothing. Instantly I realised: as we were discussing whether or not we should actually make the dive given the change in conditions, I got distracted from my usual routine of running through a normal pre-dive buddy check... or remembering to reach back and turn on my tank.

15 feet deep.

I gave up on the left fin. I needed my right hand. Crossed fins to my left hand and tried for the right fin. Right hand went to my valve... which I was thrilled to discover was sticky; a recreational shop rental tank, overtightened to prevent leaks. Kicking for the surface with my still-unfinned left foot.

10 feet.

Still no give of the valve. Still no fin.

5 feet.

It actually occurred to me, then and there, that this moment would probably kill most divers.

No buoyancy. No inflation. No fins. No exit. No air in my lungs. Nothing to fill them.

It did not occur to me that I was going to die, but that someone else might. I have talked to enough people who have survived near-misses to know that a common experience in this moment is to think, "This is where I die," but that is not what I was thinking.

While I wear no ditchable weight with my 12lbs backplate and single loop webbing, I was already thinking, "Worst case scenario, I can deploy a z-knife and cut the harness off in seconds."

I don't think that this makes me particularly bad-ass or that it makes me hard to kill or anything of the like. In that moment I was really annoyed at myself and realised that I REALLY needed to focus on working through the problem in front of me.

It didn't come to cutting anything. Even using incredibly inefficient propulsion, I breached the surface in what felt like minutes, but was only about 10 seconds. Just as I took a breath the tank valve finally opened, and my right fin slid onto my foot.

"Hey!" I called up to my two companions, who were still on the rocks, now looking, confused, down at the sea-foam around this unexpected spectacle, "Make sure your air is on!"

There is only one true emergency in scuba diving, and there wasn't much more advice I could give from where I was.

I put on my other fin as I descended out of the now more immediate danger of the roaring surf... but watched upwards like a hawk, ready to render aid in case the day wanted to continue to cascade. I watched as my one, then other buddy, burst down above me into the sea and gently descended to meet me, completely without incident.

We went for a lovely, peaceful dive. I explained what had happened during the long, steep slog back up the cliffs to the car afterwards.

I have never once forgotten to take two breaths from my primary and my secondary regulator each before splashing ever again.

Roger's account includes many cognitive biases but, most of all, it demonstrates clearly the balance between what had already been invested (time and effort) and the opportunity to get something rewarding (a rare dive at this location). Researchers Kahneman and Tversky, in their work on Prospect Theory, showed that when we are in a losing situation, we are willing to take a gamble on a little more loss - rather than a definite small loss. In this case, jumping in with marginal conditions (small loss and 'should be okay') compared to a definite psychological loss of hiking back up the hill in the heat knowing that you've missed a rare dive opportunity.

Prospect Theory and why Dealing with Risk/Uncertainty is not Simple

Many of the options we face in diving are "mixed": there is a risk of loss and an opportunity for gain. A constant tension between goals, resources and safety. Furthermore, because time is marching on, we must decide whether to accept the gamble (we cannot determine with certainty an outcome, therefore it is a gamble) or reject it - in a period of time which is often perceived to be too short to make a logical decision.

For example, you are offered a gamble on the toss of a coin.
- If the coin shows tails, you lose $100.
- If the coin shows heads, you win $150.
  Would you accept this gamble?

Most people would say, 'No', because the psychological loss is perceived as greater than the gain.[5] It is possible to determine where your own threshold is by looking at the smallest gain you would be willing to have, compared to a loss of something like $100. Kahneman and Tverskey showed[7] that on average it is about $200, with the range being approximately $150-$250. Therefore, on average, we need about 1.5-2.5x the perceived benefit, before we will even consider the taking the risk/gamble.

An interesting aspect of this is the importance of the baseline or

---

[5] Ironically, the research shows we are more afraid of psychological pain because we don't believe physical pain will hurt that much, and besides, it won't happen to me!

centre-point of the gamble. This is especially the case when it comes to losses. Consider a 50:50 gamble in which you could lose $10. What is the smallest gain that makes the gamble attractive to you? If you respond with a value less than $10, you are risk-seeking (in the financial domain).[6] If it is above $10, you are considered risk-averse in the financial domain.

What about if the odds were raised? Does your decision-making process change? What if we were talking about winning/losing $500 on the flip of a coin? Or a $2000 gamble? At some point, the gamble is just not worth it, even if it was millions. It is important to recognise that it is the centre-point or baseline for such gambles which influences the perceived psychological loss or gain. If you have millions of dollars, losing $2000 means very little compared to someone who has little. Consequently, someone who dives a lot doesn't mind missing the occasional dive; but someone who doesn't dive very often, will push the risk boundary if they think they will miss out on a dive.

Kahneman and Tversky produced a graphical model which looks at this relationship and the gradient of the curve is an important feature of this model. At the centre-point, the loss gradient is steeper than the gain gradient which means the impact of a psychological loss is greater than a gain. However, as you move further from the centre-point, the impact of loss/gain gets less and less. A full explanation of Prospect Theory can be found on the Wikipedia page (https://en.wikipedia.org/wiki/Prospect_theory).

This is why in the hypothetical example above, where a last-minute equipment failure would mean losing the dive for you and your buddy, the risk of a definite loss of the dive has a larger impact on the decision, than the 'maybe' having an issue with the equipment causing a major problem underwater. However, in both Roger Williams' example and the one immediately above, if this was a situation where the divers had been diving every day for the last 6 months and they potentially lost this dive, it wouldn't mean much to them, and so thumbing it would have likely been easier.

---

6 Domain-Specific Risk-Taking (DOSPERT) scale is a psychometric scale that assesses risk taking in five content domains: financial decisions (separately for investing versus gambling); health/safety; recreational; ethical; and social decisions.

Summary of Key Points

- Risk perception and acceptance are both personal and dynamic. This means that a risk which is acceptable to one person is unacceptable to another. Furthermore, a risk which was previously acceptable might not be acceptable now. Perception and acceptance are based on experience, environment and emotion.
- Risk is at 100% for 100% of the time. All risks are in the future, and as everything in the future is possible (unless it is impossible), we are faced with the fact that there is a 100% possibility that a particular (unwanted) event will happen. We use mental biases to assess the probability/possibility trade-off, by ignoring the 100% possibility of an unwanted event occurring and relying on the less-than-100% probability of it not happening.
- Risk savviness can be learned - but it requires an open and candid feedback loop to be effective.
- Risk and uncertainty are different. Most diving is based around uncertainty - and not risk.
- Risks in predictable stable environments can be modelled and managed - but most diving exists in the uncertain domain so cannot be quantified. As such it means that that mental shortcuts and heuristics are used in most situations in diving. These can be flawed.
- Standardisation (equipment and processes) and breaking tasks into chunks means that the uncertainty and risk present in complex environments can be better managed. This includes variations from the plan and likely contingencies. Both of which are relatively predictable in outcome but not necessarily in time, and as consequence we can reduce uncertainty.
- Prospect theory means that in mixed gambles, with the option to win or lose, loss-aversion means we are risk-averse; and where a sure loss is compared to a larger loss that is merely probable, risk-seeking is caused by diminishing returns.

Questions to consider
- Do you know the difference between risk and uncertainty when it comes to your own personal or team diving? What about dive operation within a/your dive centre?
- What are you going to do differently when it comes to dealing with uncertainty in your diving, training courses as an instructor or your dive operation?
- Do you know where your risk (uncertainty) threshold is when it comes to diving? How does this relate to your other domains like finance, health or education? Are you risk-seeking in one, but not another?

References
(1) Vann, Richard D and Lang, Micheal A (eds.) (2011) *Recreational Diving Fatalities Workshop Proceedings*, Durham, NC, DAN.
(2) *ibid*.
(3) *Third generation oral contraceptives-- the controversy*. BMJ. 1995; 311 :1589
(4) Furedi, A. *The public health implications of the 1995 'pill scare'*. Hum Reprod Update. 1999 Nov-Dec;5(6):621-6
(5) Pollock NW. Factors in decompression stress. In: Pollock NW, Sellers SH, Godfrey JM, eds. *Rebreathers and Scientific Diving. Proceedings of NPS/NOAA/DAN/AAUS June 16-19, 2015, Workshop*. Wrigley Marine Science Center, Catalina Island, CA; 2016; 145-56.
(6) Hunt, J. *Straightening out the Bends. The Stigma Associated with being Bent*. https://www.thehumandiver.com/pages/straightening-out-the-bends-the-stigma-associated-with-being-bent retrieved 8 Dec 2018
(7) Kahneman, Daniel. *Thinking, Fast and Slow* (Kindle Locations 4846-4849). Farrar, Straus and Giroux. Kindle Edition.

Additional Reading
Adams, J. (2009). *Risk*. London: Routledge.
Craig, P. A. (2013). *The Killing Zone: How and Why Pilots Die*.
Gigerenzer, G. (2015). *Risk Savvy: How to make good decisions*.
Muschara, T. (2018). *Risk-based thinking: Managing the uncertainty of human error in operations*. New York: Routledge, Taylor & Francis Group.

Chapter 5

Psychological Safety and a Just Culture: the route to improving learning

"The question that drives safety work in a Just Culture is not who is responsible for failure, rather, it asks what is responsible for things going wrong. What is the set of engineered and organised circumstances that is responsible for putting people in a position where they end up doing things that go wrong?"

Sidney Dekker

Jill Heinerth is a well-known cave explorer and wreck diver. The narrative she submitted talks about a dive in which her pre-dive and in-dive behaviours, of focusing on detail and making sure things are how they are supposed to be, were shaped during her formative years of diving education. It would be interesting to know how many instructors consider undertaking such psychological tests during their training delivery, to check both understanding and also to demonstrate the need to speak up when things are not going to plan or to step outside the expected norms.

Case Study: The courage to speak up is essential

As a young diver in the late 1980s, I sought out mentors to guide me through more advanced experiences in diving. I was working toward becoming a PADI Instructor, but there were no sanctioned courses to satisfy my appetite for what we now call technical diving. A few people in Canada were quietly mixing exotic gases in their garages, but the local shops decried decompression diving and pretty much anything beyond recreational limits. Fortunately, I found an instructor who was willing to teach a class in what he termed Advanced Wreck Diving. We would not receive a certification or recognition. There was no formally recognised synopsis, but we were promised an opportunity to grow our experience in deeper diving and decompression. I credit my instructor, Dale McKnight, for offering some very important lessons and role model behaviour that set me on a good course in my diving life.

Our course began in Tobermory, Ontario, the underwater Mecca that attracts thousands of divers a year to experience intact wooden shipwrecks in the cold fresh water of Lake Huron. After a long day of lectures and land drills with reels, we set off on a night dive inside a shallow wreck. We practiced running lines and doing blackout drills. Dale probably chuckled as we got ourselves completely entangled in the poorly-laid line. I recalled dives approaching two hours in the near-freezing late fall water temperatures. I knew he was testing us both physically and psychologically. As we worked in teams, he was learning about how we attacked problems and how we were affected by others in the group.

On our graduation weekend, we planned a dive to a wreck called the Forest City. It would be my first decompression, and my deepest dive to date. The planned dive would take us to 120 feet and would accumulate a whopping five minutes of decompression time. We carefully cut our tables and prepared equipment for an entire day, before checking the weather forecast and determining that we were ready to dive. We pre-visualised the dive and talked through all the possible things that could go wrong. We were diving on air with air for decompression. It was all we had to work with in those days. We knew we would be narced, and planned to do some skills at depth to demonstrate our ability to deal with the fogginess.

I was decidedly nervous as we headed out on the boat toward the dive site on Bear's Rump Island. I had checked my tanks and pony bottle; reset my bottom timer and backup depth gauge; and then looked at my tables one last time. I pre-visualised the landmarks of the dive and memorised the stops. Some of my teammates seemed a lot less nervous and more amped-up with adrenaline. I recall it bothering me a bit. It did not seem like the right time for celebration. We could do that when we all returned to the boat safely.

Dale gave us a last-minute briefing on our way out to the wreck, and that was when he surprised me. "You guys have all done so well in this course that I am going to offer you a special treat!" He said. "We've all prepared our Surface Air Consumption (SAC) rate calculations and have enough gas to go ten feet deeper and add five minutes to the bottom time. We can go into the open hatch at the bottom of the wreck. It is amazing to see! Recalculate your tables. You'll have to do some more deco, but it'll be no problem." He offered with excitement. My teammates let out a "whoop" of excitement and quickly turned to their manuals to find some new tables. They were jazzed about being given a longer leash.

For me, it was a completely different feeling. I had worked hard and made a solid plan that I was ready to execute. I was not prepared to implement this new plan. With only ten minutes to reach the dive site, things were happening too fast for me. I wanted to be a part of the excitement, but suddenly, I felt this horrible feeling of impending doom. I desperately wanted to be accepted by the group of diving friends and wanted to receive the praise of my mentor, but I started getting worried. Dale picked up on my discomfort and asked what was wrong.

"I just don't feel like I can do this dive Dale," I offered meekly. "I rehearsed something else, and frankly, I think this new plan is too much for me." I felt deflated and weak. My colleagues listened and tried to show me how we had plenty of gas based on our calculations. They were pressuring me to dive. "It's not that I don't feel that I have enough physical resources," I added. "I don't feel mentally ready to change the plan. I am going to sit out the dive. You have fun." Dale patted me on the back, even though I felt almost humiliated by backing out - when everyone else was so excited. I would sit on the boat while they all had fun, but I felt more like crawling under a bench from embarrassment for being so weak and incapable.

As the rest of the team continued to get dressed for the dive, I watched and tried to help out. Dale asked everyone else how they felt about the new plan and one by one they replied with "hoorahs" and hype about how awesome the dive would be. He let them get to the point of being fully dressed when he switched things up again. Ready to jump and standing on the transom, the first diver asked for permission to dive. Dale said,

"No."

Everyone was called together and told to sit down. Despite the fact we had all paid for a charter and endured an hour-long boat ride, nobody was going to dive. Dale then opened up a dialogue for a stern debriefing. One by one, he questioned why each was willing to accept a last-minute change in the dive plan. Everyone felt that it was no big deal and that they were ready and capable of diving. I thought he had recalled everyone because I was sitting out the dive. I was feeling more and more embarrassed with every moment that passed and started recognising bitter stares from my colleagues. I think they perceived they were missing the dive because of me.

It was then that my mentor offered up the most important lesson of my diving career. He said, "Jill is the only person who should go diving today - because she was the only one wise enough to stick to the plan. I wouldn't dive with any of the rest of you today."

It was like waking up from a depressive stupor. I thought Dale was going to blame me for cancelling everyone's dive - but suddenly I realised that he was patting me on the back for having discipline. He was rewarding me for good behaviour, not denigrating me for being a wimp.

We all ended up diving together that day, on the original plan. I completed my first decompression dive and the deepest of my short career. I must have checked my gauge 50 times because of the narcosis, but everything went well. I performed the skills, but more importantly, I took home a safety ethic that has served me well for over thirty years. Plan the dive and dive the plan.

Jill Heinerth's account from early in her diving career shows two elements. Firstly, the courage to speak up when they weren't happy, despite the possibility (almost certainty) that she wouldn't complete the dive and hence the course, thereby losing something which had taken a significant investment to develop. Secondly, it showed that Dale had created an environment, despite all the bravado from the other divers on the course, for Jill to be able to speak up and challenge the situation, because they believed in themselves that something wasn't right. This is psychological safety. Psychological safety is slightly different from trust though. Trust could be considered as *'Will I give others the benefit of the doubt when I take a risk?'* whereas psychological safety could be thought of as *'Will others give you the benefit of the doubt when you take a risk?'*

This chapter will look at two social environments in which learning can be improved. The first is psychological safety which primarily relates to a team or at the organisational level; and secondly, a Just Culture which also applies to the team environment, but also extends to a much wider audience, from specific diving to the whole diving industry.

Psychological safety is important, because when an individual's sense of belonging is threatened, fear reduces the brain's capabilities to deal with both the perception and processing of information. This leads to decreased situational awareness, reduced emotional intelligence leading to dysfunctional individual and team performance, and diminished decision-making capabilities - not something that you want to happen in a non-life sustaining environment.

What is Psychological Safety?

Amy Edmondson, a professor at Harvard and globally-recognised expert on psychological safety, defines team psychological safety[1] as, *'a shared belief that the team is safe for interpersonal risk-taking. For the most part, this belief tends to be tacit-taken for granted and not given direct attention either by individuals or by the team as a whole.'* For example, when a challenge to someone in the team needs to happen, the challenging team member runs a mental calculation whereby they weigh up the benefits of speaking up versus the longer-term consequences of not doing so.

As will be shown in detail in Chapter 9, the most effective teams are those which are psychologically safe. On those teams, team members feel acceptance, mutual respect and trust which means that issues can be raised in an OK:OK manner,[7] where conversations

---
7 Transactional Analysis term to describe the situation where both parties are looking for a positive outcome rather than, 'I'm okay, you're not', or 'You're okay, I'm not' or 'Neither of us are okay.'

are constructive, even if conflict is present.

You might wonder why psychological safety is so important in diving? How many events can you think of personally that could have been prevented if those all-important questions or challenges could have taken place? Think about the scenarios in this book. I know that there are a couple of narratives which are anonymous (and this is because the contributors felt there was enough social pressure without having to talk about their own failures), but the majority are named - that is because the contributors trusted me to use the events as learning opportunities for others and not tear them apart. That trust has taken time to develop - years in fact.

So, when you read the narratives in this book, think about how easy it would be for students, team members or others at a dive site to speak up about something similar happening. Jamie's narrative highlighted this self-centred approach and through reflection and discussing the event, realised that it was his attitude that he must change if the team were to operate effectively and take more informed risks.

How to Create Psychological Safety in your Team/Organisation?

The following is taken from research and practice in organisations, where they have developed a psychologically-safe environment. While it is from the corporate sector, as with many concepts concerning human performance, it is directly applicable to team diving and instructional scenarios.

Don't approach conflict with an adversarial perspective, think collaboration. We hate to lose more than we love to win, especially if that loss is psychological. A perceived loss triggers a feeling that we achieve resolution through competition, criticism, or disengagement. Success is based on win:win or OK:OK outcomes, so when conflicts come up, avoid triggering a fight-or-flight reaction by asking, *"How could we achieve a mutually desirable outcome?"*

Practice being human. The outputs of a blame culture are superficial, but beneath them there are personal, psychological needs where we want to be recognised as being competent, have values, have autonomy and are respected. If we recognise these psychological needs through positive action, then we naturally build trust and facilitate positive language and behaviours. So, whenever you are in a confrontational situation and the other's perspective is different to yours, remember that they are human, just like you.
- Just like you, this person has beliefs, perspectives and opinions.
- Just like you, this person has hopes, anxieties and vulnerabilities.
- Just like you, this person wants to feel respected, appreciated and competent.
- Just like you, this person wishes for peace, joy and happiness.

Anticipate the responses. Directly confront difficult conversations by anticipating likely reactions. To do this, you will need to collect evidence to understand others' perspectives. Don't make an assumption that your position is correct. You do this by putting yourself in others' positions and understanding their viewpoint. You are now better placed to respond from a win:win position.

Swap blame for curiosity. If team-members/students sense that you are trying to blame them, they will close up because they see you as a threat. Psychologist John Gottman's research at the University of Washington[2] shows that blame and criticism reliably escalate conflict, leading to defensiveness and — eventually — to disengagement. To change this, we need to swap blame for curiosity. If you believe you already know what the other person is thinking, then you're not going to have much of a conversation! Instead, adopt a curious and learning mindset, knowing you don't have all the facts. Professor Amy Edmondson, a world-leading expert on psychological safety, describes exactly this point in her book, *'Teaming'*, where leaders explain that they don't have the solution and want to use the experience and knowledge of the team and so ask the team for ideas.

Ask for feedback. Feedback comes in two forms. Firstly, asking the team/students how they perceived the message, how could it be improved and how they felt when they heard the message. Secondly, regularly asking questions like, *'How confident are you that you won't receive retaliation or criticism if you admit an error or make a mistake?'* gives you an indication as to a metric of psychological safety within your team/organisation.

If you create this sense of psychological safety within your own team, instructional set-up or organisation, you will see higher levels of engagement; increased motivation to tackle difficult problems; improved learning; and ultimately better performance which leads to increased safety.

Case Study: Easy to judge after the event?

Marc Crane is a very experienced technical and rebreather instructor. However, as will be shown in his narrative, experience can lead to complacency - when a small thing leads to a situation which rapidly spirals out of control. The speed by which things can deviate from, 'normal and in control' to dangerous situations is surprising to most people. The difference between the real situation and those of *'armchair quarterbacks'* - who know what the outcome will be, which makes it so easy to judge a situation after an event. As Sir Anthony Hidden QC said in summing up his report[3] to the Clapham Junction crash inquiry in which 35 people were killed and 484 people injured, *"There is almost no human action or decision that cannot be made to look flawed and less sensible in the misleading light of hindsight. It is essential that the critic should keep himself constantly aware of the fact".*

The student diver was qualified as a 60m trimix (normoxic) CCR diver and had spent the previous four days on skills development, multiple stage handling increasing comfort and awareness with a maximum depth of 55m. This dive was planned as remedial training after we made the decision not to progress with the original course, as the student was not considered ready for the full course.

The objective of the dive was to conduct a dive to the diver's current maximum certification depth of 60m with a catastrophic emergency scenario. The student was using a used CCR which had had non-critical failures and incidents in the previous days. They were carrying three S80 (11ltr) bailout stages. I was diving my rebreather and also had 3 stages. My deep bailout was only partially filled and the intermediate bailout stages for both of us were only partially filled too. The student was carrying this stage primarily for handling/management purposes, rather than to use it to breathe from on the dive.

Initial in-water check and descent to 6m were non-eventful. On arrival at the bottom, a relatively simple (unbriefed) incident occurred with the student's CCR which they dealt with, but they remained in a slightly flustered and apprehensive manner. In hindsight, the instructor should have confirmed that the student wanted to continue with the skill.

The objective of the scenario was to simulate a catastrophic gas freeflow of oxygen (O2) into the CCR's breathing loop due to the solenoid being stuck open.

The student's initial response was mostly correct, but they neglected to isolate the oxygen cylinder - allowing a large amount of oxygen to be injected into the breathing loop. This caused primary alarms on the CCR to activate. The diver had bailed out to their onboard diluent cylinder at this stage using the bailout valve. They were trying to bring the breathing loop pO2 down by flushing the loop with diluent. All the while, stress and respiration levels were increasing as we were at 60m.

As the student switched back to their loop from the bailout valve, the pO2 once again spiked rapidly to extremely high levels. The student immediately switched over to their deep bailout stage with a high ventilation rate and signalled to me to abort the dive. At this stage, the 3-litre diluent cylinder on their CCR was nearly completely depleted and this was likely to cause more problems - as it was also the source of inflation gas for the student's wing.

Due to the student's elevated stress levels, their respiratory rate was spiralling out of control and this meant that the gas pressure in the deep bailout was becoming critical. As such, I initiated an ascent and prepared to donate my regulator from my partially-filled deep bailout cylinder. With one nearly empty bailout cylinder, a partially filled bail out tank and a large amount of expanding gas volume in the student's closed breathing loop, the ascent speed was becoming increasingly difficult to manage.

I regained my ascent speed by venting excess loop volume as well as dumping the gas from my wing. We paused at 30m to regain some control of the ascent. The student, who was still breathing heavily, had nearly used all gas in my remaining bottom mix cylinder, now tried to switch to their deco mix cylinder of Nitrox 50%! This had a pO2 2 bar at this depth. I quickly stepped in and donated my intermediate gas (Nitrox 32%) from another partially filled cylinder. The decompression overhead meant that a direct ascent to 21m was not possible and with the intermediate gas also starting to run low, we were forced to try and recover the functioning, but discarded, breathing loop. I opted to donate my onboard gas supply hose to the student to facilitate a diluent flush to bring the pO2 down to a safe level. After completing the flush, the alarms stopped and the controller was visually checked to confirm that the loop pO2 was safe to breath and the diver returned to the loop to complete required decompression during the remainder of the ascent.

What I learned from this.
- Never dive partially filled cylinders, even when you think you won't need them. Gas on the surface is as useful as runway tarmac behind you when you come in to land.
- Certification does not mean proficiency -, more skills development must be conducted in shallow water with no to very little deco obligation. You achieve competency through regular training sessions and build-up dives are completed prior to big dives.
- Complacency - due to one team member diving regularly and aware of environment and equipment, with the other diver just following ('trust me' dive attitude) - even though they were probably not ready for this dive.
- Regularly service and check gear and only dive when system is working 100%

It would be easy to say that the issues which occurred on Marc's instructional dive could have been prevented, because of all of the reasons which he cited above. However, hindsight is more than

20:20, because we can see how the interactions within the system (equipment, training, experience and environment, etc) can come together in a manner which precipitates an incident. If this dive had gone a little bit differently, it could have easily ended up as a fatality and an investigation would have likely highlighted all the deficiencies in the plan and the execution. Furthermore, if this had been a fatality and it had happened in the US, an attorney would likely focus on the negative aspects, rather than the positive side of the incident recovery and problem-solving in a dynamic situation. Even if it hadn't happened in the US, the social media pundits would have picked up their metaphorical rocks and started throwing them at Marc for 'not knowing better' and judging them without understanding the situation that was faced.

That doesn't mean that Marc isn't accountable for the situation which developed. He has given his account. He has told his story and I am sure that this situation won't occur in the same manner. But if he hadn't told his story with as much context as he did, would someone else been able to learn from it?

One key to the successful implementation of safety regulation is to attain a reporting environment influenced by a Just Culture. This, to a certain extent, has been achieved within aviation organisations, regulators and investigation authorities, because they recognise the value of open learning; but it is influenced by how those organisations handle blame and punishment.

What is a Just Culture?
A Just Culture is defined by James Reason[4] as, *"An atmosphere of trust in which people are encouraged (even rewarded) for providing essential safety-related information, but in which they are also clear about where the line must be drawn between acceptable and unacceptable behaviour."*

This isn't about being a 'no-blame culture', despite what many think, because at some point you need to take responsibility for your actions. However, as you'll see from Chapter 11 (Performance-Shaping Factors), there are many situations in which error-producing conditions win the battle between efficiency and thoroughness, between risk and safety, between being able to do what you want to do and being able to afford to be able to do it, and as such, it is easy to blame without even realising it.

In Chapter 3 we saw that Human Error can be broken down into four main areas:
- slips of action (action not intended);
- lapses of memory (forgetting to do something);
- mistakes (doing the wrong thing, thinking it is right); and
- violations (where there is perceived to be an intention to break the rules).

Violations, at-risk behaviours or non-compliance can also be broken down into a number of different sub-sets too:
- unintended (thinking they are following the rules but weren't);
- situational (where the risk associated with rule adherence is greater than doing something else);
- routine (where it is the social norm to do so);
- recklessness (where no thought or care given to consequence).

Interestingly from the safety research in high-risk industries, the prevalence of recklessness, gross negligence and sabotage is pretty rare and most workers are doing the best they can with the resources that they have and are balancing competing goals of time/costs/workload. Consequently, even violations, or 'at risk' behaviours, can be used to improve learning within the organisation or group, because there is a reason why people 'break the rules'. Within diving, it is little more difficult to determine where the line between acceptable and unacceptable behaviour lies, because the difference between compliance and rule-breaking is based around an acceptance of increased risk - a level which can't easily be quantified, and within the variability of what the 'rules' say.

Unfortunately, as Sidney Dekker[5] has said in numerous commentaries, it isn't so much where the line is drawn between acceptable and unacceptable behaviour, but rather who draws it that is more important. In diving, who draws the line is often done in the social media arena for non-fatal incidents (and fatalities in some cases), where 'armchair quarter-backs' scrutinise and post comment without 100% certainty of the outcome and without the full context of those involved, in addition to the lawyers involved in litigation cases when it comes to serious injuries and fatalities. Neither of these parties are particularly constructive when it comes to learning.

Unfortunately, as Professor Nancy Leveson, a world expert on Systems Thinking, wrote in a presentation[5] for Massachusetts Institute of Technology on accident investigations,*"blame is the enemy of safety"*. She goes on in another paper to state[6] that,*"There are usually two reasons for conducting an accident investigation: (1) to assign blame for the loss or (2) to understand why it happened so that future accidents can be prevented. When the goal is to assign blame, the backward chain of events considered often stops when someone or something appropriate to blame is found...But the selected initiating event in the proximal event chain usually provides too superficial an explanation of why the accident occurred to prevent similar incidents in the future. In addition, for a variety of reasons (beyond the scope of this report), blame is usually assigned to operators and not to management or organizational and cultural flaws. A final limitation of focusing on blame, as a goal of the accident investigation process, is that the investigation process is hindered as those on whom blame may be placed, are unlikely to be forthcoming and honest about their possible role in the loss events."*

Why is a Just Culture so Important in Diving?

We should consider that the question that drives activities to improve safety when we operate inside a Just Culture is not *'who is responsible for failure'*, but rather, *'what is responsible for things going wrong'*. Even, 'Why did you do that?' infers a level of judgement which can lead to a defensive response. We are trying to find out what is the set of prescribed and organised circumstances that lead to people being in a position where they end up doing things that go wrong? Remember, divers don't get up in the morning and decide, 'Today is a great day to die!' (or get bent or injured...); their behaviour, as you'll see in Chapter 11, is a function of the person and the environment they are in.

If we look at the behaviours (errors and violations), we need to discriminate between the 'good faith' behaviours and the 'bad faith' behaviours. These latter behaviours (violations for personal gain, gross negligence and sabotage) are the focus of legal scrutiny and it is through this process that individuals are held to account. The former, 'good faith' behaviours, are focused on slips, lapses, mistakes and situational or routine violations, and the pressures/drivers that lead us to take greater risks. As such, they should be examined in the context of learning opportunities to improve the system - the results from here should not be used to punish people otherwise trust will be lost.

If we have a Just Culture in place, during the investigation (or discussions), we will start to hear context-rich stories which allow us to hear what those drivers were; what pressures they were under; what the level of skills and knowledge were and whether they were suitable for the task at hand (bearing in mind that diver training is pretty limited when it comes to developing experience); and ultimately how it made sense to do what they did. This might include why rules, guidelines or standard operating procedures weren't complied with. It is for this reason that I am not a great fan of learning from fatalities. In the majority of cases, we know what the proximal cause of death was, in time and location, but we aren't able to determine the local rationality of the situation, in effect, the sense-making. We won't know what cues, clues and drivers were missing to prevent the event from happening in the way it did.

Once we have the context-rich stories, we are able to undertake an in-depth analysis to find out why the event happened in the way it did. We should not just stop at attributing 'human error', but look much deeper. Was the equipment poorly designed and tested? Was the training inadequate? Was there a distraction? Was the checklist poorly-framed for the environment in which it was used? And so on. The term 'human error' is only of use if you want to aggregate up, but adds nothing when it comes to learning within the community.

Furthermore, we shouldn't stop looking once we have found a rule that was broken, or guidance ignored, because most people will know that such events happen and the likely reason for 'the final straw that broke the camel's back' (see Work as Imagined/Work As Done). It is really important to understand the background and context and that requires trust and psychological-safety so the whole story can be told.

By understanding how it happened, we can develop a robust process. For example, if instructors are drifting from procedures, then a process needs to be in place to prevent them from drifting too far. That can be 'rules-based', but a much better way is to look at the drivers and motivation of the individuals or teams. There might be local pressures which prevent standards from being adopted fully. Blaming the individuals without fixing the systemic problem means those latent issues will still remain.

The next step might be to develop more rules, but these aren't just the standards which organisations proscribe that should be taught to prevent those *'bad things from happening'*, but also the social norms within the socio-technical environment e.g. what is the culture of the team, dive centre or training organisation? These rules aren't about more compliance; they are about the rules which lead to more openness, and promote and support effective decision-making, and behaviours which precede positive outcomes.

Positive outcomes, which are based on recognising that divers are part of a wider system. A system which looks at the individuals and their mindset; the way they make decisions; the way they interact with equipment; the way they interact as part of a team; the way they operate as part of the instructor/student relationship; the way they interact as part of a wider social group considering their local, organisational and national cultures; the way they operate in line with national and international legislature.

Remember that safety can never be the number one priority for an individual, team or organisation all the time. Rather, a safety culture is how organisations and groups balance all the other demands which we face. For that to happen, knowledge is needed. The problem is that you can't write down everything you might face, nor can you deliver training to meet it - which means you need to be resilient, learn from failure and learn to fail safely.

Resilience is needed, because the world is a messy place. Things go wrong: kit breaks; the underwater world is not the same; the students are 'difficult'; and decisions are sometimes difficult. You only have to read some of the narratives in here which are literally life-or-death decisions. However, for us to develop resilience, we need to have an idea of how to solve problems in a dynamic environment - even if that means breaking a rule; deviating from a standard operating procedure; just making it up as you go along. because no-one told you this could happen; or just making a mistake because you are human and have physical and cognitive limitations. And for that to happen, we need to be able to talk about the errors and violations we have made, which means we must have a Just Culture in place...

What if we don't have a Just Culture?

This takes the previous journey of why we need a Just Culture - and turns it on its head and shows you what the likely outcomes are if we don't have one.

Let's start with the ability to tell open, context-rich stories. Without a Just Culture being in place, the stories told will be incomplete. They will miss crucial pieces of evidence which allow sense-making to happen. They won't talk about the rules that were broken, or the limits which are pushed, because of the external drivers and motivational factors present. As such, we end up with a story which doesn't quite make sense, although we do know that it is incomplete and that likely someone is hiding something. Lawyers love this bit! Without a complete story, we are unable to undertake an in-depth investigation. Consequently, we start to fill the gaps with our own knowledge, based on previous experiences, fuelled by cognitive biases such as hindsight bias, outcome bias and the fundamental attribution error. We identify that rules have been broken and errors made, but we are unable to work out why. But that doesn't matter, because it is easier to blame someone, because of our own cognitive efficiencies, than spend the time and effort to work out how it made sense for them to do what they did.

The outcome of limited analysis is to resort to an easy solution - more rules and regulations - especially if the leadership of the organisation are worried about litigation or liability. More rules and regulations means that when things go wrong, it is easy to point the finger and say, 'You didn't follow the rules!' However, as we've already discussed in Chapter 2, 'Work as Imagined' is different to 'Work as Done' - the latter having to deal with constant adaptation and variability. If more rules are applied and the culture is about adherence, external factors are not considered, and we don't take a system's view of the world looking for those things which might knock us off our track. Consequently, adherence to the rules becomes the goal - rather than teaching divers and instructors how to deal with the real world which is 'messy' and doesn't follow the rulebook. This limited thinking means that when problems do come up, they are unable to be solved in a manner which invokes knowledge-based thinking; and therefore the failure rate for a novel situation is pretty high.

How to Develop Conditions for a Just Culture

Under Just Culture conditions, individuals are not blamed for 'honest errors', but are held accountable for wilful violations and gross negligence. Unfortunately, given the punitive and retributive culture which exists within diving, divers are less willing to inform the community or their training organisation about their own errors and other safety problems or hazards if they are afraid of being punished or prosecuted. Such a lack of trust prevents other divers and training organisations from learning from others and being properly informed of the actual risks that divers and instructors face. This doesn't mean there is a totally "no-blame" culture present, as this is neither feasible nor desirable. Most people desire some level of accountability when a mishap occurs.

As such, a Just Culture supports learning from unsafe acts in order to improve the level of awareness concerning risk, uncertainty and safety, and helps to develop the environment in which safety-related information can be shared through social media and incident reporting. We cannot learn everything in a class, so we must learn from the real world, and that means learning from others' mistakes too.

While a fair proportion (majority?) of diving takes places outside a formal organisation, organisations set the culture for the 'real world' as divers go through their training programmes. Some agencies are known to be relaxed in their adherence to standards at the instructional level, whereas others are known for high standards and consistently high adherence to those standards - even when divers graduate from their training programmes. As such, while the following relates to organisational culture, the concepts are equally applicable to those who dive for fun, but share and host incident information online.

Areas an Organisation Should Consider with Regards to Developing a Just Culture

Divers/instructors are understandably reluctant to report their mistakes to the organisation that they are part of or employ them - if it is punitive in nature. Furthermore, the ability to report others is reduced - if the reporter believes that the individual will just be fired, without anything changing in the system. (See Lanny's account in Chapter 10, 'Leadership and Followership' for an example of this).

To encourage them to do so, these organisations must first recognise that 'to err is human' and that we are all fallible; make this recognition visible; and then should publish statements summarising the fundamental principles of a Just Culture which they will follow. Additionally, they must ensure that these principles are applied at all levels of their organisations, especially those in senior and influential positions in the organisations. 'Walking the talk' is essential if trust is to be maintained throughout the organisation:

- **Confidentiality**. Divers/instructors are reluctant to draw attention to errors made by themselves or their colleagues, primarily due to personal embarrassment, but also because they don't want to be seen as a 'snitch' on other instructors. They must be confident that their identity, or the identity of any person implicated in the report, will not be disclosed without their permission or unless this is required by law. An assurance should also be given that any subsequent safety action taken will, as far as possible, ensure the anonymity of the persons involved. This can pose a problem in the diving community, because it is relatively small. Consequently, fatalities or serious incidents are often hard to hide when it comes to those involved. Furthermore, within an organisation, it is hard to hide where the information came from, because there are only certain individuals who will have known what has happened. However, every effort should be made to maintain confidentiality; and at the same time, provide some means of learning to the community, not just focusing on the outcomes, but also the context.

- **Punitive Action**. A diver/instructor who breaks the law or breaches a regulation or agency policy through a deliberate act or gross negligence cannot expect immunity from prosecution. However, if the offence was unpremeditated and unintentional, and would not have come to light except for the report, he/she should be protected from punishment or prosecution.
- **Removal of certification to teach**. The circumstances of an investigation may indicate that the performance of an instructor is below an acceptable level - this in itself is an issue - what is acceptable when it comes to performance?! Such an outcome may indicate the need for further training, or even the removal of the instructor's certification to teach. However, two things should be recognised when this happens. Firstly, such actions must never be punitive; and secondly, the instructor must recognise that this is about the organisation helping them develop -not about punishing them. If the instructor is seen to be punished for anything other than gross negligence or deliberate acts, then trust will be lost and 'Work as Done' will be hidden.

The following narrative from a dive safety officer currently working at a major university, shows how social and professional pressures, and the lack of both a psychologically-safe environment and a Just Culture, can seriously hamper diving safety. One of the biggest contributors to an environment which doesn't support learning from failure is a steep authority gradient, where the experience, knowledge and behaviour from the senior member of the team prevents critical feedback or challenging to take place. As we'll see in Chapter 10 on Leadership (and Followership), reducing this hierarchy-based barrier is essential for high-performing teams.

Case Study: An authority gradient limits learning

I'm a dive officer in charge of a fairly large dive program at a leading university. It was during a routine training update that I noticed one of my divers begin to squirm and look decidedly uncomfortable as we talked about how and why we report diving incidents. I made a mental note of the body language and continued the discussion. We talked about incidents, near misses, and hazards, and why reporting them was critical to our ability to learn how we might improve our diving, make our work safer and even improve our research outcomes for our university. We talked about it from the perspective of those further up the organisational chart who have special duties of care to all of us; and how it is not fair to them when we withhold information about such events. These are the people that need to know when things don't always go the way they should. If they don't know the realities of our day-to-day operations, they cannot make the best decisions about policies, funding and other resources. We work for a large university with most of our diving being scientific/research project diving, and resources are typically scarce.

We broke for lunch and I stood for a moment, feeling like I was forgetting something, and then remembered. Just as I turned around, I heard the diver say, "Uhm...I'm so sorry ...I should have told you this a long time ago." And so the story goes like this:

The plan for the dive was to deploy two divers from the research vessel, who would descend down a shot-line and each diver would begin laying a

50m transect line – one to the North, one to the South. Each diver would then swim back along the entire 100m transect, stopping at randomised points to collect data on the West side of the transect line. Each diver turns around and repeats this along the East side of the transect line. Once done, each diver reels their 50m line back up, moving back toward the shot-line. Typically, this dive takes about an hour.

After they had started laying their respective transects, Jessie saw the other diver once or twice as they swam past each other. Then, later in the dive, as Jessie had just started reeling in the line, the other diver appeared and, using hand-signals, asked if Jessie was okay. Jessie signalled an okay back, and assuming the other diver would stay and assist, looked away for a moment and then looked back to see the other diver was gone. Jessie shared with me that the okay signalled to the other diver was not very accurate. "Maybe if it had been someone else I would have said, 'No'," Jessie told me. "Or if I realised they weren't going to stay and help me finish the dive. But this was my PhD supervisor, who is pretty intimidating. I didn't want to seem weak."

The lead-filled transect line that Jessie was reeling in was very heavy - and lugging it through the kelp in the moderate surge and swell was taking its toll. Jessie was reasonably fit and strong, but would not be described as a large diver. "To be honest, I was also a bit scared and a bit stressed. It was late in the day, dark, noisy, and really surgy. I also knew I was getting a bit low on air, but knew I still had enough to retrieve the line and get back to the surface with plenty to spare, so I figured I would just tough it out. Then quite suddenly, I discovered I was entangled in both kelp and the lead transect line." The entanglement included the knife on Jessie's lower leg. Jessie thought briefly about trying to get to that knife, but then rejected the idea. Not only was it part of the entanglement, but Jessie didn't think that the line could be cut.

At this stage, Jessie was well and truly tangled, and physically struggling with the ridiculous mess of transect line, kelp, reel, and the ever-present surge tossing everything around like a washing machine.

And then, in the middle of the spin cycle, Jessie ran out of air. Expletives have been deleted!

"I wasn't entirely shocked, I guess I knew it was coming, but I admit I was really scared. I don't rightly know how I got out of it. I know I was sucking on nothing. Somehow, I managed to calm myself down, get somewhat free of the mess, and make it to 5m to the surface, though I was still a bit tangled up in the reel. I have no memory of it, but I must have orally inflated my BC on the surface. One of the other divers was snorkelling over to check on me, and they grabbed the reel and line and yanked the rest of it up to the surface."

Jessie got back to the boat and told the rest of the team about the entanglement and running out of air. "I was feeling pretty cranky at being abandoned, but I didn't say that part," Jessie told me. "Why not?" I asked. "My supervisor is really pretty scary," Jessie shared. "I just didn't feel I could express that. The other team members seemed fairly upset about what happened, but not my supervisor. But my supervisor did pull me aside later and tell me that I didn't have to dive the next day. However, he didn't acknowledge that he had left me, and didn't suggest he was sorry. After that, I've become more cautious diving with this team. I pick my buddies – and we dive as a real buddy team."

I asked Jessie what could be done better, what might be included in pre-dive briefings, and the like. Jessie told me there was no pre-dive briefing, only a quick discussion on how to collect the data. No safety information about the dives was included. Jessie went on to say, "No one asked me if I was comfortable before the dive. If I had been asked that, I probably would have shared that I was a bit anxious about the conditions. But I also see my role as essential - I can't not dive. That whole hierarchy/supervisor thing is a big part of this." Jessie also shared that the boat trip across to where they would be diving had probably contributed to the fatigue and stress. Jessie and one other member of the team had vomited during the crossing. But this wasn't seen as anything of any real relevance. Seas can be rough. Sometimes we vomit.

I also asked Jessie what might improve reporting. "Well, that's a problem. It is just the whole culture of the group – it is implicit that you have to harden up – and that's how we do things. If you can't do it, we will replace you. I didn't want to get the reputation of being a wimp. To *improve this, the supervisory level must explicitly prioritise safety. They don't. Data is number one. Safety is down the line. And for me, yes, I know we are supposed to report this stuff. But I wasn't ready for it to blow up into a huge dramatic thing. It should be, but I hadn't processed it enough myself to handle that.*

Jessie had given me a lot to work with. But where to start – the dive plan, the briefing, the debriefing (lack thereof), the team's complicity, the non-existent buddy system, the complacent response to the event, the failure to report…and on it goes. The blatant and obvious issues had my full attention for several minutes. But then I dug deeper and got curious. What are the more forensic pieces of this?

To say this team has fallen into the trap of normalisation of deviation is obvious. But what about all the hints along the way that were missed? How can any of us on any operation identify when conditions are changing, and what our margin of manoeuvrability is? Can we see the bad stuff coming? In Jessie's example, what were the quiet little red flags that hovered in the peripheral vision of the divers on this team? What were the weak signals that everyone missed – that bad stuff was about to happen?

Jessie's inability to speak up in the diving community isn't unique; and the fact that this could only be raised as a confidential incident report within the university and permission was given to publish this - but only anonymously. An inability to speak up isn't limited to the diving community either. Nurses are unable to speak up in operating theatres; co-pilots are unable to speak up in cockpits; and drillers are unable to speak up on the drilling floor of an oil rig. If we want safety and performance to improve, we need to increase levels of psychological safety and create a Just Culture in the diving community. Both of these support learning from failure and it is only through failure do we improve.

Organisations can lead the way when it comes to developing a Just Culture, and leaders within the community can create the environment for psychological safety. In addition to the guidance in this chapter, more information will be provided in Chapter 10 on how leaders and teams can create such a positive environment.

In summary, we need to break down the following barrier to learning: people, especially experienced individuals, are more afraid of judgments by their peers, than they are of those who are further from the 'frontline'. To do this, we need to make ourselves vulnerable by talking about the personal mistakes we have made.

Summary of Key Points
- Psychological safety is a key trait of high-performance teams. It is defined as *'a shared belief that the team is safe for interpersonal risk taking.'*
- To develop psychological safety within a team requires members to demonstrate vulnerability by talking about their lack of knowledge, lack of skills and failures, mistakes and violations they have made. This vulnerability also extends to teams/organisations when working in, across and between larger groups.
- If learning from failure as a way of improving performance is to be truly embraced, then errors and certain 'at risk behaviours' need to be examined in a curious manner and not a retributive one. However, that doesn't mean that gross negligence, sabotage and violation for personal gain are considered acceptable behaviours. These are what underpin a Just Culture.
- Through a curious approach to deviations, individual and team performance, and consequently safety, can be improved because 'latent pathogens' within the system i.e. systemic issues, will be exposed - which means they can be addressed. 'Fixing' the individual at the sharp end by punishing them (socially or through disciplinary action) without addressing the systemic issues means the problem remains and another individual will succumb to the social/environmental drivers.

Questions to consider
- When was the last time you considered the ability of junior or inexperienced team members to speak up in your team or instructional set-up?
- How do you know that students or team members are able to speak up?
- When you look at an incident or accident, do you quickly jump to the conclusion that the divers did something wrong, or do you look at the bigger picture/context and try to work out their local rationality/sense-making?
- If you are an instructor, when was the last time you talked about something that didn't go to plan *for you* on the dive that you are currently debriefing? (More on this in the teamwork chapter on debriefing.)

References
(1) Edmondson, A. *Psychological Safety and Learning Behavior in Work Teams*. Administrative Science Quarterly, Vol. 44, No. 2 (Jun., 1999), pp. 350-383.
(2) Benson, K. *Transforming Criticism into Wishes: A Recipe for Successful Conflict*. www.gottman.com/blog/transforming-criticism-into-wishes-a-recipe-for-successful-conflict/ Retrieved on 8 Dec 2018.
(3) Hidden, A. *Clapham Junction Accident Investigation Report*. London. HMSO. 1989.
(4) Reason, J. 1997. The Components of Safety Culture: Definitions of Informed, Reporting, Just, Flexible and Learning Cultures.
(5) Dekker, S.W.A. (2009) *Just Culture: Who Gets To Draw The Line?* Cogn Tech Work 11: 177. https://doi.org/10.1007/s10111_008-0110-7
(6) Leveson, N. *Analyzing Accidents and Incidents with CAST* https://ocw.mit.edu/courses/aeronautics-and-astronautics/16-63j-system-safety-spring-2016/lecture-notes/MIT16_63JS16_LecNotes6.pdf retrieved 8 Dec 2018
(7) Leveson, N. Stringfellow, M. Thomas, J. 2011. *A Systems Approach to Accident Analysis*. sunnyday.mit.edu/safer-world/refinery-edited.doc retrieved 8 Dec 2018.

Additional Reading
Dekker, S. (2018). *Just Culture*. 3rd ed. Boca Raton: Chapman and Hall/CRC.
Dekker, S. (2014). *The Field Guide To Understanding "Human Error"*. Boca Raton, FL: CRC Press.

Zwieback, D. (2016). *Beyond blame: Learning from failure and success.* O'Reilly
Edmondson, A. (2012). *Teaming: How Organizations Learn, Innovate, and Compete in the Knowledge Economy.* New York: Wiley, J.
Edmondson, Amy C. *Strategies for dealing with failure.* HBR. <https://hbr.org/2011/04/strategies-for-learning-from-failure>
Gilbert, C., Journé, B., Laroche, H., & Bieder, C. (2018). *Safety Cultures, Safety Models: Taking Stock and Moving Forward.* Cham: Springer International Publishing.

Chapter 6

Decision-making in Diving: 'Choices' are not what many perceive them to be

"When any one asks me how I can best describe my experiences of nearly 40 years at sea, I merely say uneventful. Of course, there have been winter gales and storms and fog and the like, but in all my experience I have never been in an accident of any sort worth speaking about. I have seen but one vessel in distress in all my years at sea. I never saw a wreck and have never been wrecked, nor was I ever in any predicament that threatened to end in disaster of any sort. I will say that I cannot imagine any condition which could cause a ship to founder. I cannot conceive of any vital disaster happening to this vessel. Modern shipbuilding has gone beyond that."

Captain EJ Smith, the Captain of the Titanic.

The following account is from Ryan Booker, one member of a team of four experienced cave and technical divers, three of whom were also recreational diving instructors. Their goal was to get one of the team members diving after spending several years recovering from a serious injury. The outcome? Goal achieved, but with serious risks and a very close call.

Case Study: How easy is it to say no?

After several false starts, and several years of painstaking recovery, this was the day. We were going diving. The gear was ready, we were ready.

We'd taken into account the issues his accident had left him with. Less mobility. Less strength. We had twin 7s instead of twin 12s. We had a scooter. We had a solid team who'd all dived together many times before.

We surveyed the site.

Our first chance to abort: It was a spring tide and running fast. More than usual, and past the normal slack window.

Second: It was dirty water. Rain during the lead-up had dropped the visibility significantly.

Are we ok with this? Of course. We're experienced. We've been looking forward to this for years. Why back out now? Three.

We're geared up. We're in the water. "We still good?", "Yep, stay close". Four.

Descend.

May as well be zero vis. The buddy teams are separated. Five...

We abort and ascend.

"What should we do?" Six.

One buddy team: "We're getting out". Seven.

Buddy team with injured diver: "Still good?" "Yep." Eight.

We descend. Stay close. Touch contact. Scooter for a while, in the direction of some interesting features we know of. The current is strong. Stress is high. We decide to abort. Again.

We break touch contact to shoot a dSMB. We can just see each other. We end up on a navigational pylon in the middle of the boat channel, the dSMB tied around it. Not where we expected. There's a ladder. I grab it. The injured diver surfaces a little off the pylon. Scooters back. I'm really glad we had that scooter. He wouldn't have made it otherwise.

We signal that we're ok. I take the scooter and tow him back to shore.

We get out.

We have quite the debrief.

Hindsight is 20/20.

This was a classic "goal-oriented" failure. We had built the event up so far, and had already made so many attempts, that we simply couldn't be dissuaded until it was almost too late. We had so many clear reasons to abort the dive, and opportunities to do so, but persisted - to almost catastrophic results. We achieved the goal, but it's hard to think of it as a success in any other metric.

We all knew it was a bad idea, and we all sensed the escalation. Two of us had a slightly lower threshold or perhaps pig-headedness. But we all knew. Yet none of us took control with any confidence.

It was a failure of planning, of leadership, of followership. A failure to speak out. A failure to listen to the non-verbal cues. An overconfidence in our own abilities.

We learned a lot. Thankfully with limited consequence.

As Ryan's account highlights, sometimes humans aren't very good decision makers! Most of the time, we make acceptable decisions. On a few occasions, we make amazing decisions. But the 'choices' people make when they are caught up in the moment are rarely choices: rather they are a product of the experiences they have had previously (good and bad); the knowledge they have gained from experiential learning; from the information they have gained from learning in a passive manner such as reading or watching videos; and finally, from the hard-wired genetics and physiology which makes up the human body and brain. Understanding how decision-making actually happens is essential if we are to improve our own performance and safety in diving.

This chapter will describe the different decision-making models and processes we use (Skills/Rules/Knowledge, System 1/System 2, Naturalistic Decision-Making and Biases & Heuristics); their strengths and weaknesses; how to overcome some of the cognitive limitations we have through the use of checklists; and, ultimately, give you the skills to make more effective decisions both topside during planning, but also underwater while on the dive.

Decision-Making

Decision-making has been defined as the process of reaching a judgement or choosing an option to meet the needs of a given situation. It can be broken down into the following main areas:- understanding the situation at hand/defining the problem; determining a potential course of action or the option(s) available based on the information immediately at hand; selecting and executing that option and then undertaking some form of review process to determine if the decision was effective in terms of the goals set; and then, repeating until the goals have been met.

This might seem like common sense, because decisions happen every minute, every hour and every day of our lives; and yet many of them, we don't even realise we are making as they are made subconsciously and they are subject to biases and heuristics (mental shortcuts) - even those which take many days or weeks of deliberation to come to a conclusion, once we have weighed up all the 'facts'.

The environment, task or time available means that different decision-making techniques are available and can and will be used. The ability to recognise the strengths, weaknesses and biases of the different techniques leads to an effective decision-maker who can undertake critical thinking. It is important to note that the ability to be a critically-thinking decision-maker doesn't just reside with the leadership. One of the key skills for an effective follower is to be able to honestly and robustly apprise their leadership and peers to ensure that decisions are in line with the current goals.

In high-risk industries, there is significant research which identifies that poor judgement or ineffective decision-making were contributory factors to accidents. For example, between 1983 and 1987, research showed that these factors contributed to 47% of accidents in aviation[1]. In the oil and gas domain, *Piper Alpha* and *Deep Water Horizon* disasters both happened due to ineffective decision-making. However, we need to recognise that hindsight bias is easy to apply when examining accidents and near-misses, because we have more facts than those involved. Daniel Kahneman uses a term which sums this up nicely, "What you see is all there is..." - (WYSIATI) - to highlight that when we make decisions in real-time, we only have the externally-generated information that we perceive as being important or relevant and we apply previous experiences to make sense of that information; once we have made sense of the information, we apply it to make a decision. So, when something goes wrong, fundamentally, at that moment of decision-making, it makes sense to us to make it, as we have based it on the information that is currently available to us in that moment i.e. on what we know. This is known as local rationality.

Consequently, to make better decisions, we need to understand the limitations of the decision-making processes we use, what external or internal factors can influence a good or bad decision and learn tools which help us improve those decisions.

Understanding these limitations, developing and deploying ways around them was one of the reasons why Cockpit (now Crew) Resource Management training started to be embedded into aviation training programmes in the 1980s. Following the success of such programmes in that domain, a number of different Non-Technical Skills training programmes have been developed in other domains:

- Healthcare. Non-Technical Skills for Surgeons (NOTSS), Anaesthetists Non-Technical Skills and TeamSTEPPS.
- Maritime. Bridge Resource Management (BRM) and Human Element Training (HELM).
- Oil and Gas. Well Operations Crew Resource Management (WOCRM) programme.

The only such programme developed specifically for recreational, technical and cave divers is the one I have developed and deployed globally via, 'The Human Diver' and you are reading the only text book devoted to this topic.

Mental Models

The world is a really complicated and complex place and we humans would prefer things to be much simpler. So, what we do is create mental models which act as a way of reducing reality to something which is 'good enough'. A road atlas or SatNav are examples of models which are 'good enough', because we don't need to have a high-fidelity image of all the bumps, turns, lane layouts and signage to go on our journey. This simplified model of reality allows us to drive hundreds of miles across the country without too much of a problem or without too much mental effort.

A cave map does the same job: it provides the cave diver with enough detail to get from the entrance to the exit in a safe manner, highlighting areas of interest. However, for them to be effective, there needs to be some form of translation available. I am not a cave diver and so if you showed me a cave map, without a key to explain the symbols, the map (model) would have limited use.

Our mental models do the same thing. They provide a simplified model of the world which allows us to undertake activities without diverting all of our cognitive resources to the situation at hand. This reduction in mental workload means we can do other things, like dive and have fun in the process.

As an example of how models develop over time: we are driving our car and waiting at cross-roads to turn right across the oncoming traffic. This already invokes a mental model and one which might not be valid for you. If you are not used to driving on the left-hand side of the road, this would be counter to your mental model of 'turning across traffic' because turning across traffic means turning left!

As the traffic is coming towards us, we are looking for gaps to pass through. We don't know the speed of the traffic coming towards us, nor do we know the exact distance between the cars, but we have a mental model of what a 'big enough' gap is supposed to be, based on our previous experiences. When we were novice drivers, the gap we would use would likely be much larger than one we would use now, because we have more experience and have reduced the uncertainty involved. We find 'the sweet spot' for these models by failing and making mistakes and having a feedback loop which then informs our future decision-making processes.

So how does this relate to diving? When we ascend and want to stop at a certain depth to complete a decompression stop, we dump gas from the Buoyancy Compensation Device (BCD) or wing to arrest the ascent. The amount of time which we hold the dump valve open to let the gas escape is based on previous experiences, either during training or on 'fun dives'. Over time, we refine this action so we can pre-empt the dumping process (i.e. the time the valve stays open and the depth below the stop when we start opening the valve); and we stabilise at the right depth 'without thinking about it'. However, if you change the parameters, like being much heavier because you are now diving multiple nitrox-filled cylinders instead of a twinset or twinset with helium mixes, then the amount of gas which escapes when you hold the dump valve open for a 'normal dive' is much more and you stabilise early or sink because too much gas has escaped. I know this because it happened to me during my advanced trimix class during the initial skills and ascent training phase. Instead of helium-based mixes in the twinset on my back and the bottom stage, they were filled with Nitrox 32% which weighted considerably more than the helium-based mixes.

As divers we need to recognise the mental models we use all the time. They exist topside when communicating with others; when we are in the water on a dive and interacting with our buddies; or when we are observing the world. These mental models are essential for humans to live in the world we do. Our 'fight or flight' responses are based on mental models which have been created over millennia of learned behaviours and we can't easily turn them off. Training can help reprogram them, but it takes significant effort to unlearn and then relearn, especially if we are in an alien environment - like diving where previous models might not be valid, like having a regulator mouthpiece detach from your regulator. Your lips say there is something there but there is no source of gas!

Cognitive Biases and Heuristics

What are the answers to the following two questions?
- A bat and ball cost $1.10. The bat costs one dollar more than the ball. How much does the ball cost?
- If it takes 5 machines 5 minutes to make 5 widgets, how long would it take 100 machines to make 100 widgets? 100 minutes OR 5 minutes?

These questions are part of a *Cognitive Reflection Test*. Research using Stanford University students showed that 90% of them made a mistake in at least one of the questions. How did you do? The answers are at the end of this section.

The reason for the high error rates is that we take mental

shortcuts when we make quick decisions, shortcuts which are based on previous mental models. In the first question, we make a mental jump from $1.00 and $1.10 as being a 10¢ difference, and therefore that is the answer. In the second example, we are looking at repetition of numbers. In a similar way that if I flip a fair coin 10 times and I get 10 heads, the normal response would be for a head to be the answer for the 11th flip because we expect it to happen that way. Often we say 'assumptions make an ass out of u and me', but in many cases they don't and we need to understand which the critical ones are so we can slow down.

Unfortunately, or fortunately depending on how you look at it, there are hundreds of cognitive biases which we are subject to. The positive side is that these biases allow us to operate at the pace we do: filtering and ditching apparently 'irrelevant' information, so that we can spend more time on more 'important' information and actions. The negative side is that sometimes the filtering process and the constant use of assumptions means we miss critical information and we end up with the wrong outcome. Most of the time, the assumptions we use are valid. However, divers aren't too good at looking at the reasons behind the outcomes we have, often attributing it to skill - when in fact it was luck that an adverse event didn't happen.

The way we can prevent biases and heuristics catching us out is to recognise when critical situations are likely to occur and to raise our game when it comes to monitoring the situation; the WITH model in Chapter 11 (Performance-Shaping Factors) covers this in more detail. A correctly-formatted brief will help with decision-making and increase situational awareness e.g. by briefing a minimum volume/pressure of gas which we want to end the dive, and a rough time we think it will happen, we can start to raise our awareness as we get closer to that time or pressure. However, it requires us to understand the rate at which our breathing gas pressure drops while at depth - so technical skills and competence are also required. The brief might also include something which covers previous experience which might shape or frame decision-making, a topical point if you consider

Michael Menduno's event in Chapter 12 (Learning from Failure).

The following narrative from cave diver and retired instructor, Clare Pooley describes a cave diving incident in which such knowledge could have reduce the likelihood of the stresses faced by the team in a sustained zero-vis exit from a cave; and at the same time, there was a recognition within the team that something wasn't quite right and so they ended the dive early. As with many incidents and near-misses, there are numerous positive and negative actions which take place and we need to make sure we don't just focus on the negatives, but also look at the positives. For example, how many consider the 'obvious' major contingency (failed scooter/DPV) as part of their plan, but how many consider if it is the most critical? Using a DPV in a cave isn't just about going faster and further, there are some fairly major implications that need to be considered when it comes to failures.

Case Study: Blind Exit with Scooters

It was a great day in Florida when I returned to dive a cave I had dived several times before. This time I was returning with my buddy, who had accompanied me on previous dives, and two other very competent divers one of whom I had done a lot of quite advanced cave diving with; and the other who I had dived with a few times – although not in a cave. They had been doing some diving together that week. They had not dived this cave before.

On previous dives, we had reached the limit of swimming. This time, we had brought scooters to see some new caves. The plan was to enter in two teams, scooter for a predetermined distance and then drop the scooters and swim until gas limits were reached. We looked at the maps and worked out that this should get us to the end of the cave.

We had to take a boat to the cave and, on tying it up at the dock, I put on my drysuit only to break the neck seal. I had a spare, back at the house, and rather than force me to miss the dive, everyone agreed to return with me to get it. Leaving two people diving and taking the boat away was not a safe option. This put our timing out by about 45 minutes and so, having been delayed, we entered as a four - rather than as two pairs with a period of time between us.

Two of the borrowed scooters were very poorly weighted, sinking like a stone when let go, but the divers using them felt that they would be able to cope.

I led us in, my buddy behind me, then the other pair with the most experienced bringing up the rear. The first 20-30 minutes was familiar cave and it felt a good dive with the struggles on the surface forgotten. The new (to me) cave was duly reached but there was time on the trigger remaining, so I pressed on. The cave became a different shape, low and wide with the line tucked in quite tight on the right, quite close to the floor. For those who do not cave dive, I should explain that divers do not hold the line when cave diving but should remain close to it and aware of where it is at all times, so that it can be reached should light or visibility suddenly fail.

We had perhaps four or five minutes left on the scooters when I saw a signal from behind. The diver right at the back was signalling a scooter drop. I was slightly surprised by this – but more surprised that when I looked back at him: the visibility was markedly worse behind us than in front. A team of four with propellers on scooters, raising small amounts of silt through prop wash in the low cave and bubbles from an open circuit dive hitting silt on the ceiling, was creating far more disturbance in the cave than I had seen before. I realised that his suggestion that we drop the scooters early was a great one.

We dropped the scooters, and the stage bottles we had been using, and pressed on into the cave. The cave soon opened up again and we went on to have a great dive. We did not make the end of the line, but all were content to turn when we did. It later transpired that the dive was not thumbed on a gas limit being reached but a comfort level – the diver felt we had gone far enough.

The order of the team was reversed on the way out – I was now last and surprised to see, even in the bigger cave, how much our bubbles had disturbed from the ceiling. This part of the cave was not dived much, and sediment was falling from the ceiling with our exhaust bubbles. Four divers going in and now four divers coming out was affecting visibility and

I soon couldn't see the lead diver at all.

We made reasonable progress until we returned to our stage bottles and scooters. I picked mine up and waited for the signal to set off. As each diver passed through the cave for a second time more and more particulate was falling from the ceiling and more silt was being sucked up by the props on the scooters. As the narrow part of the cave approached, we were forced closer to the bottom and then the inevitable happened – a diver ahead misjudged things slightly and hit the bottom. The silt came up, went through the prop of his scooter, and the poor visibility went to zero.

I knew that the line was down low, close to the floor and now on my left. I had my hand on it in seconds – as did other members of the team ahead of me (although I did not know this at the time). Thus, one hand on the line, the other hand holding my scooter as high as possible to avoid contact with the cave floor, I started to head out.

After a short time, I was surprised that the visibility was not improving. Normally, after an impact, divers will soon emerge from a cloud and be able to make progress again. What was happening was that the heavy scooters my buddies had were dragging in the cave and taking the problem with us. Smacking my manifold into the ceiling for the umpteenth time, I started to do the maths and it was not good. At best, we were exiting at about 1/20th of the pace we entered the cave. Whilst we had extremely good gas reserves planned, no gas planning would allow for an exit 20 times slower than entry.

There were no options but to press on. Slide one hand along the line, another hand in front of the face to ensure I avoided the sharp rock on the ceiling. Occasionally, a hand on a buddy's arm where the cave permitted. I'd been in zero viz a number of times before and the team was functioning well, but this was a different issue due to the gas volumes available, travel times and the fact that we were continuing to destroy the viz by our very presence in the cave.

Eventually (around 20 minutes) the cave opened up following a restriction and the line was away from the floor. The visibility immediately improved sufficiently to allow us to swim and then, after a few more minutes to scooter.

Exiting with 80 bar in a twin set which was just in reserve also proved to me the value of conservative gas reserves – particularly on scooter dives where there can be such a difference in travel times. Most scooter gas plans are made on the basis that the scooter may fail and you may have to tow or swim. Going from scootering to touch contact on exit is such a large difference that I am not sure any gas plan would have allowed us to exit the whole distance in this way. Our buddy's call to drop the scooters early due to the conditions he could see from the back of the team was a very good call – and saved us probably another 20 or so minutes.

For me it was one of those "grass is greener, sky is bluer dives". It taught me a number of things, but probably the biggest is that problems can sometimes be building behind you and to always have an eye on your exit.

System 1 and System 2

Two researchers, Kahneman and Tversky, developed a theory which described decision-making under the context of behavioural economics and considered that the brain worked using a two-part conceptual system imaginatively called System 1 and System 2.

System 1 is about fast, intuitive and automatic decision-making based on biases, heuristics and mental shortcuts. There is very little control involved and most of the time the answers are good or rather they are 'good enough'. System 1 is used most of the time we make decisions and so the 'choices' we make aren't really choices. System 2 is the more logical and methodical way of processing information. While you might think that System 2 would help us make more effective decisions, it has a couple of downsides. Firstly, it takes considerable time to collect the data; process it so its relevance and importance can be determined and then a plan of action created before a choice is made; the action is executed; and feedback observed. Time, that is often not available in modern life, and normally not available when underwater with a finite gas source either. Secondly, System 2 requires mental energy to process. Humans are very efficient creatures and anything we can do to reduce mental effort is a good thing. We could say we are lazy or efficient, depending on whether you are positive or critical! Crucially, System 2 needs to be kicked in when there is a decision which can't be easily reversed.

This is why we often describe those involved in accidents, incidents or near-misses as being complacent, because they were doing something without thinking about it. The dictionary definition of complacency is, *"self-satisfaction especially when accompanied by unawareness of actual dangers or deficiencies."* However, that doesn't necessarily help us improve our decision-making processes leading to improved diving safety.

The way I explain the concept of complacency to get people thinking about the process and not just the outcome, is to say that if we do something which uses mental shortcuts and we don't have an adverse event, that would be called efficiency by many people. Whereas if they do the same actions, informed by the same previous experiences, and they have an adverse event because something has changed, then complacency is normally attributed to the activity! Erik Hollnagel coined the term, 'Efficiency Thoroughness Trade-Off' whereby there is a constant balancing act between quality and time/resources and we only find out the balance was wrong! There is so much on this topic, that Erik wrote a whole book about it![3]

Some might argue that complacency and normalisation of deviance are the same, but I don't believe they are. Normalisation of deviance involves a gradual drift from 'safety' with new baselines being set over a period of time, which are considered to be 'safe'.

The conflict we face about right and wrong actions is because we are subject to two biases called 'outcome bias' and 'hindsight bias' - and they massively impact our future decision-making processes. If nothing went wrong, then it must have been okay! What needs to happen to correct this mindset is to have a debrief which doesn't just look at outcomes, but also the process. In effect, look at how we got to where we are. Four high-level questions I teach my students to use during my human factors/non-technical skills classes to help facilitate this learning are:

- What did I do well? Why?
- What do I need to improve on and how am I going to fix that?
- What did the team do well? Why?
- What does the team need to do to improve and how are we going to fix that?

It is essential that those questions are answered in a specific manner rather than general terms e.g.

"Team communications was good." - Bad.

"The way John asked an open question to see how much we understood the brief and what we were going to do at the bottom of the shot was great. It picked up the fact that Billy was supposed to partially inflate the lift bag and he wasn't aware of that fact." - Good

More will be covered in Chapter 9 in the Teamwork section on briefs and debriefs as a way of improving decision-making.

Naturalistic Decision-making

The work which Kahneman and Tversky undertook was mainly done in controlled scenarios using college students, in circumstances where as many of the external factors and drivers were removed from our normal decision-making processes e.g. running late, limited money, external peer pressure/social conformance, experience outside the direct task at hand and so on. The idea being that by isolating external factors, the biases and behaviours could be identified. This was ground-breaking research, but it doesn't easily relate to much of the real world where numerous factors, pressures and drivers are present. Drivers and pressures which skew our decision-making processes and outcomes. Cue the work by Gary Klein and his associates which developed a concept called Naturalistic Decision Making (NDM)[4].

The theory they put together was that decisions weren't made in a logical, systematic manner where options were weighed up and rated, but rather they were based on observations of cues and patterns and how these compared with previous experiences, mental models and expectations. The closest 'fit' would be chosen (subconsciously) and the actions associated with that 'fit' executed. This is another example of where mental models come in and why their accuracy to reality is important.

What became apparent from their research was that novices had a limited set of experiences and mental models to compare their current reality against. As such, it took them longer to determine and then choose what was an important cue or clue to help with the decision-making process. Furthermore, if they didn't have a close fit, they would try the best they could to make something fit. These tie in with the work from Rasmussen who described knowledge-based decision-making where the error rates were in the order 1:2 - 1:10. Experts on the other hand, could observe a scene or situation pick out the most important elements, quickly make a decision based on the fewer elements, execute the task and have a better idea of what 'success' looked like. Experts were also quicker to stop a course of action when it wasn't going to plan and then restart their analysis and execution process. Captain Sullenburger captured this nicely with his quote following his successful ditching on the Hudson River:

"For 42 years I've been making small regular deposits in this bank of experience, education, and training. On January 15 the balance was sufficient, so I could make a very large withdrawal."[5]

Klein's work was originally based on firefighters and military commanders and how they made decisions in the 'heat of the moment'. Ironically, when first questioned, the leaders said that they hadn't 'made' decisions - but just did what needed to be done.

Using more directed questioning, it was apparent that the most effective fire chiefs were able to determine cues and clues from the way the scene was developing, from the colour of the smoke, the wind direction, the location of the fire, the building materials etc. This gave them some patterns to match against their previous experiences and execute an 'action script'. What was interesting was that the experience could be passed around the team through the use of effective and targeted debriefs after each fire was fought. These were lessons both identified and learned, and therefore could be shared within the team for the next fire. By having a common goal for improving the firefighting performance of the team, because lives depended on it, the teams knew it was advantageous to talk about what worked and why, and what didn't work and what they would do differently next time. Iterative learning within the team accelerated the individual learning processes and improved their own and the team's performance.

In the context of diving, this could be an 'expert' diver observing the current pick-up and change direction which would indicate that they would need to turn back sooner, rather than follow the initial plan which was based on either gas consumption/remaining or time duration. A novice is more likely to follow the plan, unless they encountered such situations before. Contingency planning does help provide some 'fat' in the system, but doesn't help with making a sound decision; it only mitigates a poor (in hindsight) decision. The rear diver in Clare's narrative above highlights how an 'expert' made a very sound call, because they could 'project' what was likely to happen if they didn't drop the scooters there.

Using Checklists to Improve Decision-making in Critical Circumstances

System 1 behaviours are there to provide mental shortcuts in well-practiced situations and save time. However, sometimes we need to intentionally slow people down, so they don't assume something is in place. That's what checklists do. They intentionally create System 2 behaviour when it is critical that something is done correctly first time around.

Checklists, specifically, written checklists, don't have a great reputation in diving, especially technical diving. This may have come from the past where divers were expected to know everything from memory and be self-sufficient. That same mindset of perfectionism is still present in healthcare with surgeons. The surgeon behind the *World Health Organisation Safe Surgical Checklist*, Atul Gawande, is quoted as saying *"that when questioned, more than 90% of surgeons, if they were a patient, wanted their surgical team to use a checklist, but 20% actually used a checklist on every occasion.[6]"*

However, checklists are not the panacea they are often made out to be. They need to be effectively designed; they need to fit into the operational environment in which they are going to be used (too big, too bulky, on an iPhone/Android phone); and they need to be based on the technical competence for the average user. They should not be used as a liability limiting tool which can be used to say the diver ticked the box, but didn't execute the task; therefore, it was their fault the event happened in the way it did. A quote which often comes up is from *Rebreather Forum 3* where David Concannon, a lawyer specialising in litigation in the diving industry, said that in all of the rebreather fatalities he had investigated, he had not found a checklist on the diver or in their kit bag. My counter to that is: that every aircraft which crashes will have a checklist present. The presence of a checklist won't prevent every fatality; but it will massively reduce the likelihood of one occurring, as long as it relates to the configuration and operation of the equipment and the fatality is not health-related.

My view is that for critical checks, there should be one common checklist across ALL diving organisations - be that a verbal checklist or a written one. The reason for this is because consistency of repeated actions reinforces what the action should be and if something is missed, then it is more obvious, both from another's perspective and also from self-awareness. If one agency teaches ABC (Air, Buoyancy, Clips); another teaches BWRAF (Buoyancy, Weights, Releases, Air, Fins); another GUE EDGE (Goal, Unified Team, Equipment match, Exposure, Decompression, Gases, Environment), then what check is done when mixed teams or diving operations take place? The challenge is that each of the agencies wants to have their own brand when it comes to products...

Guidance for checklist design

My experience, and that of others I have spoken to, is that when going through CCR training, instructors advise their students to develop their own checklist based on the manufacturer's manual. While this limits liability and might help develop an understanding of the reasons behind the items in their own checklist, it does not help with accountability within the team. If your checks are different to mine, I don't know if you've missed a step or it is intentionally not there. However, I have been asked on a number of occasions to give some guidance on how to write a checklist:

- Checklists should be no more than 7 lines long. If there are more than 7 items, then create a new checklist for a different phase.
- The words in each line should be mental prompts and not full sentences.
- The checklist needs to be accessible at all times it will be needed.
- Verbal checklists for solo divers WILL fail. Verbal checklists in a team are less likely to fail.
- Checklists need to be designed within the time and environment they are going to be used. By that I mean, having a full page of text for a final check when diving from a boat means it is less likely to be carried out than a few critical items.
- Only operationally relevant and timeline specific details should be included. A pre-jump check should not have 'Bubble check' after entering the water written in it!

Crucially, there is a specific mindset required to use a checklist. That mindset says, *"I don't know when I will fail to do a memory check, but I will, so I will use this checklist."* If you are interested in learning more about checklists and checklist design, consider reading *The Checklist Manifesto* by Dr Atul Gawande.

Thumbing the Dive isn't Easy, Even as an Instructor
The following narrative from Andy Davis, an advanced trimix instructor based in the Philippines, and from his student show how having two different perspectives can be beneficial when understanding the 'flawed' decisions which took place. 'Flawed' is in inverted commas

- because hindsight makes it so easy to determine why things went wrong! As with all of the case studies in the book, look at them not with the benefit of hindsight, but rather what cues and clues would you look for to prevent such an event happening to you and how would you overcome the mental biases we all have to complete a task which is important to us. Decisions made in the armchair are nowhere near as complex and difficult as those which need to be taken when all the drivers and pressures are placed upon.

Earlier this year, I conducted a 72-meter, open-circuit trimix dive off the coast of the North-West Philippines. It's a dive that I'd done many times previously when conducting trimix qualification courses.

The dive is onto the wreckage of a US Navy AJ-2 'Savage' carrier-based nuclear bomber. It's a small dive site, with only the wreckage standing alone on an otherwise desolate sandy bottom. We typically only dive the site in very fine weather, as that stretch of coastline is very unprotected during the monsoon season storms, and the available dive boats are relatively lightweight local boats and unable to handle anything beyond marginal sea conditions.

My student for this dive was a fellow that I'd mentored extensively over several years and we had established a close friendship. He worked in several different countries and had very tight windows in which to accomplish training dives. On his previous trip to Subic Bay, we'd had to abort our attempt to dive that site, because of high seas which had involved hanging around on the dive boat all day and hoping for the wind to calm. It didn't.

I knew the student was very eager to dive that particular wreck and also complete his trimix qualification. He didn't put me under any direct pressure, but I knew we had very few opportunities left to dive that site before the monsoon season arrived and we'd be unable to get outside the bay for another six or seven months.

Everything went according to plan in the preparation for the dive. We had cylinders of deco and back-gas, analysed and marked, from our previous attempt ready to go. Our kit was already packed in crates for the boat. We'd spent hours planning, assessing and agreeing the dive parameters, deco schedule, contingencies and risk mitigation options. The dive boat departed shortly after dawn so that we could avoid the stronger afternoon winds typical for the late-spring season.

When we arrived at the grid-reference for the site, there was a long rolling swell of about 1-1.5 metres and a moderate surface drift. The boat ladder was smashing up and down in the water as waves passed. It would make water entry and exit more problematic in sidemount configuration, but this was something we could effectively plan around before we started.

The boat crew deployed the shot-line and marker accurately on the GPS mark. I had confidence in their mark and ability to deploy accurately based on my previous experience with them. The shot-line was a lightweight affair, with a 6-kilogram weight under a large plastic buoy, linked by a set length of 8mm nylon-braided rope. I would personally have chosen something more substantial, but we were chartering from another dive operation and this was their standard routine.

The first trio of divers entered the water and descended. They were diving CCR and DPV with an intention to conduct a long bottom time in preparation for an upcoming expedition. We allowed 45-minutes before my student and I kitted up and entered the water. This should ensure we'd pass the first group as they ascended through their deco schedule; providing some extra measure of mutual support between teams.

As we descended through the blue water to our target depth it became apparent that the other group hadn't returned up the shot-line. When we reached the bottom there was no wreck to be seen. However, it immediately became apparent that the shot-line weight had dragged itself across the sea floor.

The combination of a large buoy and moderate swell was lifting and dragging the meagre 6kg weight cross the sand. We had maybe 15 metres of visibility and the channel in the sand caused by the dragging weight extended far beyond eyesight. If the aircraft wreck was anywhere nearby, then we'd see indications of it, especially the large schools of fish that typically inhabited the wreck, or smaller items of debris. None were apparent.

At this time, we had to make a decision on the best course of action.

The previously- discussed contingency was to deploy a 30-metre finger spool and conduct a circular search around the base of the shot-line. If that didn't achieve success, we'd abort the dive and surface according to our planned schedule.

I was clear-headed at depth, as we'd used trimix to keep our narcotic depth under 30-metres. Nonetheless, I began to second-guess our planned contingency. I was acutely aware of the cost of the dive for my student, coupled with his previous disappointment and our limited opportunity to complete the dive again for the remainder of the year. The sand-trail indicating the direction that the shot-line had been dragged seemed to make a reel search unnecessary. However, at the same time, I was disinclined to swim away from the line without an assured method of return.

I made an atypical decision to manually lift the shot weight and swim back along the drag-channel pulling the entire line assembly and buoy behind me. My rationale was that it couldn't be too far, and it would be simpler than having to recover, or cut-away, a finger spool when the bottom time got short.

I signalled my intention to my student and we set off along the drag channel. I had inflated my sidemount BCD to compensate for the 6kg of weight I was carrying. Nonetheless, I swiftly became aware that dragging the line involved considerable exertion. We swam further and further along the drag channel, but the wreck failed to appear.

After covering perhaps 150 metres, I had to signal my student to assist me dragging the line. The distance was far longer than I expected and my level of exertion much higher than I'd typically tolerate on a technical dive.

It didn't occur to me to abort or re-consider my plan at this stage. I had become very task-fixated on finding the aircraft wreckage; almost desperate not to disappoint my student. We continued together, dragging the shot- line, for perhaps another 100 metres before I really became aware that I was suffering from some CO_2 retention. My head felt like it was spinning, my breath was short, and my chest felt compressed.

I hadn't fully considered the level of exertion that I was subjecting myself to and had over-estimated the capacity for trimix to offset and alleviate gas density / respiration issues. A 30-metre narcotic depth was not nearly sufficient to compensate for dragging a long shot-line for such a distance at that depth and against the surface tow on the buoy itself.

We still had a third of our planned bottom time remaining, but an instinctive warning had illuminated inside my now CO2-fuddled mind. I dropped the shot-weight, being careful to dump the surplus buoyancy from my BCD in the process. We took another look around and could only see the drag-channel stretching further into the distance. A team gas-check confirmed that we were over our estimated Respiratory Minute Volume (RMV) rates and would be into our reserves if we persisted any longer at depth.

We signalled to ascend and recovered up the shot-line, completing our scheduled decompression without further incident – although it wasn't until well through our deeper and middle 50% stops, before I felt fully recovered from the CO2 hit.

Once back on the boat, we took a GPS mark for the actual location of the shot-line. It measured over 450 metres away from the actual mark where it was dropped. Even accounting for us dragging the shot perhaps 250 metres during the dive, it was obvious that we never came close to reaching the wreck.

The first trio of CCR divers surfaced over 30 minutes after us. They'd abandoned the shot-line, but used DPVs to follow the drag trail to the wreck. Even with that propulsion, they'd had relatively little time on the wreck, before conducting a blue-water drifting deco ascent; eventually surfacing nearly two kilometres from where they'd entered on the shot-line.

The same event is recalled by the student, Peter Stubley:

The descent down the shot-line in blue water is, for me, one of the best aspects of ocean diving. The anticipation of what I will find at the bottom of the line, was increased that day, as there should have been a nuclear bomber at the end of the line. When we reached the bottom, it was only sand as far as we could see. There was a tinge of disappointment; however, I'd learned to dive with a university club in the UK in the early '90s when GPS was in its infancy, so was quite used to diving 'HMS Nearby'. When I saw the drag marks of the shot in the sand going into the distance, but no sign of the 'shoals of fish directly above the wreck', I knew that the chance of finding the 'Savage' would be slim. The surface conditions and the small weight could have dragged the shot a long way from the wreck in the time we waited to drop in. I was half-expecting Andy to produce a reel from nowhere, as he has done before, so was surprised when he signalled to me, then picked up the shot-line and started carrying it in the direction of the drag-marks. I was worried that this was sub-optimal, but I wasn't going to argue with Andy underwater, especially as I wanted to see the 'Savage'. During the time we were carrying the shot, I was calculating how long we'd have on the plane before we'd need to start our ascent. The 'time on plane' eventually decreased such that I'd figured even if we did find it, we'd have no time to look at it.

When Andy dropped the shot-line, I knew that I wouldn't see the plane this dive. This was confirmed when almost immediately after, he thumbed the dive: it was at this point when we checked our gases, that I realised I had not swapped over my side-mount regulators, and that I had breathed way more of my left tank than my right tank. This caused me a fair amount of anxiety, as I knew I'd be in a poor position to support Andy if he needed any of my reserve gas after all his effort carrying the shot. His RMV is lower than me, but I hadn't done half the work he had. I was much happier when we switched to our 50% mix, as we had a lot of reserve, and it was during those shallower stops that I started to calculate how much I'd spent to see some sand; the relief was that it only cost me money for gas, and nothing more precious.

As we can see from both Andy and Peter's accounts, there were numerous biases at play which meant that the point at which the dive was ended was much later than it should have been. However, we know what the outcome was and therefore have 100% certainty as to the way the situation would develop. This 100% certainty is not available to the divers at the time. All we can do is recognise that goal-fixation can drive behaviours and that an authority gradient and social conformance will reduce the ability of those involved to speak up. This is especially prevalent when in an instructional setting, because of the investment in time and/or money and the want to end the class with a certification card. The sharing of accounts like these helps the community develop their decision-making processes and reduces the communication barriers.

A known problem to speaking up is when standards don't exist or when standards do exist, but the leadership have drifted from the original intent and meaning and have set a new 'standard' which is now taken as the 'truth' or the way to do something. Such drift is normal as we have a tendency to move towards more risky situations. This term is known as 'the normalisation of deviance'.

Normalisation of Deviance - being a deviant is normal

This is a term which has become more prevalent in social media as a way of explaining poor or suboptimal behaviours in divers. The term comes from Diane Vaughan's book, *'The Challenger Launch Decision : Risky Technology, Culture, and Deviance at NASA'*, where she highlighted the organisational acceptance of deviance from accepted safety standards over time, such that when a critical decision was made concerning launching STS-51 on 28 Jan 1986: *"...the key to accepting risk in the past was what I called "the normalization of deviance": having accepted anomalous O-ring performance once, precedent became the basis for accepting it again and again. The normalization of deviance was a product of NASA's organizational system: the connection between environment, organization, and individual interpretation, meaning, and action."*[7]

Unfortunately, the drifting associated with 'Normalisation of deviance' is normal human behaviour. Amalberti, a human factors researcher, highlighted in his article, *'The Paradoxes of Almost Totally Safe Transportation Systems'*[8], that there is a natural tendency to migrate towards risky behaviours because of the pressures associated with finite resources e.g. finance/time/manpower and workload pushing the operating position away from the original rules, processes and regulations put in place. Humans are adaptable, working towards the goals which are laid out. This means that safety margins are eroded.

Humans aren't very good at judging absolutes. For example, I can tell you if the water temperature is warmer or colder than something else, but I can't tell you the temperature with a high degree of accuracy.

Or, I can tell you if I perceive if something is safer than something else, but I can't tell you whether it is actually 'safe'. This relative judgement can cause problems as we erode the safety margins which have been built into a system. Figure 5 shows the progression across small changes until an accident happens. After the accident has happened, we can see that we have deviated a long way from the original standard and the social commentary often follows, *"How could you have missed how far you had deviated?"* when in fact the deviations that were being judged were the minor ones between each new baseline that was set. In hindsight, the major deviation is obvious!

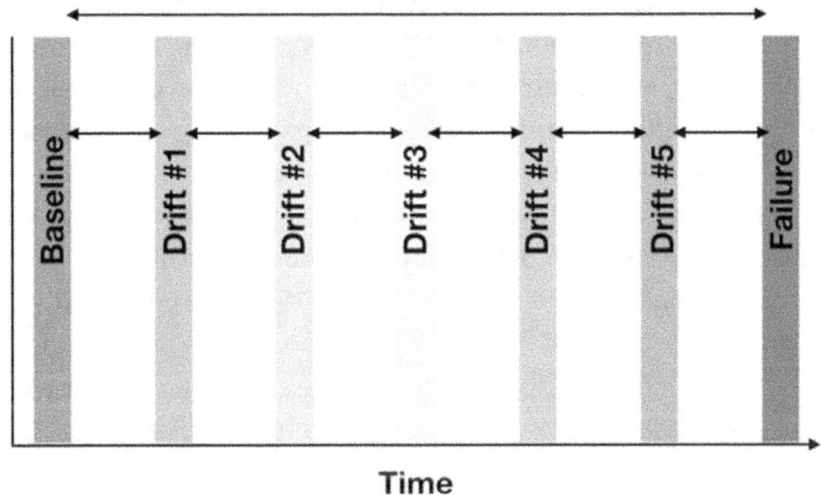

Figure 5: Small deviations are not recognised during continual operations, but when something goes wrong, the major deviation is obvious.

Cook and Rasmussen in their paper, *'Going Solid'*[9] describe how the variation in performance of the teams within organisations takes them unwittingly closer to a point where accidents and incidents are more likely. Some organisations are depicted by large fuzzy circles, highlighting large variations in standards, procedures and outcomes with poor internal feedback; whereas others are shown by tight, intense circles with minimal variation across operations. They describe how High Reliability Organisations (HROs) reduce this variation and deviation by having high levels of consistency and standardisation combined with a psychologically-safe environment which facilitates robust and open feedback to continually improve operations, changing work-as-imagined/work-as-prescribed to be closer to work-as-done. This means that while these organisations still don't know precisely where and when adverse events will happen, they are able to operate in higher-risk situations with the confidence that:

a: the risks are less likely to be materialised, and

b: that if an adverse event does happen, the teams are able to respond in a consistent and effective manner.

Given the above, as divers we need to recognise that the behaviours associated with 'normalisation of deviance' are in fact normal human behaviours and not those of 'stupid people'; and consequently, we should create environments where we can challenge others for drifting and, therefore, keep each other and ourselves accountable. This requires standards to be defined and known, and a psychologically-safe environment is present to allow the challenge to take place. However, the requirement for standardisation creates a tension against the premise that diving is a recreational activity and we should be able to do what we want without being told what to do.

As a community, we should also recognise that innovation isn't the same as normalisation of deviance. To undertake exploration, there is a need to actively push the boundaries. However, this should be done in a conscious and informed manner, as opposed to drifting without a realisation of how far procedures or 'safety' have been compromised. This can be hard when goal-fixation reduces the objectivity of the activity.

Summary of Key Points

- Decision-making isn't as simple as we think it is. We filter, discard and ignore significant amounts of information and data, because we don't think they are relevant. We take numerous mental short-cuts based on this filtered information. Most of the time the decisions we make are 'good enough' for the situations we are in. However, on a few occasions, it doesn't work out very well and someone gets scared, injured or killed.

- If we can understand the strengths and weaknesses of our decision-making processes, then we are more likely to make more effective decisions. We shouldn't just focus on the outcomes, but rather look at the processes we used and the information we perceived to help inform future decisions.
- Stop and think if you are about to make an irreversible decision and engage System 2 to purposely slow your thought processes down.
- There are tools which we can use to improve decision-making: checklists, briefs and debriefs. However, checklists are not a panacea. They need to be well-designed and not just deployed as a liability limiting exercise for a manufacturer or training agency. They need to be used with the correct mindset - the mindset that says, "I am fallible. I WILL make a mistake at some point. Slowing down and checking critical configurations are one way to reduce the likelihood of a fatality."
- When things are going to plan, and you are using skills- and rules-based decision-making processes, it doesn't really matter that you don't understand the 'why' behind the activity you are doing. However, as soon as you diverge from the plan, you are into knowledge-based decision-making/performance territory and the likelihood of an error goes up massively - if you don't understand the why.
- Normalisation of deviance is a normal human behaviour. We constantly migrate towards more risky behaviours due to external pressures based on limiting our workload (physical and cognitive) and the financial/time constraints we have to operate with. If we don't end up with a negative outcome, outcome bias provides a feedback loop that says what we are doing is acceptable or 'good enough'.

Questions to consider
- When was the last time you looked at a dive, or an instructional dive, and really looked at how you made the decisions you did and discussed them with the rest of the team?

- When you look at your diving, do you see informed innovation, or do you see drift and normalisation of deviance?
- If you are in an organisation, dive centre, dive team, what prevents you from speaking up when you see drift?

References

(1) Flin, R. ,*Safety at the Sharp End* (Kindle Locations 959-960). Ashgate. Kindle Edition.
(2) https://www.merriam-webster.com/dictionary/complacency retrieved 8 Dec 2018.
(3) Hollnagel, E. (2009). *The ETTO Principle: Efficiency-Thoroughness Trade-Off; Why Things That Go Right Sometimes Go Wrong*. Farnham, GB: Ashgate.
(4) Klein, G., 2008. *Naturalistic Decision Making*. Human Factors, 50 (3), 456–460
(5) Sully: A Hero's Story. https://www.telegraph.co.uk/films/sully/a-real-heros-story/ retrieved 8 Dec 2018.
(6) Gawande, A. Reith Lectures. https://www.bbc.co.uk/programmes/b00729d9/episodes/player, Reith Lectures, December 2014. Retrieved 8 Dec 2018.
(7) Vaughan, D. *The Challenger Launch Decision* (Kindle Locations 86-88). University of Chicago Press. Kindle Edition.
(8) Amalberti R. *The Paradoxes of Almost Totally Safe Transportation Systems*. Saf Sci 2001;37:109–26
(9) Cook, R, & Rasmussen, J. (2005). *"Going solid": a model of system dynamics and consequences for patient safety*. Quality & safety in health care, 14(2), 130–134.

Additional Reading

Craig, P. A. (2013). *The Killing Zone: How and Why Pilots Die*. New York, NY: McGraw-Hill

Gawande, A. (2014). *The Checklist Manifesto: How to Get Things Right*. Gurgaon, India: Penguin Random House.

Hollnagel, E. (2009). *The ETTO principle: Efficiency-Thoroughness Trade-Off; Why Things That Go Right Sometimes Go Wrong*. Farnham, GB: Ashgate.

Kahneman, D. (2015). *Thinking, Fast and Slow*. New York: Farrar, Straus and Giroux.

Klein, G. (2011). *Streetlights and Shadows: Searching for the keys to adaptive decision-making*. Cambridge, Mass: MIT Press.

Answers to the Cognitive Reflection Test:

A bat and ball cost $1.10. The bat costs one dollar more than the ball. How much does the ball cost? **The ball costs $0.05**

If it takes 5 machines 5 minutes to make 5 widgets, how long would it take 100 machines to make 100 widgets? 100 minutes OR 5 minutes? **5 minutes**

Chapter 7

Situational Awareness: Just because it's there, it doesn't mean you've recognised its significance

"There can be no doubt that situation awareness is potentially one of the most important topics facing ergonomics, along with workload, error trust, stress, mental models and feedback."

Stanton, Salmon, Walker and Jenkins[1].

Case Study: 'Exploration fever' rears its head again
Anton van Rosmalen, a cave explorer and professional risk expert, recalls his third visit to Grotte de la Source, France when they finally got to actually dive it. Diving this cave requires the serious efforts of a large group of 20 – 30 people that are willing to help to carry the gear and set the dive up. Previous attempts had been thwarted by either a team that were scared by the complexity of getting to the water and the bigger complexity of getting a potential injured person outside again; or the poor conditions that were discovered after they had to (literally) blast the entrance open in order for them to be able to get their equipment to the water. As such they were pretty eager to finally get in as the conditions were great...

I was diving with my recently-acquired and very small KISS manual closed-circuit rebreather (mCCR); and my buddy Jan was diving his massive RB80 passive addition semi-closed rebreather (pSCR). This RB80 is also the type of rebreather I had been diving with until recently and the unit I had also been trained on. The key difference being that the mCCR injects a preset minimal amount of oxygen into the loop to account for metabolism in rest, but also requires the diver to manually bring oxygen levels up to the required level - once it has deviated from the preferred level. The oxygen level is adjusted to keep the oxygen at the correct pO2 for decompression and, more importantly, to support life. The pSCR will automatically refresh breathing gas and comes much closer to OC diving with a (predictable) pO2 drop.

The diluent gas for my KISS was 10/70 and Jan was using EAN40 as the drive gas for his RB80. Before diving, we went through all normal procedures which included me flushing my unit with O2 in order to check the calibration of my oxygen sensors. 10/70 was chosen to reduce the logistical burden of having multiple gases, as well as being able to cover any depth up to 95m which is the maximum we expected to dive on this trip.

We started our dive and crossed the first 20 metres of the crystal-clear pool and followed the old metal line down to the start of the sump. As I left the surface, my pO2 was close to 1.0.

The cave starts with a bit of a vertical restriction. I managed to squeeze through easily enough and found myself in a very big room that marks the start of the main gallery at a depth of 15m. As I descended, my counter-lungs were compressed by the increasing ambient pressure, forcing me to add diluent to the loop through the Auto Diluent Valve (ADV) by simply inhaling deeply to deal with the decreasing loop volume.

While I waited for Jan to arrive in the main gallery, I started to look around and saw openings in the walls at various locations. However, when Jan did not arrive within a few minutes, I decided to return to the restriction where I saw him signalling that he was unable to pass as his unit was too large. I ascended to a depth of 3m passing the restriction, so we could discuss what to do next. During the ascent, I vented my unit due to the gas expansion. In addition, the ascent also lowered the pO2 in my loop due to the reduction in ambient pressure.

After a brief discussion, we decided to end the dive. However, just as we started to go back, I noticed another opening, just above the location where I had previously seen the side passage in the main gallery.

I briefly signalled Jan and told him to stay where he was. I took my reel and started to descend in the side passage, where I found another somewhat restricted hole that seemed bigger than the main restriction. As I descended, I added more diluent to my loop by inhaling though the ADV. I used this process and did not manually add oxygen (nor did I check my pO2 levels) as I had my hands full with the reel, and because I had to inflate my drysuit in the vertical position I was in while passing the restriction.

I arrived into a very silty, but big enough passage at a depth of 12m and continued my exploration, feeling quite excited to be laying line so close to the entrance. After 20m or so, I arrived at the start of the main gallery and tied into the main line ready to end the dive and join Jan.

Once I tied in, I finally took some time to look around. Despite being happy that I had laid new line, I felt that something was wrong. Only at this point did I notice that I was feeling a bit out of breath and lightheaded. I looked at my oxygen sensors and saw my pO2 had dropped down to 0.12, a level barely capable of supporting life.

I immediately started injecting oxygen into the loop and brought my pO2 up to 1.2 where it should have been all along, cursing myself for letting exploration fever, peer pressure and lack of experience on this particular unit get me this close to a major incident where, if I had gone hypoxic and passed out, I would have likely died as no-one was nearby to help me.

It is easy to look back on Anton's event and say, 'He should have been paying more attention.' Hindsight is a wonderful thing, because it allows us to identify what the key factors were and how they contributed to the positive or negative situation developing. Often, we say, 'The root cause of this was a lack of attention'. While this might be technically correct, as we will see in this chapter, our attention span is limited; and even when experts undertake an activity, they dismiss what are apparently irrelevant features that help them make more effective decisions. Once you've read this chapter, come back to the start and review the incident with a different set of glasses - one which shows what Situational Awareness (SA) is, and why it appears that Anton 'Lost his SA'.

The Finite Capacity of our Brains to Perceive, Process and Project

Situational Awareness is a finite capacity which can be easily lost when other tasks or interests which appear to be more important or relevant are the focus of our attention. The problem is that given the way our brains are wired, it is difficult to identify that we have 'lost situational awareness', because it is only really apparent that this has happened after the event as we look back in time.

Anton's narrative describes a situation which I am sure many readers will have experienced before: the mind or focus coming back to a reality which is different to what you thought you were experiencing. In this case, the task loading, pressures to complete the exploration and elation at finding a new passage, all took Anton's attention away from what was a critical task: ensuring that additional O2 was injected into the breathing loop to deal with the additional amount being metabolised by his additional physical and mental workload.

In 2007, Paul O'Connor, a researcher working with the US Navy in Pensacola, FL published a paper looking at US Navy diving[2] incidents and accidents. His research showed that nearly 40% of incidents and accidents had situational awareness as a contributory factor; the next highest contributory factor was leadership and supervision at nearly 30%. In the sport's diving research, there isn't anything which looks at contributory factors in such a manner.

So, what is situational awareness? In 1995, researcher and academic Mica Endsley wrote a paper titled, 'Toward a Theory of Situation Awareness Dynamic Systems'[3] in which she described how the human mind was able to perceive data through our senses; process it to determine its relevance to now; and then, depending on experiences and training, project into the future about what was likely to happen. These outputs would then feed into the different decision-making processes we use; and because we had executed on a decision, our state or the state of the environment would change, a change which we would pick up and the system would carry on as a loop. In her paper, Endsley defined SA as, *'Situation awareness is the perception of the elements in the environment within a volume of time and space, the comprehension of their meaning, and the projection of their status in the near future.'*

I have recreated a model based on her research to highlight those factors which influence how situational awareness is developed based on the perception (level 1), processing (level 2) and then projecting (level 3) of information, as well as how the design of the 'system' can impact the quality and effectiveness of both situational awareness and decision-making. The overlap between situational awareness and decision-making is because the output of the situational awareness process is decision, and the input of a decision-making process is information gathering. This model is at Figure 6.

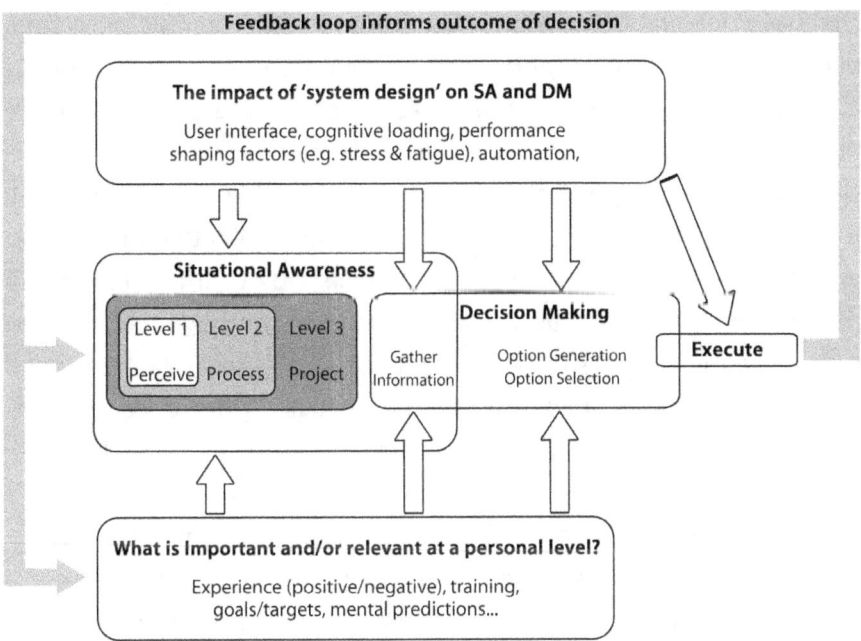

Figure 6: Factors Influencing Effective Situational Awareness and Decision-Making

At the centre of the model are the three levels of Situational Awareness.

Level 1 - Perceive

Level 1 - This could be thought of as gathering information. Using all five senses, the diver is perceiving information which makes up elements of the situation. Examples in diving include:
- Feeling a drysuit squeeze;
- Feeling increased pressure in the ears;
- Seeing the current picking up;
- Seeing a pO2 value displayed in the HUD by colours;
- Hearing bubbles which aren't related to the normal exhalation process.

What should be noted here is that it is the direct sensing and perceiving of the data - not what it means. Given our limited mental capacity to hold a small amount of information in our working memory, only 7 elements plus or minus 2, we can easily get distracted by tasks which we perceive to be more important or relevant. This attentional blindness or cognitive tunnelling has been shown in a number of experiments, the most famous by researchers and authors, Chabris and Simons involving 'Invisible Gorillas'. In their experiments, they showed that when people are given a fairly simple task, it is possible to miss something really obvious in the scene, because the focus of attention is spotlighted on something else. Due to the limitations of the senses and the efficient filtering systems we have, the data we perceive and then pass to Level 2 for processing is massively reduced. For example, the eye has more than 120 million photoreceptors, but only 1.2 million nerves transmit information to the brain where it is further filtered.

As an example of this filtering/discarding in real-time, again we go back to driving and distracted driving due to mobile phone use and texting. While these activities do indeed reduce the attention afforded to driving, all driving is distracted. You cannot focus on and process every bit of data which your senses are picking up. Most of it is binned as not being relevant until your subconscious (or conscious brain) picks up something during the scanning processes and says, 'Look over there, it's important'. Given this reduction in data during both the sensing and processing stages, it is no wonder we miss important information. Now consider that when we dive, we have to take into account the new environmental data being picked up which reduces out capacity.

Level 2 - Process

Level 2 - This is the ability to process the information which has been perceived. Bear in mind that the data has already been filtered, so something which is relevant might have been rejected from this process. Level 2 is about determining the relevance of the data to now; turning it into information based on previous experiences; training; abilities; and the current goals and expectations which are informed by mental models. In the examples given above, Level 2 situational awareness would mean:

- Drysuit and ear squeeze. The diver is descending;
- The diver is now drifting along the bottom faster, or they have to work harder to swim into the current;
- A series of flashing colours in the HUD of the CCR depicts the pO_2 of the breathing loop - a sequence different to the expected baseline;
- If the bubbles aren't associated with the exhale, then there must be a leak somewhere.

However, for this to work effectively, there must be some mental model against which the sensed information can be processed. If you have never dived in a drysuit before, you might end up descending a fair distance, before you pick up the cues that the suit is getting tighter. This means that your control of buoyancy will be coarse. If you don't pick up that your ears are being pressured until too late, you might not be able to clear them without causing distress in the outer/middle ear. If you don't know what the correct lighting sequence is for a high pO_2 situation (not all HUDs display in the same way), then you don't know what the red flashing light means. If you haven't tuned your ears/brain to listen for additional bubbles, you might miss the non-exhale related bubbles, discounting them as just 'noise'.

Humans are experts at pattern matching. So, for experienced divers in the relative domains, each of the examples above would appear obvious. However, that is because mental models or 'schema' have been constructed over time, which allow us to create a match - without even thinking of it. Therefore, unless you have a pattern to match, it is likely you will make a mistake, either because you missed the significance or because you attributed the wrong model to the perception. The attribution of wrong models can easily be demonstrated through the numerous optical illusions which can be found on the internet.

The mental shortcuts and jumps we complete help save time and mental energy, but they also lead to errors if the perceived information is not coherent with the reality. Furthermore, team situational awareness adds another dimension, because while each team member has their own elements of SA, there is also the shared mental model within the team. A model of team SA is shown below and you can see that team SA is where the four team member's elements overlap, but that this doesn't mean that it aligns with reality, which a number of the team are missing information about. This is a static model, in the real world, the circles and overlapping areas are changing size based on the same factors which influence individual SA.

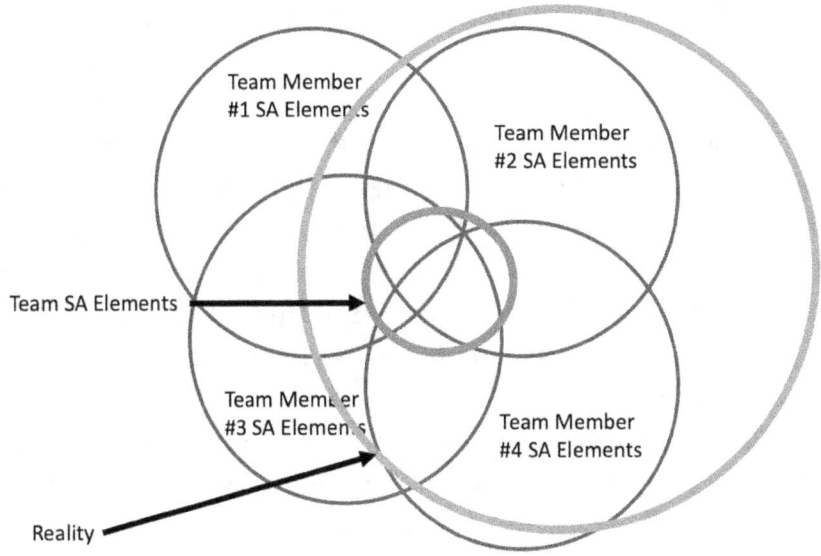

Figure 7: Team Situational Awareness Model

Research in 2010 (*Did You See the Unicycling Clown? Inattentional Blindness while Walking and Talking on a Cell Phone*[4]) showed that by sharing cognitive resources across the team, issues could be spotted which were missed by individuals. In this case, when operating on their own and task loaded by operating a digital device, 75% of subjects missed a clown who was riding a unicycle through the college grounds. However, when two subjects were together, only 25% of them missed the clown. The reason being that the chances of both subjects being distracted at the same time are reduced. However, that doesn't mean that teams won't make a mistake when it comes to ineffective situational awareness. 'Confirmation bias' can seriously hamper our ability to determine what is the correct model to understand what is happening now.

In 1994, two USAF F-15 fighters conducted a visual identification of two Black Hawk helicopters operating in Northern Iraq as they had been told that they were Mi-24 Hind aircraft and according to Snook in his book *'Friendly Fire,',*[5] *'There is little doubt that what the F-15 pilots expected to see during their visual pass influenced what they actually saw.'*

In the words of one of the pilots, *'I had no doubt when I looked at him that he was a Hind. The Black Hawk did not even cross my mind when I made that visual identification'* (p80). Unfortunately, following the (mis) identification process, the pilots fired on the Black Hawks, destroying both of them and killing all on board. These were professional aircrew, but their mental models had been compromised by the information which they had been fed from the intelligence briefs and the Airborne Warning and Control System (AWACS) aircraft that there were unidentified aircraft in the area which were transmitting an incorrect identification code.

The same issues of missing relevant cues can be faced when diving as many accounts in this book have shown e.g. all three narratives from Chapter 6 (Decision-making) have examples of a reduction in SA at the team level leading to poor decisions.

One way in which team and individual SA can be improved is through the use of briefs and debriefs. The former to outline what should happen; the latter to close the loop when it comes to learning and developing new or enhanced mental models. Both of these techniques are covered in more detail in Chapter 9 under teamwork.

Level 3 - Project

Level 3 - This is the ability to project a mental model of what is likely to happen in the near future based on perceived information, the current state and previous experiences. This is why, in hindsight, it is easy to determine that something would have happened; but in real time, it isn't so easy unless we have experienced it before.

A simple non-diving example is running into the back of another car at a road junction - something I have personally done, but only once! I was waiting to turn left while leaving work one day and there was one car in front of me also turning left. I looked to the right, saw that there was a large gap, so got ready to move, I looked forward, saw the car in front start to pull away, I looked right again to make sure the gap was big enough for the two of us (it was) and then I gently pressed on the accelerator and hit the back of the car in front! I perceived that the car had moved: I compared that to a mental model that said the gap was big enough and so I expected the car to turn into the main road. It didn't. My mental model did not match reality. They had decided the gap wasn't big enough and so didn't pull out. I have since changed my behaviour to ensure that the car does in fact move before I move forward!

Looking at the diving examples above again, we can show what Level 3 SA would look like:

- If I don't arrest the descent soon, I am going to end up with a major drysuit squeeze or barotrauma if I don't clear my ears.
- If the current has picked up and we are going further down current, we need to turn around earlier than the planned bottom time, so we make it back to the exit point with gas reserves intact.
- The HUD the diver previously used only displayed a red LED for low pO2 situations, whereas his current CCR has red for both high and low pO2, and it is showing high pO2. The diver continues to inject O2 into the loop to 'increase' the pO2 from a hypoxic situation. (This scenario is based on a real-incident - which unfortunately led to a fatality).
- If the bubbles aren't from the exhale process, there must be a leak somewhere. Assuming a twinset, isolate the side which the diver thinks the bubbles are coming from and signal their buddy. If diving with a single cylinder, signal their buddy and prepare to ascend to the surface.

The scenarios above are relatively simple. What about looking at the weather/sea state while on the boat and working out whether you can get across the boat safely, through the gate and then back on again if the weather stays the same? What about if a diver surfaces with an injury or has DCS? Does your assessment of the situation before you get in the water still hold true? What about the scenario that Clare and her team encountered in the cave in which the clues were subtle and may not have made sense to someone not as experienced? In fact, consider any of the scenarios within the book and think about how you would need to look at a scene differently to determine a likely outcome?

Being involved in dynamic situations means it is very hard for novices to apply a correct projection to the situation. This is because unless they have experienced a similar situation before, they are likely to make flawed decisions based on the following biases we all use:
- availability bias - to say that there isn't a risk because we haven't encountered this problem before.
- confirmation bias - means we will find information or data to support our thought processes based on previous experiences.
- outcome bias - to say that the last time we did something like this, it was okay.

Experts are much more capable of having successful outcomes in Level 3, because they have more mental models against which to compare their current perceptions and likely outcomes. This process of perception and associated heuristics (or mental shortcuts) links with Naturalistic Decision Making discussed in Chapter 6 in which schema and mental models are used to make intuitive decisions based on the ability to run mental simulations against them. The more models the individual has, the more timely the decisions.

Klein and his associates also showed that experts require less elements to initiate the task execution process, which might mean the difference between life and death in high-risk situations. The models don't have to be exact, but close enough to provide a match; and the gaps are then filled in with assumptions based on previous experiences. You are likely thinking of the phrase, 'Assumptions make an ass out of u and me'. This is true, but only in a few circumstances. Most of the time, assumptions make our lives much easier!

In addition to the normal cognitive limitations of the human mind when operating on the surface, divers have to consider both the physical and physiological implications of operating in a submerged hyperbaric environment. Not just that there are additional tasks to complete like buoyancy control, decompression management, effective propulsion to minimise the chance of reduced visibility and underwater navigation in a three-dimensional space - an environment for which our brains are wired for, but also the influence of high-pressure gases on decision-making and situational awareness. The following narrative from Astrid de Jager, a marine biologist living on the Caribbean island of Bonaire, shows how nitrogen narcosis (and likely CO2 narcosis) can impact diving safety and performance by reducing our ability to think clearly, even for simple tasks.

Case Study: In hindsight, hunting lionfish at 60m on air wasn't such a great idea...

It was a bright and sunny day; the water was calm and clear and circumstances were ideal for diving. Nothing exceptional if you live on Bonaire. We were on our way to the Windjammer, one of the many shore dive sites on Bonaire, but one of the few sites where it's actually worth going a bit deeper. At a depth of 170-200 feet, one can find a large schooner that sank a bit over a century ago. Divers cannot go there except with an approved local guide; and it so happened that my buddy was an official windjammer guide. During his last dive he had noticed a large amount of lionfish hiding out around the reef. Our mission for the day: catch as many fish we could.

I don't consider myself a very experienced diver. I got trained in 2005, became a dive professional in 2009 and enrolled in technical diving training a year later. I had been diving sidemount since the system was introduced on Bonaire, and way before any organisation I knew offered training. By the time of the incident, I approximately had 2000 dives under my belt, but most of them were in Bonaire's warm and clear waters, and I had been doing sidemount and decompression dives for some five years, climbing the steps to extended range diver and decompression procedures instructor. I had done the Windjammer dive about five or six times before, and knew the dive site reasonably well. Like I said, I wasn't very experienced, but experienced enough to be comfortable with this dive.

My buddy for the dive was my husband, who also happened to be the instructor that taught me on most of my tech classes. He is an experienced diver and dive instructor and has been (tech) diving under numerous different circumstances, including the North Sea. Based on his seniority, he was technically in charge of the dive, but given our relationship neither of us gave that too much of a thought.

Like most of our 60m dives in those days, my buddy and I used sidemount, with air as our bottom gas and EAN40 and EAN70 as deco gasses. Our choice was based on training and availability: neither of us was trained in trimix (not to mention the sky-high prices for a trimix fill on the island), and 200 bar EAN70 was easier to get than 200 bar O2. Bonaire lacks cold water, heavy currents or other reasons why carbon dioxide build-up adds noticeably to the narcotic effects. Still, on air at 55m, gas narcosis is more than a potential danger, so we agreed to stick together and monitor each other closely.

The start of the dive was uneventful. We checked our gear and swam out to our descent point. The plan was to descend to a maximum of 60m for a maximum of 25 minutes, or until either of us used a third of the bottom gas. We descended a couple of metres, did an s-drill, after which I clipped my longhose 2nd stage and stayed on my necklaced 2nd stage. We descended to the wreck, spotted our prey and started hunting.

Although we stayed fairly close to each other, both of us got caught up in the hunt. At one moment I noticed I had breathed 100 bar from my tanks, and we were at 15 minutes bottom time. I decided not to switch tanks now, because I noticed a new nest of lionfish - I would switch after we caught those. 5 minutes and 35 bar later I signalled to my buddy to start our ascent, and so we did.

Halfway to our first gas switch, I noticed breathing became harder. Internally swearing, I reached for my longhose second stage - I had neglected to change tanks, and the one I was breathing from was down to the last breath. At which moment I found out, that I had clipped the regulator in a rather inconvenient angle, and I couldn't instantly unclip it. After a few highly uncomfortable seconds - during which I debated alternatives like swimming to my buddy (I would never have heard the end of that) and making a rapid ascent from 130 to 100ft and switching *to EAN40 - I was able to unclip the regulator and breath again. The rest of the dive was uneventful, aside from a slightly elevated heart rate. My buddy never noticed a thing.*

My internal reflections on the event: first of all, this was one of the last deep dives I did using air. I know all arguments for and against doing dives deeper than 40m on air, and I'm not choosing sides. However, personally I'm too easily affected by gas narcosis to do a deep dive on air and perform any other task than simply diving. Hunting lionfish at that depth on air was - for me - a bridge too far.

As far as equipment considerations go, from that moment on I started using my long-hose regulator during the deeper part of the dives, and clipping the second stage to the necklace when changing at depth. This would keep it accessible at all times.

But most importantly, I started working on my buddy team protocols, both together with my husband and with other divers I buddied up with. When faced with a problem, a potentially life-threatening one, my first thought should have been to go to my buddy for help. He was less than 10m away. And at some point, my buddy would have noticed I was struggling, and come to my aid. Instead I forced myself to solve the problem independently, because I was afraid of a little teasing. Not quite the team spirit we should be looking for during any dives, and especially not at this level. We've improved much since.

Astrid's account highlights that once we start to reduce our cognitive abilities to manage SA and 'rational' decision-making, then things can start to go wrong quite quickly. Fortunately, many adverse events in diving don't end up as a serious injury or fatality. However, this can then work against us, as this can lead to normalisation of deviance (see Chapter 6) and changes our perception of the risk/uncertainty which we face. In Astrid's case, there was also contributory effects of peer pressure/social conformance which prevented the optimal solution - go to her buddy when low on gas, rather than keeping the problem to herself.

If we look at the need to be able to project what might happen, another reason why the sharing of such information concerning compromised equipment is essential is because her team mate might have been low on gas and their mental model/solution would have been to use Astrid as a donor - if an emergency developed. In fact, a very similar scenario came up in a two-day human factors class I delivered in 2018, when one of my students described being on sidemount, in a cave, shooting video & stills as part of a four-diver team and they forgot to change their sidemount regulators, because they were task loaded. Again, they did not say anything at the time, but they did at least cover it in the debrief after the dive. The point I made during the class was that unless the team knows all the resources they have available to them, i.e. breathable gas being a key team resource, they cannot make the best decisions available to them. For example, in the event of an out-of-gas situation, the victim might have gone to her instead of another diver who had been managing their gas more effectively, and then the problem gets worse - because an additional change will be needed later.

In aviation, Crew Resource Management was developed to increase the fidelity of the shared mental models held by the flight deck crew, cabin crew and Air Traffic Control. The same applies to diving and non-technical skills where one diver might have a critically important piece of information that they should share with the team, because it impacts the plan or possible contingencies in the future.

'Losing Situational Awareness'

Knowing what situational awareness is, is important, because it shows how perceived data is processed by the senses and brain to produce information and knowledge. However, knowing when you're more likely to 'lose it' or that you've 'lost it' is probably more important when it comes to safety and performance.

The research shows that perception or information gathering (Level 1) is the biggest issue when it comes to 'losing' situational awareness. 'Losing' is in inverted commas, because it is difficult to know that you have 'lost it' until after the event. In one study, 143 aviation accidents were examined to determine what level of situation awareness failure was implicated for pilots and air traffic controllers. The authors found that 78% of the accidents were down to issues relating to level 1 (i.e. not having enough or the correct information needed to make sense of the situation.) Furthermore, the most common level 1 error is a failure of scan (35% of all SA errors; Jones and Endsley, 1996[6]). Far fewer problems (17%) occurred when all the information had been gathered, but was then misunderstood and only 5% were related to failures to think ahead when the situation had been correctly interpreted. While these data refer to aviation and ATC, there is no reason to suspect that divers would be any different when it comes to information-gathering and processing.

There are some common 'clues' that can be used to determine if individuals or the team has 'lost' situational awareness:
- ambiguity;
- when information from two or more sources does not agree;
- task fixation or focusing on one thing to the exclusion of everything else;
- uncertainty or confusion about a situation;
- lack of required information;
- failure to maintain critical tasks (e.g. monitoring gas reserves, decompression obligations or location within the dive site/cave system);
- failure to resolve discrepancies;
- contradictory data;
- a 'bad gut feeling' that things are not quite right.

The following is something all divers should be aware of though: '*lost situational awareness*' is only possible to classify after an event. By this, I mean that while the event is happening, your knowledge of the event is increasing. However, if it ends up as an adverse event, because you missed a critical element of information, then you apparently had less knowledge of the situation. The problem with such a statement is that you cannot know everything; and, therefore, focus on what you perceived, at the time, too important and/or relevant. Your situational awareness isn't lost, it was just pointing in the (apparently) wrong direction.

As situational awareness is very much dependent on the capacity of the working memory, it is affected by distractions, interruptions and having your senses overloaded. For the majority of diving situations, this isn't too much of an issue. However, if divers need to make critical decisions/actions (e.g. observing an instructor/guide give guidance or direction, following a line in a cave, assembling a rebreather, undertaking a decompression gas-switch, analysing gas, etc.), reduced awareness can have serious or fatal consequences. Consequently, knowing when an interruption is 'safe' is a key skill to have within a team, a skill which needs to be developed. Another part of understanding when attention must be paid is to have a level of technical competency about the task at hand, and so that it can be clearly understood what the consequences of missing a critical step or a flawed decision can lead to in the end.

It has been recognised that dispensing errors occur when healthcare workers are disturbed. A number of studies have taken place showing how the introduction of a control, such as wearing a vest with, 'DISPENSING DRUGS. DO NOT INTERRUPT', written on them has improved safety. One study from Ireland[7] showed a 98% reduction in dispensing errors and 85% reduction in disturbances, whereas others were much lower (35%[8]) but still significant especially as the majority of interruptions were not clinically-based. This same 'boundary' process can be applied in diving through effective teamwork by letting others know a critical task (e.g. rebreather assembly, is underway and only to disturb them if there is a very serious issue.)

Novices are particularly likely to have their task performance disrupted by distraction. As a diver becomes more skilled, then he or she will be able to perform tasks in a much more automatic fashion; and, as a consequence, less concentration is required to perform the task (i.e. the load on working memory has been reduced.) In addition to novices being more susceptible to distraction, instructors/guides should be aware that stress can cause a reduction in cognitive abilities (see Chapter 12) and as such novices are more likely to miss critical information - because their attention is taken up by nervousness and stress. Using closed-loop communications and open questions are two ways of ensuring that the listener has both heard and understood the meaning of the message being conveyed (see Chapter 8).

Case Study: Was the twinset depressurised?

The following narrative comes from an experienced cave diver who was taking their banded and manifolded twinset cylinders in to a dive shop to conduct a visual inspection, before they went on a dive trip the following weekend. To facilitate this, they knew that the cylinders needed to have the bands and the manifold joining the two removed. Obviously, this meant they had to be drained too. Unfortunately, due to a number of factors which happened over a period of time, not all was as it was expected to be.

To drain the cylinders, I opened the valve on the right cylinder and the gas was drained slowly. I didn't think to use the left cylinder valve to expedite the draining. Once drained, I loaded the cylinders into my SUV, and while I was doing this, I had a niggling thought that I should open the manifold valve to ensure that both sides were drained, but seeing as the manifold was never normally closed, I ignored this little voice of concern. The cylinders had previously been used 12 months prior by me and hadn't been used by anyone else.

When I arrived at the dive shop to undertake the visual inspection using their workshop facilities, I spoke with the owner and went into the backroom to start the inspection. I started by removing the bands and then began to loosen the nuts on the isolator bar. At this point I noticed some resistance while unscrewing the bar. I assumed that the resistance was due to the cylinders being slightly uneven, but I proceeded anyway. As the wrench turned the nut on the left side of the isolator, there was a large and very obvious discharge of gas focusing mine and the owner's attention on the cylinders. The shop owner looked at me from his desk and very clearly said, "You need to be very, VERY careful right now." Without hesitation, I opened the left side valve and the remainder of the gas escaped through the hole in and around the DIN valve dust cap.

How in the world could something so obvious occur? It would be easy to say complacency, but that doesn't explain how it made sense in a manner which prevents future events from happening.

So why didn't I open the isolator valve when the "voices in their head" told me to do so? The simple reason for this is that I never use the isolator apart from during in-water shutdown drills - so why would it be anything other than open? This is despite them not being used for 12 months and that was by me. Fundamentally, there wasn't a memory which said the isolator valve had been closed so why would I open it or check that it was open as it wasn't part of my normal sequence for checking valves?

Why didn't I stop trying to remove the isolator bar even with resistance? In the past I have had cylinders which were unevenly aligned and so there is some resistance when moving the nuts on the isolator bar. In hindsight, it was obvious that there was pressure in the cylinder, but this potential configuration wasn't in my head as I had already drained the twinset before I left the house.

Why didn't I ask for help? I had done this before on numerous occasions before, having certified under the Visual Inspection Program and wanted to do it again on my own. And, if I'm honest, asking for help (admitting I was unsure), may have dented my pride a bit.

Sometimes we need to listen to that niggling voice over our shoulder saying, 'Look out, things aren't what you think they are.' Our subconscious sees more than we do!

Summary of Key Points
- Our sensory and cognitive processing systems have a limited capacity to deal with the vast amounts of data in the real world. As a consequence, we ditch the majority of that data because we do not perceive it to be relevant or important.
- What we focus on is based on goals, experiences, expectations

and mental models. Without an understanding of relevance or importance, we will not perceive it.
- Sensing is not the same as comprehending. Just because something is in your field of view, it doesn't mean you will notice and comprehend its relevance.
- Systems (in the wider context of system) can be designed so that it is easier to identify relevant and important information through the application of recognised human factors principles.
- *"It was obvious"* is normally informed with hindsight bias. If it was that obvious, the adverse event wouldn't have happened!
- 'Lost situational awareness' is really only able to be determined after the event. To improve situational awareness, there needs to be a debrief to understand what was more relevant or important than the task that was missed.
- Most errors are caused by poor perception leading to a sound decision based on flawed information, therefore improving situational awareness skills is essential.
- Understanding how situational awareness is developed and lost is essential to improving decision-making.

Questions to consider
- The last time you 'lost' situational awareness and missed some important and/or relevant information, where was your attention pointing? Why was that more important than the task at hand?
- The last time you got your situational awareness back, what was the trigger to bring you back to the room? Could you have spotted those cues/clues earlier?
- When was the last time you sat down with your dive team/buddies and discussed what each of you had seen on the dive and how that compared to each others' perception of the dive? Sharing stories and perceptions improves the performance of the whole team.

References
(1) Stanton, N. et al., 2010. Is Situation Awareness All In The Mind? *Theoretical Issues in Ergonomics Science*, 11(1-2), pp.29–40.
(2) O'Connor, P., O'Dea, A., & Melton, J. (2007). A methodology for identifying human error in U.S. Navy diving accidents. Hum Factors, 49(2), 214-226.
(3) Endsley, MR. (1995). Toward a theory of situation awareness in dynamic systems. Human Factors: The Journal of the Human Factors and Ergonomics Society, 37(1), 32–64.
(4) Hyman, I., Boss, S., Wise, B., McKenzie, K., & Caggiano, J. (2010). Did You See The Unicycling Clown? Inattentional Blindness While Walking and Talking on a cell phone. Applied Cognitive Psychology, 24(5), 597–607.
(5) Snook, S. A. (2000). *Friendly fire: The Accidental Shootdown of U.S. Black Hawks over Northern Iraq*. Page 80. Princeton, N.J: Princeton University Press.
(6) Jones, D. and Endsley, M. (1996) Sources of situation awareness errors in aviation. Aviation, Space and Environmental Medicine, 67, 507– 512.
(7) Uko-Udom B. Introduction of Drug Round Tabard and Checklist to Reduce Interruptions and Error in Medication Administration. [MSc Thesis]. Dublin: Royal College of Surgeons in Ireland; 2014.
(8) Westbrook JI, Li L, Hooper TD, et al Effectiveness of a 'Do not interrupt' bundled intervention to reduce interruptions during medication administration: a cluster randomised controlled feasibility study BMJ Qual Saf 2017;26:734-742.

Additional Reading
CAA (2014) *Flight-crew human factors handbook. CAP 737*. Gatwick: Civil Aviation Authority. www.caa.org

Chabris, C. F., & Simons, D. J. (2010). *The Invisible Gorilla: And Other Ways Our Intuitions Deceive Us*. New York: Crown.

Snook, S. A. (2000). *Friendly Fire: The Accidental Shootdown of U.S. Black Hawks over Northern Iraq*.

Chapter 8

Communications: If only people could communicate clearly!

"The single biggest problem in communication is the illusion that it has taken place."

George Bernard Shaw

Case Study: Communication helps build the mental models
The following account from Garry Dallas, an Instructor Trainer with thousands of hours in caves, highlights the impact miscommunication or no communication can have when it comes to diving in a team where implicit assumptions are the norm and the significance of the issues identified are not passed over. Communication is about facilitation of the shared mental model within the team. When that communication breaks down, the model is incomplete.

Early afternoon, on a calm, slightly overcast and breezy day in north Wales at Dorothea quarry, my friend and I began a descent to 105m to explore the floor of this lovely open quarry. We couldn't have wished for better conditions, while camping over the weekend, with so much equipment to take up and down the steep gradient, known as Cardiac Hill, which many divers struggle to deal with, before or after a dive. The dive ended with, "Thanks for that! Don't know what I'd have done if it wasn't for you, I owe you one!"

Everything seemed to go as planned logistically-wise and we even had Sherpas to help move equipment from the top of the steep hill to the water's edge and back again.

Knowing my friend was very comfortable with the depth on open circuit trimix in sidemount, as he had done so many beforehand, I too felt comfortable with his mindset and skills to go diving with him. He was not only trained by me for technical diving, but also for cave diving, so I didn't ever feel like I was, or ever had to look after him; although my first instinct when I dive with anyone, of any qualifying level, is to be very aware of them regardless.

The dive was planned with suitable mixes, along with primary and backup decompression schedules. To complete the dives, we had six 200 bar tanks. Lean left, rich right for our stage and travel gases, with bottom gases as per our normal sidemount configuration. Despite having the same kit configurations, we went through our detailed buddy, equipment and gas checks, so everything was clearly understood. This finished with a final question, 'Are we happy with everything and happy to continue with the dive?' At this point, I noticed a slight hesitation in my buddy's response and asked if there was a problem. My buddy replied, "Nah, no problem". We then spent a few minutes relaxing on the surface and made our way over to the buoy.

All seemed to go well as we descended down the shot-line on the 32% travel gas. During the dive we stopped at 5m to do our final safety checks. Oddly, my buddy seemed a little less comfortable in his buoyancy control on this occasion, but I held my position and after a few moments, he was stable and gave me a good clear, "OK" that he was comfortable again and we continued our descent. We switched just shy of 40m to our bottom gases to take full advantage of the allowable time at depth. At this point, I again noticed an unusual amount of stress appearing in my buddy, something which was very unlike him. After another brief stop and confirmation, "OK" we descended together.

We hit turn pressures, thumbed the dive and started our ascent.

At 60m when we switched sides ready for the gas switch at 40m, my buddy's buoyancy became erratic, not as controlled as he usually was on a dive like that and I couldn't understand why. I was in exactly the same equipment as he was. It appeared like he was struggling, and it became more and more difficult for me to understand his erratic hand gestures. He was breathing more quickly and working harder. We arrived at 40m for a gas switch back on to 32% where I checked the gas pressures on all his tanks. I noticed that he had much less pressures than anticipated in the tanks on his left side and this is where the problem may lie. I gave him some weight by giving him one of my tanks to compensate for his lack of weight on his left side. He felt much better at this point and seemed to calm down, but he was still a little uncomfortable as he gestured.

He began pointing to his second stage regulator in his mouth, indicating there was something wrong. The decision I needed to make: let him carry on with what he was currently breathing or switch our travel gas cylinders, as I was more qualified to deal with failures. I decided to switch out, taking his tank and replacing it with mine and switching regulators. This appeared to sort the problem right away. We continued our decompression stops allowing for extra time at the final stops where we switched to our high-oxygen content mixes. We exited without any further issues.

As usual, we debriefed the dive. It's part of our continual improvement process, whether the dive goes as planned or not. During the debrief, it became apparent that something very interesting happened. Something I personally wasn't aware of and more to the point, something he didn't consider to be of interest to me. During our pre-dive checks, he noticed a slight overpressure on his second stage regulator coming from his 32% travel gas mix. All the other regulators were working perfectly, except this one. Feeling that it was of little consequence at the time and deciding he'd rather not call the dive and have to de-kit, walk up the steep hill, swap regulators out and start all over again, and then delay the team by waiting for half an hour while he did this, he decided not to say anything. He had also not balanced his gas very well during the bottom phase of the dive, resulting in more buoyancy in his left cylinder leaving his right heavier. He didn't consider this to be too important as we ascended the wall together and so didn't say anything to me.

My reflections on the dive:
- I was busy thinking about equipment, going through our pre-dive

checks and relying on my buddy's previous meticulous conduct. Although I noticed something, I didn't act on my suspicions and make the call myself. Probably and unconsciously dismissed the reply, "Nah, no problem" too quickly, not realising he might be subjected to peer pressure.

- A problem that exists on the surface, inherently grows the deeper or longer you dive. Not just a physical problem, but a psychological one too. The fact he noticed the problem, played on his mind throughout. This cascades into a faster breathing rate, accentuating the problem further and so on.

- The art of "dealing with the problem" is another way of saying "task load management". As the problem, physical or mental accentuates, so does the task-loading. Impressively, some of us can multi-task on the surface to some degree, how well we manage the same underwater, the complexity and its knock-on effect, is another story, like this one.

- Peer pressure. This is my friend and I taught him from open water level, having over 1000 hours underwater, dozens of cave dives, commercial qualified too. Yet, he felt the pressure to perform perfectly when amongst his peers, even though I taught him differently.

- Not checking his bottom gas pressures correctly, leading to a much lighter cylinder on his left side. Had it have been his right-side cylinder, the two problems of lighter cylinders on opposing sides would have cancelled each other. He was not underweighted for the dive.

Garry's account highlights the importance of picking up on small details and non-verbal cues as they may cascade and multiply - so that the effects are disproportionate to the original problem. However, the narrative also highlights the impact of hindsight bias and confirmation bias when we look back at an incident. Once we know the outcome, it is easy to join the dots, working backwards through time and find the reasons we were looking for. The constant challenge faced by divers is determining 'what is good enough' and balancing the investment of time/resource/skills against 'quality'.

Communication Underpins Technical and Non-Technical Skills

At its core, communication is about us getting information from one party or system to another party or system with the minimal amount of, or no, confusion to ensure understanding takes place and the intent is maintained. As George Bernard Shaw said, *"The single biggest problem in communication is the illusion that it has taken place."* Therefore, we need to understand what the barriers and enablers to effective communication are if we are to ensure that the message and intent are clearly understood, and the associated action(s) are executed.

A key concept to recognise as we work through this chapter is that communication is often assumed to be human to human; whereas in fact it also includes human to system, system to human and system to system. Therefore, don't just assume it is verbal or non-verbal language, but also how dive computers or rebreather controllers/HUDs display information to the diver or dive team, or how organisations communicate to their membership and training staff or how the community communicates through media that don't allow the subtleties or nuances which are obvious when face-to-face with someone else.

To examine the barriers and enablers to communication, we need to look at how communication and a check of understanding takes place. By doing this, we can see where the potential gaps in communication will occur and address them before they become critical.

The Communications Process - Barriers

At its very basic level, communication is a process and the following diagram of a simple communications model shows this process as it goes from thinking about ideas; to encoding them; to transmitting them; to crossing the barriers; to receiving, decoding, checking of understanding; and then executing the associated action(s).

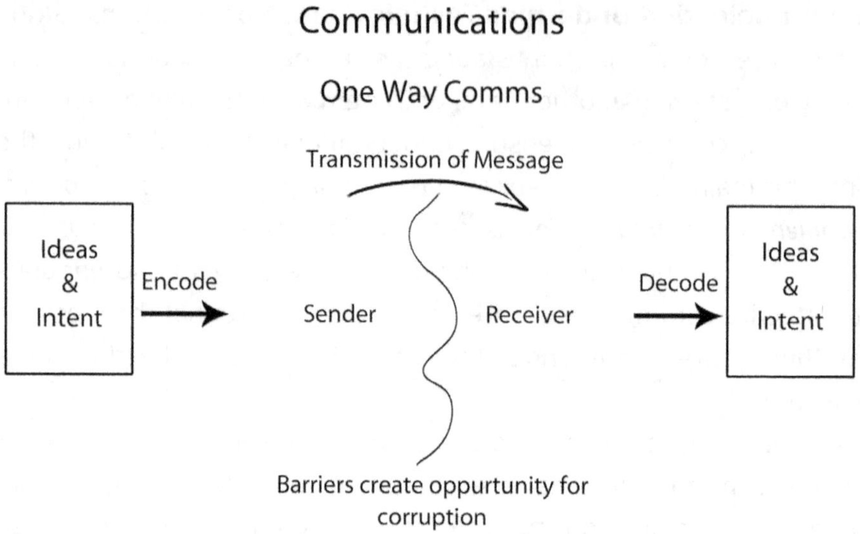

Communications

One Way Comms

```
                    Transmission of Message
                    ─────────────────────▶

┌──────┐                  ⎫
│Ideas │                  ⎬                      ┌──────┐
│  &   │ Encode           ⎪                Decode│Ideas │
│Intent│ ──────▶  Sender  ⎬     Receiver  ──────▶│  &   │
│      │                  ⎪                      │Intent│
└──────┘                  ⎬                      └──────┘
                          ⎭

              Barriers create oppurtunity for
                        corruption
```

Figure 8: One-way communication model

During each step in the process there is an opportunity for error to occur i.e. the real outcome wasn't the expected outcome - there was a deviation. Of note, the processes identified below are all impacted by Performance Shaping Factors (see Chapter 11) and therefore we need to be cognisant of amplifying the errors due to external and internal factors.

- Encoding. The encoding process is where the thoughts are turned into messages (words, sentences, instructions). The barriers at this stage might be as simple as not having the vocabulary needed to develop the message. There might also be an assumption about what the listener already knows. Consequently, these data are not included in the message to be transmitted. In diving, such an omission might be not telling the divers which way the wreck is orientated and, therefore, which way to turn to visit the bow or the stern. From an equipment manufacturer's perspective, it might be about how a specific caution/warning message is written/displayed, to ensure its meaning is understood. For example, contributory factors in an incident involving a diver from the National Park Service Submerged Resource Center included the

fact that the handset message was not clearly understood by the diver following a detected system fault, and the significance of HUD indications were not immediately obvious to the operator.
- Transmission. During the transmission phase, a number of factors can reduce the effectiveness of communication. These include physical barriers (physical dislocation, being underwater), social barriers, culture, language (technical and social) and personal factors. They all have the ability to corrupt the message in a technical sense or change the intent of the meaning.
- Reception. The listener receives the message and starts to decode it by applying their previous experiences, mental models and cognitive biases. Many of these are informed by situational awareness, specifically expectations and framing effects. An example recounted to me from a senior counter-terrorism (CT) police officer was how does one define floors in a building when responding to threatening situation? In the UK, floor 1 is normally the ground floor; Floor 1 could also be the first elevated floor with Level 0 being the ground floor. When time is critical, assumptions are the norm, but this can lead to serious problems if the assumptions are flawed.

This simple model is known as one-way communications and it certainly has advantages because it is quick, simple and requires little in terms of preparation i.e. vocabulary doesn't need to be explained beforehand. However, the downside is that there is an implicit assumption that the listener has an understanding of what is being said.

In addition to being a simple form of verbal communications, this concept is normally how many display systems work. They give you data and/or information; you have to put that into a context to create knowledge; and then you have to do something with it. The following example shows how information, which is displayed to the diver, can have very different meanings if the context is not understood.

Your submersible pressure gauge (SPG) gives you data and you have to do something with that information if you are to stay alive underwater. However, there are a couple of pieces of information which are being given to you with potentially conflicting information. The front cover of most SPGs has a red segment shown behind the needle. Depending on whether this is a metric gauge or an imperial one, the red or highlighted segment is at 50 bar or 500 psi. This is supposed to provide a warning to divers that they are low on gas. However, 500 psi equates to approximately 35 bar. Furthermore, 50 bar in a 7 litre cylinder is different to 50 bar in a 15 litre cylinder. Finally, 50 bar at 75m in a Ali 80 cylinder is very different to 50 bar at 6m in the same sized cylinder. Consequently, an additional level of processing is required to understand the context and turn 'transmitted' and 'received' information into something which is useful. As you'll see from Michael Menduno's incident in chapter 12, carrying over context from dives can lead to very serious consequences.

One way of ensuring that the message is understood by the listener is to provide some form of feedback loop, so that the transmitter and listener both heard and understood the message. Putting up an 'OK' signal (thumb and forefinger in a circle) doesn't do this; all it means is that 'I am OK', but 'OK' to what? By getting a critical message to be repeated back can help, but we still have potential for message corruption. The problem with a simple repeating of the message back is that it doesn't check comprehension; it really only checks the effectiveness of the short-term memory of the listener. Looking for non-verbal cues which are incoherent with the verbal message can help identify problems.

The most effective way of checking the message has been clearly understood is by asking the other person to confirm their understanding of the message using their own words. This means the listener has to have both heard the message and its intent, because they have to recreate the message which can only happen if you understand the message. Of course, the feedback message can also be corrupted. If it all gets really difficult underwater, just get your wetnotes out and write the message! It is funny to watch divers spend time with hand signals trying to convey a meaning, when in fact it would have been quicker (in hindsight) to have got their wetnotes out and write out what the question/problem/message was.

A simple example of an unexpected outcome comes from a discussion I recently had with Emma Farrell, owner of Go Freediving, based in the UK. They recently ran a beginner freediving class where the students were told a number of times the order of what would happen when they got in open water for their buoyancy check. Their instructions were along the lines of, 'Enter the water. Put your legs together, arms by your side and don't fin. Take your snorkel out of your mouth and exhale completely. Then we will see how you float vertically in the water.' So, they entered the water, the instructor again briefed them what they were supposed to do, and as the instructor said, "Snorkel out", a student didn't take the snorkel out of their mouth, rather they went horizontal and started swimming away from the side and out into the middle of the lake. They had taken the communication to mean, 'Snorkel out into the middle of the lake' not 'Take the snorkel out of your mouth'. As described earlier, sometimes getting them to recount what they are supposed to do in their own words (not parrot fashion) and explaining why they are doing something is the most effective way of ensuring comprehension.

The downside to two-way communications is that it takes an additional level of communication which takes time to execute. Furthermore, there is an additional mental overhead as the listener has to process the information, re-encode it and then transmit it back to the original person. Finally, when physical barriers are in place, like being underwater, additional resources like wetnotes and more complex hand signals are needed to ensure the loop can be closed. Below is the first model with the feedback loop in place.

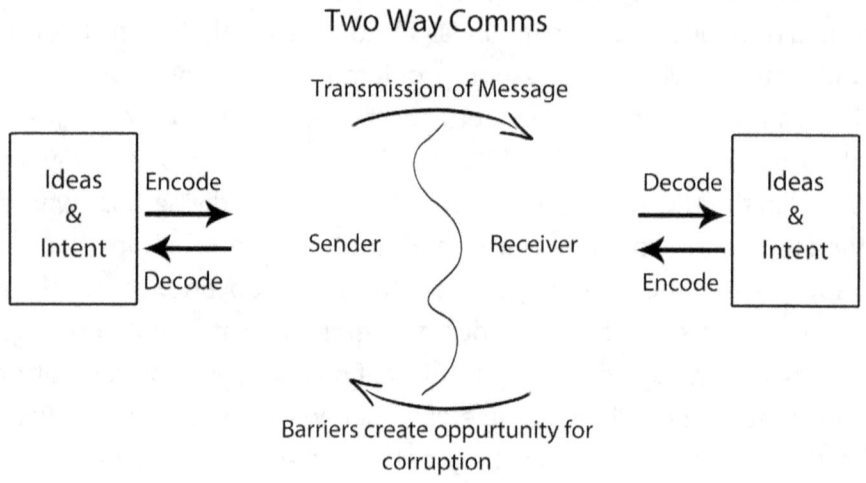

Figure 9: Two-way communication model with feedback loop

Non-Verbal Communications

Communication takes place via words, the way those words are used and body language. Our culture and personal development has taught us how to extract the meaning from communications, and importantly where to prioritise meaning if there is discourse between these elements. For example, if someone, who had a fierce expression on their face, were shouting, but their words were, *"I love you, please will you come to dinner with me"*, we would likely not accept the invitation. Therefore, if we want to communicate effectively, we need to make sure that we are aware of our body language and facial expressions.

As an example of how wrong it can get, I ran a GemaSim-based simulation exercise with a number of surgeons. The GemaSim missions are set up with four astronauts flying a prototype spacecraft and two observers; missions take 45 mins and the debrief is between 60 and 90 mins. The training day was set up for one simulation and debrief in the morning, lunch, then the second mission in the afternoon. The leader for the first simulation was a very animated female surgeon, I'll call her Debbie, who was constantly talking and giving direction to her team. Sat next to her was another female surgeon - I'll call her Jane, who was quiet and not very dynamic. On the other side of the table flying the other consoles on the spacecraft were two male surgeons. The mission went well and the debrief was constructive with many lessons identified, both for the next mission after lunch but also for their clinical environment.

For the second mission, I chose Jane to lead. After about 10 mins, Debbie kept on trying to usurp Jane's leadership. So, I gave her a piece of paper which said that her 'intercom system' was broken and she was no longer able to communicate with the team until I said she could speak. Despite Debbie now being quiet, the rest of the team hadn't noticed she was 'offline' and Debbie was now getting frustrated for three reasons. Firstly, she could see that the team weren't dealing with the failures they were encountering, and she believed she could help. Secondly, I had taken her 'voice' away and so she couldn't let the others know what to do. Finally, no-one had noticed that she was offline.

Shortly after I had failed Debbie's intercom system, Jane looked over and saw a 'pissed off' expression on Debbie's face. At this point Jane just shrugged her shoulders and carried on, not asking Debbie what was going on and if there was anything they could do to help. I was curious about the lack of engagement and so was glad that we were operating in a surgical training room which allows the mission to be video-recorded. When we got to the debrief, I asked Jane why she had looked over, shrugged her shoulders and didn't appear to care about what Debbie was up to. Her response was, *"I looked over and I could see she was pissed off with me. So I thought, if she's pissed off with me, I am not going to speak to her and I'll just carry on without her."*

I was shocked that the power of non-verbal communications could have such an effect in such an environment. So were the rest of the team - not least Debbie who was completely unaware of her facial expressions and body language and the effect that this was causing on the team performance. The problem with non-verbal communications is that unless we are really aware of our emotions, the discourse between non-verbal and verbal communications can break down trust, which as we'll discuss in the next chapter, is a cornerstone to effective teamwork.

The Communications Process - Enablers

Understanding which enablers are effective is essential if we want to create a positive effect. For example, just telling someone to stop doing something - without giving them an indication of what 'good' looks like, will only create frustration.

Since 2016, I have been a trainer in the Process Communication Model™ which is based on the concept of perceptions, psychological needs and the way we communicate via verbal (words) and non-verbal communications (gestures, facial expressions, tones and posture)[1]. This training has provided me with an ability to recognise miscommunication and distress by the words used and also how they are being said. In fact, listening to the 'process' can give you a greater insight into how to connect with someone, prevent miscommunication and invite ourselves and others out of distress when predictable patterns of behaviour are experienced.

Drawing an analogy with in-water technical skills, consider a diver who hasn't got good trim or propulsion skills, but their buoyancy is good. Telling them to stop silting the bottom out won't work unless you tell them what good trim is, what good finning techniques are, and most importantly, how to develop and maintain these technical skills.

The same goes for non-technical skills. From the non-technical skills model previously described in Chapter 1, we can see that the aim of effective communications is to develop situational awareness which allows better decisions to be made, and if we consider the roots of CRM/Non-Technical Skills to be about creating a shared mental model, then teamwork, leadership and followership all rely on effective communications too.

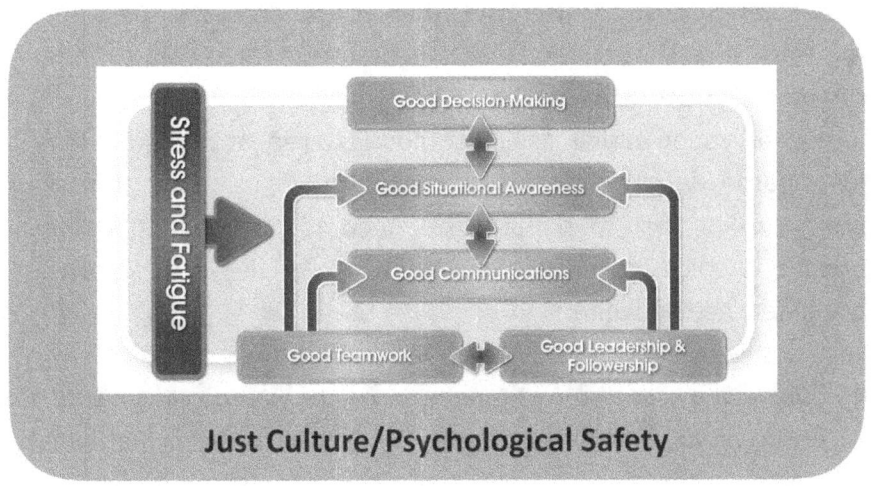

Figure 10: Model of Non-Technical Skills, Psychological Safety and Just Culture

Like decision-making, there is much more to effective communications than telling someone something. As such, there will be a number of tools described below which will enable effective communications thereby improving performance and ultimately safety.

Check of Understanding

Within the many briefing tools which are out there, one of the final topics or headings which resides in them all is 'Check Understanding' or something similar. Obviously, there is no point in going to the length of holding a brief to impart knowledge if we don't actually pass that information on. Not unless you are doing the brief for a tick-chasing exercise to limit liability that is!

Notwithstanding this, most checking of understanding takes the form of, *"Did everyone understand that?"* of which the normal response is, *"Yep..."*. The problem with a closed question like that is two-fold. It is easy to say 'Yes' and social conformance takes over such that the under-confident person can't speak up for fear of 'being different' if everyone else has said 'Yes'. The second is that an immediate response of 'Yes' doesn't really check the understanding of the message. In a fair number of situations, a robust checking of understanding is not needed and doesn't matter, but when critical decisions are made on this transferred understanding, then it is important to have confidence the message is indeed understood.

As we've seen earlier, asking someone to repeat back what they've just heard doesn't test comprehension either, just their short-term memory. For that to happen, we need to use open questions - questions which cannot be answered with a single word e.g. consider the difference between:
- *"Does everyone understand their role on this dive?"*
- *"We have a complicated task ahead, I'd like you to explain what you are going to do with your team, 15 mins after we hit the bottom... John?"*

By constructing a question that can't be answered 'Yes' or 'No', then the listener has to recall the information out of a sequence and then recreate the narrative. This isn't easy to do, because it requires active listening to take place and as we have described previously, we don't like to expend mental effort if we don't have to.

One way which leaders can improve the likelihood of retained information is to apply the 'Pose, pause, pounce' technique. Pose the question; pause so everyone has time to think about it; and then pounce on someone. The second question above was formatted in this way. Note, that if the name of the person is said first, then the rest of the team stop paying attention as they know the rest of the sentence/question isn't for them. Furthermore, by going randomly around the group instead of following the circle of people from one side to another, then the team have to be more alert as they don't know if they are going to be asked next!

Questioning Techniques

Whenever you frame a question, think about what your aim is. Are you trying to:
- Check specific facts, number, data e.g. *"What is the gas pressure in your cylinder?"* or *"What is the maximum bottom time you have*

planned for this dive?"
- Elicit more information about a communication which just took place or to check understanding e.g. *"How did you come to that maximum bottom time?"* or *"Where would you like me to be in this photograph and how will I know I am there?"*

The different questioning techniques (closed question, leading questions, answering a question with a question and open questions) all have their place. As time is precious, asking open questions when they aren't needed is inefficient and frustrating for others. However, there is a trade-off between efficiency and thoroughness, and we have to use experience and feedback (verbal and non-verbal) to determine the most effective techniques to use.

Assertiveness

While assertiveness is a character trait and is facilitated by a psychologically-safe environment, there are things we can do to improve the likelihood that those who have a concern are able to speak up when they need to do so. Assertiveness doesn't mean being rude. It is about being respectful and recognising professional and technical competencies based on experience and learning, and at the same time, confident that the information held by one party is important and needs to be aired in a constructive manner.

The PACE model which follows, was developed in the latter-half of the 20th century in the aviation community as a way of increasing the likelihood that co-pilots or flight engineers could speak up in the event that they had noticed some critical information that the captain hadn't noticed or processed, or that the captain hadn't recognised the significance of the information. The reason the programme was developed was because when cockpit voice recorder data was examined, it showed that other crew members had the important information, had even told it to the captain, but that the captain had over-ridden the position presented - with the loss of the aircraft.

If we think about the goal of CRM/Non-Technical Skills as being to create a shared mental model amongst the team, if we aren't able to assert and then impart important information, the mental model will be incomplete and flawed decisions are more likely. To show its applicability across multiple domains, the PACE model (and other assertiveness techniques) have been transferred to the healthcare domain where authority gradient is a real problem in the clinical environment and patient safety has been compromised/lives lost as a consequence.

The PACE Model

PACE stands for Probe, Alert, Challenge and Emergency and follows an escalation process. The aim being that it is easier to make small escalatory steps than a large one. Key to the success of the model is that as each level is acted upon, the response from the person being challenged is assessed as being appropriate to the challenge being made. If the response is acceptable, then the process stops; if not, it goes up a level. Another key to its success is the recognition within the group that such escalatory processes are needed and that if other team members are saying something a number of times, then something is likely up. That requires some self-awareness which can be missing in ego-driven/task-focussed individuals and the lack of clear standards as to what is acceptable behaviour.

- **Probe.** The first part of the assertion process is to get the attention of the person to whom the challenge is being directed. To do this, the speaker asks a non-confrontational question and makes a statement. The idea is to appear curious or inquisitive e.g. a divemaster to instructor, *"I think that this diver might have a weighting and buoyancy issue."* The response should be, *"Oh, ok, how did you find that out?"* or *"Sounds like we need to do a weight check."* However, if the response is not in line with the challenge e.g. *"Don't worry, it will be fine, I've given him 10kg..."* - then the process escalates.
- **Alert.** At this point the challenge is becoming a little more forceful and so the tone and the language used needs to be more direct. *"I*

recommend we do a weight check. It will save us time in the future and the student will be able to grasp the concepts more easily if they don't have to worry so much about their buoyancy." Again, the challenger is looking for an appropriate response, which could be something like, *"Ah, yes. Why not? Can you do that for me?"*

- **Challenge.** If the response was still not appropriate, then the next step is to formally challenge the individual with direct language and using an evidence-based argument, making reference to existing guidelines, rules and processes. *"That diver cannot start this dive without doing a weight-check as it is against the risk assessment and SOPs we have."* This provides the challenger with the authority for making the challenge. It is more than an opinion: it is based on an established process or procedure. This isn't about being an ass; the SOPs and risk assessments are there for a reason. However, many consider that such documents/processes are there to limit liability, rather than improving safety and performance.
- **Emergency.** If the response to the challenge isn't acceptable, then we move to the final step in the process and there are no more options available after this. This level might mean physical intervention to stop something happening, or the use of a specific command word like," STOP! DON'T GET IN THE WATER!" Because this is the final step, the challenger needs to be really sure that a), their worry is genuine; and that b) there is both a time and mechanism to stop the activity from progressing.

The PACE model certainly has application in more formalised diving environments such as instruction or scientific diving, but the concepts are also equally applicable to recreational, technical and cave diving. The problem with the less formal environment is the lack of standards, rules and processes to provide the evidence and allow 'lines in the sand to be drawn'. Risk and safety are personally constructed and are based on perceptions. If a line doesn't exist, in the form of a SOP or process, then it makes it very hard to escalate and conduct a challenge on someone else. Ultimately, you can choose to not get in; but if you are team-diving, the implications will be felt by others, despite the mantra, *"Anyone can end a dive, for any reason and at any time."* For example:

- Probe: *"Looks like current is still running. I'd hate to be swept off the line, nor be able to make it to the wreck seeing as it's my only dive this month."*
- Alert: *"Wow! Look at the buoy being dragged."*
- Challenge: *"What do the tide tables show? Surely this can't be right?"*
- Emergency: *"I am binning this dive for me. I am not getting in. Just not worth it."*

One way to reduce tensions in a less formal environment is to use humour. However, make sure that the target of the humour isn't the person themselves, but rather the situation, what is being done or the action. In the example above, *"If you jump in with that current running and get blown off, we'll see you back onshore. But I think you'll be getting a red/white flying taxi to get you there!"*

PACE works when the majority of the people within the group or team are aware what should happen, because they can bolster the challenges being made, either by adding more humour or by providing more evidence / force behind the challenge. Ultimately, we can decide to not take part in the activity, although when 'working' - this isn't quite so easy. Look at Becky Kagan Schott's narrative in the leadership chapter (Chapter 10) to see how external pressures associated with her job made it hard (but not impossible) to challenge the wanted outcome.

Relationships are based around effective, collaborative and cooperative communications where conflict is often downplayed. However, as a number of experts in the field, like Dr Nate Regier (author of *'Conflict without Casualties'*) and Kim Scott (author of *'Radical Candor'*) have shown, conflict is essential within high-performance teams. As well as dealing with conflict in a constructive manner, high-performance teams are also recognised as being cognitively diverse. The reason for this is because while diversity means that conflict is more likely, it also means that the likelihood for 'group-think' is reduced, and innovation and development are more likely. To deal with conflict in a positive manner, a psychologically-safe environment must exist.

In diving, being able to apply *'Radical Candor'* means that you are both caring and challenging in the way you provide feedback (see the next chapter on the DEBRIEF model), because you genuinely believe that what you are saying will have a material impact on their lives and lead to better informed risk-based decisions. The difficulty for the person being challenged is that we often fall foul of four psychological myths when it comes to emotions and feelings:
- I can make you feel bad;
- I can make you feel good;
- You can make me feel good;
- You can make me feel bad.

All of these are untrue. Whenever someone says something to you which we feel isn't positive, remember that we are generating those feelings inside of us; it is not the other person or the message that is creating negativity or positivity. If someone says something overly critical, respond with, 'Thank you, I'll reflect on that' and then move on. Don't challenge them there and then as it will descend into a defensive/aggressive exchange. I get that this is incredibly hard, but it is really worth it because emotions cloud our critical reflection and that means we don't improve or develop as a consequence.

Case Study: The failures are often further back in time.
Steve Lewis, a cave, CCR and technical dive instructor, describes an incident where it would be easy to focus on the proximal issues at hand - running out of gas at depth on a CCR due to starting the dive with limited gas reserves, and not being able to deploy the bailout stage regulator due to an incomplete pre-dive check, but if we take a wider view on developing situational awareness, sharing mental models and the impact this can have on future events, we can see

that the pre-dive communications weren't as clear as they could be. Especially when it comes to a critical piece of information regarding the state of the lines in a mine, which the team were surveying.

In 2016, some nine years after we lost a team member in quite odd circumstances during the first Mine Quest expedition, we were back in Bell Island Mine with renewed enthusiasm and prospects. Our primary task was to prepare the mine — a massive network of passages and galleries covering several square kilometres of dive-able overhead — for guided underwater tours. It was the second to last day of Mine Quest II and my dive was among the last shifts of the day. My job was to survey one last section of the "tour circuit" adding directional line markers to a line placed the previous day, and collecting distance/depth/orientation data as I went. The visibility in the final passageway was unexpectedly appalling and — as arranged — I'd sent my assistant/buddy on ahead to a rendezvous in the main shaft with two other team members.

Checking the oxygen pressure on my rebreather it was obvious that there was insufficient gas for me to finish the job, get to the rendezvous, complete the safety stop required by our SOPs, and to return to the surface breathing from the rebreather in CCR mode. In addition to beginning the dive an hour or so earlier with only a partial fill of pure oxygen, there was only enough air diluent for the planned dive and only a small contingency volume. In addition, the remaining diluent wasn't even enough to run the unit in semi-closed mode, finish the task at hand and get to the surface. As such, I would have to bailout at some point and finish the dive on open circuit. This wasn't a problem as I had a bailout cylinder filled with more than 2000 litres of breathable gas; more than enough to cover any contingency on the dive including a CO2 hit. Since there were also cylinders of contingency gas staged at regular intervals on the permanent navigation line in the main shaft (Number Two), I felt comfortably safe at this point. As it was, the nearest additional cylinder of nitrox, complete with regulator and SPG was no more than 80 metres away.

At exactly this point in time, the line I was following slackened in my hand as I attached a line arrow. A tie-off some distance ahead had come loose. Whether my buddy had kicked it off, or whether I had pulled it off was irrelevant at this time: there was enough free line to be a potential hazard in restricted visibility. I did discover later that the line had been placed incorrectly, but the team responsible for that had neglected to share the fact with me before I started my dive as we did not have a standard handover brief between teams.

I put down my notebook, my survey slate, and a handful of line arrows (all attached to each other). I did not secure any of this to the line, but placed them beside a point where a solid line wrap had been made behind me. It was secure and, even in the silty water, I could see the glow of my light reflecting off the slate. I checked my oxygen partial-pressure: I'd run out of pure oxygen and the unit could no longer maintain the desired set-point of 1.2 bar. It was time to bailout.

During the pre-dive preparations, my buddy and I had assistance "suiting up" from a couple of volunteers standing in the water with us. I usually decline help donning kit but, on this occasion, acceded. Unfortunately, the clip holding the second stage attached to the bailout bottle had been tucked under a strap and another bolt-snap had been laid on top of that. During my rush to get this dive and its tasks completed, I had not worked through the SOP pre-dive checklist with my volunteer, which included a deployment of the stage regulator.

On the face of it, my dilemma was easily fixed, but I could not unclip the second stage; the clip was inaccessible. The expedition's SOP was clear that essential bits of kit attached to bolt-snaps had to have a break-away. In the event of a bolt snap locking or (as was this case being out of reach) one sharp tug and the line securing the piece of kit to the clip would break and the kit would be usable. I tugged the second-stage and it stayed put.

In his thought-provoking book, 'Oneness with All Life', Eckhart Tolle writes:

"Whenever you are upset about an event, a person, or a situation, the real cause is not the event, person, or situation, but a loss of true perspective that only space can provide. You are trapped in object consciousness, unaware of the timeless inner space of consciousness itself."

I have practiced "mindfulness and oneness" for much of my life. On this occasion, I observed what was happening from somewhere in the water off to one side, and outside my "body," and took notes. Primacy is always to have something suitable to breathe. I sank to the floor — stirring up more silt — hoping that doing so would support whatever was clipped over the bolt-snap holding the second-stage I needed tight to my chest. The visibility was now zero. Before closing my eyes and calming myself, I looked at the CCR's handset — barely visible — and immediately switched to semi-closed mode of breathing. After maybe three or four cycles, the diluent ran dry.

I was still focused on freeing the clip to my open-circuit regulator. From my mindful observation point, "I" wondered when I'd stop fucking around and pull hard enough to free the break-away. It seemed like five minutes, was likely less than 30 seconds, but eventually, I tugged, and the second stage was in my mouth and I was breathing EAN30.

I tied off the line, never did find the tools I'd left at the previous tie-off (despite feeling around for them for a couple of minutes making poor visibility absolutely worse) and swum forward unable to complete my task, but somewhat wiser.

When Steve recounted this story to me at TekDiveUSA16 over breakfast one morning, I knew that I had to tell the story to the wider diving community. Interestingly, Steve's initial submission to me didn't include the incomplete handover between the other team and me, and yet to me it is a crucial part of the story. The gas planning and stage clip issues are important, but they became really significant because of the line.

Often we ignore miscommunication as a contributory factor, because it happens so often, and as such it becomes 'normal'. One of the reasons for this is because communication isn't really covered in dive training - there is an assumption that we can do it, and yet you can see from multiple narratives in this book and from your own personal experiences while diving and in 'normal' life how critical accurate communications are.

The sections prior to Steve's incident talked about concepts and tools around communication, but didn't cover briefs, debriefs or how to communicate something specific in a short period of time. Briefs and debriefs will be covered in the next chapter, teamwork, but the following tool will help you transfer critical information from one person/one team to another in a short period of time.

SBAR

One of the most critical times in healthcare is handing over a patient from one team to another, or from one person to another when time is of the essence. This is a difficult task, because the originator of the message will have developed a mental model and implied knowledge based on their experiences over the last X minutes/hours and they now need to pass that knowledge quickly without going into too much detail but at the same time covering the salient points. Other situations where critical information needs to be passed is when a junior staff member is communicating to a senior or more experienced healthcare professional about something they are unable to do, or looking for guidance. In this case, there must be enough information provided which allows the receiver of the information to challenge the situation or ask for more information to make the diagnosis or solve the problem. In both cases, there can be a significant challenge when filtering and condensing information, so it is in the 'Goldilocks state' - not too much information, not enough information, but just right.

As a consequence, the healthcare community developed a communications tool called SBAR (Situation, Background, Assessment and Recommendations) which would allow the current situation to be quickly explained; the background to the event and how it developed in the way it did; what the current person/team's assessment of the situation; the rationale covering both confirmatory and disconfirmatory evidence; and a recommendation about what should happen next. The recommendation should also include what success looks like, so that progress towards the goal can be tracked. By using a framework, the 'transmitter' would know what to say and the 'receiver' would know what is coming next so as not to interrupt, but also use the narrative to build a mental model of what has happened.

The following is the medical framework used by a number of UK hospitals and trusts and shows how the message is constructed and what details included.

Situation. My name is....I am a.... (role) on ....ward. I am calling about ....(patient name). The reason I am calling is....

Background. The patient was admitted with.... (Diagnosis) on .... (Date). The patient's relevant medical history is.... Their condition has changed in the last.... minutes. Patient is now .... (give details of current condition).

Assessment. This is what I think the problem is......./I am not sure that the problem is, but the patient is deteriorating/seems to be unstable. Provide evidence using clinical information.

Recommendation. I would like.... (state what you would like to see done). Ask: Do you need me to do anything now? Determine timescale of review and call back time. If timescale too long, who is an alternative to contact.

This technique is incredibly useful in abnormal or emergency operations to ensure that critical information is passed in a timely manner; for example, rescue scenarios where specific information is needed to help the emergency services or medical cover provide the best service/care possible. However, SBAR can also be applied in less tense situations, like the incomplete handover between Steve and his team outlined in the previous narrative.

If you are going to use this in a 'normal' situation, you don't have to mention the words directly e.g. "The situation is..., the background is..." - but rather a natural conversation. In Steve's case this could have been a simple handover between the previous team and Steve. "Steve, just be aware that the last tie-off might be loose, it didn't feel quite right, but we were low on gas and so didn't have the time to check it. The vis is really bad there, so take care, you don't want to be wrapped up in that part of the mine." All of the important elements are there, but it doesn't appear as a forced and structured conversation.

Case Study: If only you knew how much effort was needed to free a hook

The following narrative from Heather Choat Armstong, a CCR instructor operating in Hawaii, shows how assumptions can lead to adverse events on a dive and that if prior information had been shared, the level of workload might have been anticipated, reducing to less of a surprise and increased gas consumption. Hindsight bias gets everywhere - which is why tools like SBAR or a standardised briefing format are useful for passing on critical information. It helps the speaker to ensure the information is included. It helps the listener, because they know what information will be coming and if it isn't provided, then they can ask. Effective communications help build coherent shared mental models of the current and expected future situation, that leads to better decisions.

The WW2 wreck Rhein lies in a remote area of the Gulf of Mexico, with the nearest land mass being the Dry Tortugas. I first dived the Rhein on open circuit in the summer of 2002, and continued to dive her several times a year on small group charters of 4 divers out of Ft Myers, FL. In early 2006 I made the move to CCR, and soon was visiting the Rhein and other Dry Tortugas wrecks on larger live aboard type dive boats. In the late summer of 2009, with several hundred CCR hours under my belt, I again visited the Rhein this time as crew on the MV Spree out of Stock Island, FL.

The Rhein was the first stop of a multi-day deep wreck trip aboard the Spree, a 100' converted aluminium crew boat carrying about 12 paying passengers plus crew. I was a "mate" for this trip, charged with setting and recovering the tie in for the vessel. In the early morning of the first day, we arrived on site at the Rhein and while the boat motored into position, my dive partner and I geared up to splash and secure the hook for the day's diving. Once the hook went over the side, we followed it down and proceeded to wrap it securely around an I-beam on the deck in approximately 60m/200' of water. After securing the hook we had a nice tour around the wreck and then an uneventful decompression.

As was typical for these trips, we had planned two dives per day: one in the morning and one in the afternoon. I began the day with steel 3L cylinders on the rebreather filled to about 220bar (3200psi) each of oxygen and trimix diluent. Having done quite a few dives not only on this wreck, but also on others in the same depth range, I had learned that after the first dive I would have about 180bar (2600psi) remaining. Since the 3L cylinders are rated for 182bar (2640psi), this would mean they were essentially "full" and since our gas usage was only about 35-40bar (500-600psi) each of oxygen and diluent per dive, we had plenty for two dives per day without refilling.

After the clients were all back on the boat from the afternoon dive, my partner and I splashed for our second dive, to recover the hook. In the course of the recovery I learned that tying in was a lot simpler than untying for a vessel the size of the Spree, and consequently I used more gas than usual filling the wing in the course of moving the hook around. Once we'd finished untying, we tied hook into the line, as the boat had untied from it, and proceeded to begin our decompression. We had ascended to about 46m (150'), and when I dumped gas from the wing I overcorrected and found myself beginning to descend again. I attempted to add more gas back to the wing and found that I had no on-board diluent left. At this point I had begun to descend rather quickly, and the gas in my counterlungs was compressed to the point that I was no longer able to take full breath. I could not add volume to the counterlungs, nor gas to the wing from my on-board gas supply which was empty. Next option, I tried to plug in the deep bailout to my mixed gas bypass valve. I deployed the hose and found that there was now too much ambient pressure so that I could not remove the cap from the valve. By now I'd descended about 10m (30') and I could only take about a quarter of a breath at a time. My partner stayed right with me and continued to try to render assistance. At this point I gave up on the mixed gas bypass valve, and I bailed to open circuit. After taking a couple of breaths to steady myself, I began inhaling from the bailout, and exhaling into the loop to create lung volume. Once I had established breathable volume and recovered back onto the loop, I orally added some gas to the wing, and my partner and I were ready to begin our ascent again. We discovered that in all the excitement we had drifted away from the shot-line and could not see it, so we deployed a lift bag. We ascended back up to our last stop to pick up deco where we left off. About the time we reached 46m (150') again, I realised that my wetnotes were in my hand when everything went to hell before, and I had dropped them. My partner had also managed to lose his wetnotes too. Lucky for us we spent a lot of diving in this depth range, and pretty well knew the schedules, so we continued our ascent with an estimated schedule.

During the course of our decompression, we re-acquired the shot-line, and everything was going fine until the 6m (20') stop, where my partner ran out of diluent and we proceeded to repeat the whole process, albeit less dramatically this time as he was able to use the shot to stabilise his depth. As we were only a few minutes from finishing our estimated decompression, he decided to go ahead and surface. He was a little rattled once on the surface and was kicking to stay up. I told him to orally inflate the wing. After being made positively buoyant, we then began our wait for the boat to come and pick us up. As luck would have it, one of our friends decided to take a swim over and check on us, and he recognized pretty quickly that things were not good. He hailed the boat, and had the rib come to pick us up. We got my partner out of his gear and into the rib, back to the Spree, then the rib came back for me, and made a third trip for the equipment.

In the end, no one was injured beyond a bad fright, and after taking the following day off from working dives, we both subsequently crewed on many more trips to that area on the Spree.

Heather's account highlights a number of mental biases involved in decision-making. Some of these could have been mitigated by having a simple conversation based on the question, *"I've not freed the hook of a boat this size before, what's it like?"* But even a question like that is made difficult by the biases we hold and based on previous experiences the typical mental response would be, *"I mean, how hard can it be?!"*

Summary of Key Points

- Communications underpins the effectiveness of a high-performing team. The leader and team members might have excellent situational awareness with the ability to see what is going to happen, they can make robust decisions using previous experiences, but if they are unable to communicate those ideas and concepts to the other team members, then failure is almost guaranteed.
- If we understand the barriers and enabler to effective communications, we can do something about improving one of the most critical elements to safer diving.
- How we say something is often more important than what is being said. Non-verbal communications can have an impact far greater than we think and so we need to create coherence between what we are saying and how we are saying it.
- Determine what the purpose of the question is before you ask it. If it is about generating curiosity, then ask an open question which allows you to dig into the details and check understanding; closed questions are really only suitable for simple yes/no or numerical responses to check values. Closed questions have a limited ability to check comprehension. If you want to really check understanding, don't say *"Does anyone have any questions? No? Good, let's move on!"* as you've automatically closed the communications channels down.

Questions to consider

- When was the last time you asked an open question as part of a 'check understanding' part of a brief or discussion?
- How easy is it for your team or staff to speak up and challenge you or others in a leadership position about something going on? Why not consider looking at the PACE model and talking it through with your team to help improve communications?
- How often do you complete a brief with students, dismiss them, and then watch them gather round in a huddle to discuss what they think they are going to do?

References
(1) Process Communication Model. https://www.processcommunication.eu/index.html

Additional Reading
Feuersenger, E., & Naef, A. (2012). *If you want them to listen, talk their language: Communication, motivation and success in business and personal relationships using the process communication model.* Waikanae, N.Z: Kahler Communications Oceania.

Regier, N. (2017). *Conflict without casualties: A field guide for leading with compassionate accountability.* Oakland, CA: Berrett-Koehler Publishers, Inc.

Scott, K. (2018). *Radical Candor: Be a kick-ass boss without losing your humanity.* Griffin.

Chapter 9

Teamwork and Teaming: Doing more with less

"Great teams consist of individuals who have learned to trust each other. Over time, they have discovered each other's strengths and weaknesses, enabling them to play as a coordinated whole."
Amy Edmondson, from McChrystal's "Team of Teams"

I thought hard about where to put this case study because, as you read it, you will see that it transcends leadership, teamwork, situational awareness and performance shaping factors, just like many incidents and accidents do. My first thought was that it should go into leadership section as instructors are leaders too; but there are more issues relating to team, especially as the instructor is part of the 'student development team'. This team is often forgotten about, but it is important if real learning is to happen, not just rote learning. Instructors and instructor trainers are leaders - which means one of their key roles is to serve the students in their development. While their role is often defined as teaching students to pass a course, their role should be to teach their students to dive safely for when they leave the course and the instructor is not present. From feedback I have received from students and instructors, the 'team' which receives most of the focus is the 'team of students' and how they should perform; but, as demonstrated here, being a 'team' involves far more than 'just diving next to each other' and should involve the instructor.

Unfortunately, the quality of instruction is not always great and the lack of ability to provide robust feedback on those who are at the top of the industry, especially 'names', means that issues like this will continue to propagate, because of the social power of these individuals. Interestingly, from discussions I have had with senior training agency staff and others within training agencies, much of this resistance comes from the agencies who don't want to lose a 'name'. The irony is that having a 'name' isn't doing the agency any favours! It is for this reason that this narrative is anonymous, and the instructor(s) was not named by the contributor, but the learning opportunities for all are real.

Case Study: Teams don't just happen because you say, 'Dive in a team'.

The dynamics and pressures present in this course were not ideal for my learning as I am dyslexic and normally complete my technical training on a private or semi- private basis, as I need a little more time for processing and reflection. There were 4 students, 3 instructor candidates and 3 instructors on this class. One of the instructors (Instructor #1) was also an instructor trainer/examiner who is a 'name' in the industry.

Day one didn't start well. Instructor #1 did not introduce himself to anyone; nor did the students or instructor candidates introduce themselves to each other. Instructor #1 assigned dive partners and told us to pair up ready for dive one which would be a skills dive. During this self-introduction process, it became apparent that there were students, instructor candidates and instructors in the group - something we, as students, were not expecting.

As I put my unit together, I noticed there was a problem with my head and oxygen sensors and told this to Instructor #1. He was irritated at me for not being better prepared. This is despite the fact that the unit had just come back from a manufacturer's service; I had run a full check before the trip; and the unit had functioned normally at home before I left. Instructor #2 had a spare head and I put the unit back together with that. Instructor #1 then said the group would be team diving - something that I had not done before as I spent most of my time solo diving.

We started dive one and I couldn't get my partner, student #2, to team up with me. Student #2 is also an independent diver used to diving alone, and also unused to team diving. During the debrief, the instructors, unsurprisingly, highlighted a lack of team diving! Instructor #1 said that the teams needed to stay closer together and instructor #2 specifically told student #2 to pay more attention and swim with their team-mate. During the post-dive checks/debrief, I picked up that there was some water in my breathing loop.

Instructor #1 commented on my configuration and had me change my bailout setup and rigging. I do this; it is a learning course, even though I have no experience of this new set-up which includes swapping the bailouts from all left (my normal configuration) to all right. I dry my unit, assemble it and then run tests. They all pass.

Day two started out with a deep dive to practice skills and to demonstrate the time/deco calculations associated with the class. The drills we were to do were discussed, reviewed and then Instructor #1 directed the class to get gear ready. I had already built my unit, but I couldn't find my mask. Instructor #1 asked me, "Where is your back-up mask?" I replied that it had been damaged in transit, so I didn't have a spare. I borrowed another mask, which further upset the instructor. Instructor #1 states that this was to be a 100 min dive, with the run-time and deco-time being such that we surfaced at 100 mins.

We entered the water and student #2 left me and I become an independent diver once again! I decided to swim over to pair up with another diver in group. As the dive progressed, I sensed water rattling in the loop. I didn't believe the unit was flooded so stayed on the loop. Instructor #1 lost track of time and the associated deco, so we surfaced after 100 mins. During the bottom phase, I had noticed we had run past the ascent time, but given my previous experiences with Instructor #1, I decided not to say anything. No-one else on the dive said anything either.

During the debrief, the question came up about extending beyond 100 mins and Instructor #1 said he just missed it, and no explanation was given as to why. Student #2 and I were reprimanded for not diving together. I was getting frustrated with my assigned dive buddy as he was not taking any responsibility for diving with me as a team- mate.

This exchange further irritated Instructor #1 with his frustrations being directed at me.

Hesitantly, I reported that my unit had more water in it. Instructor #1, made it clear he was frustrated with me, questioned several areas of how I ran my checklists and tests. I replied that every step had been followed and all tests were successful. Instructor #1 alluded that I should, "check your mouth piece". I did this promptly. The mouthpiece was custom-fitted for my bite and then placed on the factory DSV, with a tie wrap. I didn't see any issue with the mouthpiece or its fitting to the DSV.

At lunchtime, I found my mask at 'lost and found'. Instructor #1 briefed the team about the upcoming dive which was to be a boat dive. We were to be dropped off to complete a 55m (180') dive and complete the deco up the wall. A few drills were to be performed and dive times were to be monitored. We were again reminded to remain in our buddy pairs. The dive was to be led by one of the instructor candidates. Instructor #1 discussed with part of the class that this would be a 'team' dive using 'team bailout'.[8] In this case, the bottle to be shared was the 50% bottle. However, I had no experience of this concept; the idea was not explained clearly; and we weren't sure which diver would be carrying the 50% bottle.

The dive began badly. The boat drop was not where it was supposed to be; and the instructor candidate began swimming in the direction they believed to be the intended exercise area. The current started to pick up until it was a noticeable force into which we were swimming. As the instructor candidate continued searching for the correct dive site, I believed the goal of the dive had changed from an instructional dive to 'find the dive site'. All of the divers were now spread out with no real buddy system in place. After about 15 mins into the dive, I noticed gurgling again in my rebreather, and this continued to worsen during dive.

As the current picked up, our workload picked up as well. This was not made easier as Instructor #1 and the [instructor] candidate kept pushing us into the current to find the dive site. After about 35 mins, I tasted sorb for the first time and the breathing resistance was increased too, so I found it difficult to breathe. Shortly after this, I realised that my diluent

---

8 Team bailout is where the bailout is shared amongst the team to reduce logistical burden although for a 60m dive, this isn't necessary given that each diver should be capable of carrying two stages, either both left or left-right.

was empty, and I quickly switched over to my bailout. However, in the process, and due to my stressed mental state, I forgot to close the DSV when I bailed out. This causes the loop to flood.

I was now on open circuit using the bottom mix gas. After a few breaths, Instructor #1 realised that I had bailed out with my loop open. My team-mate was at least 30m away. Instructor #1 rushed over to assess the situation. We were at 53m (175') on bottom gas with a 35 min deco obligation assuming a CCR ascent and 1hr 15 mins of ascent using OC. I was ushered to 21m (70') where instructor candidate #2 had a bottle of 50% and this was handed to me. After this was consumed, instructor candidate #2 provided another 50% bottle, until the deco was complete during the ascent. I returned to the boat along with the rest of the students and candidates, and was placed on 100% O2 for 30 minutes, with no DCS. Once on the boat, I was chastised by Instructor #1 for having water in my loop and not closing loop when bailing out.

Back on shore, the source of the leak into my loop was caused by an incorrect tie wrap being used to hold the mouthpiece to the DSV - it should have had a metal reinforcing band inside the wrap. Mine didn't. I never knew this, and Instructor #1 had never mentioned this earlier. Replacing the tie-wrap with a metal-lined one solved the issue.

We then held a long debrief. However, the focus was on my actions and not the role/performance of the instructor candidate, nor Instructor #1 losing focus/control of the class; and the fact that both Instructor #1 and the instructor candidate were task-focused on finding the dive site.

Day three didn't start much better. Instructor #1 started a classroom discussion, and this was the first instruction we had during the class. Open discussions followed along with practice drills. Instructor #1, now obviously irritated with me as he called me derogatory terms, put me through a barrage of drills. The difference now was that I was given instruction and through this proper direction and instruction, I performed all the tasks to a standard acceptable by Instructor #1.

Days four to seven of the course continued with drills and a final experience dive. All of which happened without incident.

This case study saddens me, because it highlights that a knowledge of human factors and non-technical skills should be core to instructor development, especially when it comes to authority gradient and the impact it can have on student learning, student performance, team performance and, ultimately, safety. A steep authority gradient was one of the key reasons why Crew (Cockpit) Resource Management programmes were brought into aviation - young, knowledgeable co-pilots were unable to challenge old-school, 'crusty' captains about their decisions and this inability meant that information which could have saved the aircraft was not made available or ignored, leading to the loss of many aircraft and those on-board. The incident in Chapter 1 with the AOW diver and Jamie's reflection's in Chapter 2 show that the presence of a steep gradient isn't uncommon. Trust is a key component of a high-performing team and you cannot have trust where there is a steep authority gradient.

It would be easy to 'blame' the instructor for not doing a good job at the start. However, the student also made a number of mistakes - some of them based on knowledge which should have been known beforehand. This incident could be used to write a complete chapter, but consider the following factors in your own instruction or when you are a student:

- The student didn't declare that he was dyslexic and the impact this might have on the learning environment.
- The instructor didn't create a psychologically-safe environment, so students could fail and learn from that failure, even if that meant asking a 'stupid' question. There is no such thing as a stupid question, only the one you wished you had asked.
- The lack of defined pre-course standards in terms of competence meant that instructors often have to spend early dives correcting/picking up issues and not teaching course skills.
- Following his experience on day one, the student didn't trust the instructor to impart the knowledge needed and ensure the knowledge was in place before the students entered the water. This trust deteriorated until day 3 when the dry-runs were carried

out and instruction was actually carried out.
- The instructor wasn't humble in their own failures which increased the psychological barriers to challenge them if something didn't go to plan or wasn't expected.
- The student didn't bail out earlier on the second dive of day 2, based on social conformance, because of the previous feedback from Instructor #1.
- Incomplete knowledge by the student regarding the metal-lined tie-wrap and assumed knowledge regarding this by the instructor. Specific language was needed for 'checking' the tie-wrap.
- Changing stages from 'all left' to 'all right' introduced mental stresses that weren't needed. Especially if the student is going to go back to 'all left' after the class. The learning during the class should be relevant to post-class diving and should not be focused on the instructor's personal preferences.
- 'Team bailout' and team diving needed to be defined and knowledge developed before jumping on a 60m dive. As was shown, the reason to have bailout is to be able to use it when needed.

What is Teamwork?

There is a general consensus in the research literature that a team consists of two or more individuals, who have specific roles, perform interdependent tasks, are adaptable, and share a common goal. To work effectively together, team members must possess specific knowledge, skills, and attitudes (KSAs). In the context of diving, these KSAs cover both technical skills (e.g. videography, surveying techniques, line-laying and photogrammetry), but also non-technical skills such as the skill in monitoring each other's performance, knowledge of their own and teammate's task responsibilities, and a positive attitude toward working in a team. These latter KSAs are a key component to effective teamwork.

Public speaker and expert on team performance, Simon Sinek adds to this with his definition of teamwork as, *"A team is not just a group of people who work together. It is a group who trust each other."* While diving is a recreational activity and the term 'work' is used, we shouldn't get hung up about this. 'Work' can be anything which is used to create something else (e.g. a dive experience, a 3D model of a cave, the exploration and identification of a new wreck, the documentation of underwater life and many other things which are produced as an outcome from a dive.) However, as we saw from the first narrative in this chapter, we can see that teams don't happen, even if you say, *'You are now a team';* there is a process by which each team goes through which allows the both technical and non-technical skills to be developed. This developmental process is experienced by most teams and as long as we understand that journey, we can better manage the stresses and barriers which prevent high-performing teams from flourishing.

Teams exist across a multitude of areas in diving where the goals are obvious:

- Project specific exploration teams like the J2 project led by Bill Stone.
- Cave-diving survey and exploration teams like the WKPP, the Wet Mules or the Karst Underwater Research team.
- Technical dive teams focused on wreck identification like 'Dark Star' or 'Divers of the Deep'.
- Scientific dive teams like the National Park Service Submerged Resource Center or the Woods Hole Institute.
- Cave rescue teams like that which executed the cave rescue in the Tham Luang cave in Thailand.
- However, teams also exist in the 'fun' and training environments:
- Technical dive teams formed by divers who are undertaking or have undertaken training through organisations like GUE, UTD or ISE like the one I am still a member of, 'Team Foxturd', which was formed in 2007 when Gareth Burrows, Howard Payne and I started our training with GUE.
- Training teams within dive centres e.g. the owner(s), instructors, dive masters and guides.
- Student teams who come together to complete training, a team formed of students. However, another team exists in this

environment too, the instructor plus the students is another team, a team which is often forgotten.

Teams can be ad hoc or formed on a more formal or structured basis. Although no data exists to prove this, I believe that the majority of diving takes place in an ad hoc or group (not team) basis rather than team diving. I believe that I was lucky because my diver training really started in 2005 when I met a group of divers who were interested in 'Doing It Right' (DIR) diving. In 2006, I took GUE Fundamentals which started me on the road towards effective team diving. Given my military aviation background, such a route wasn't unexpected, and I must say that the lack of 'team' in the diving I had done up until that point frustrated me. I also recognise that when I go diving outside of a team, I find it uncomfortable, because I don't have that shared mental model which means I understand what the team is going to do, how we are going to communicate, what the ascent plan is...this is not unexpected, if you know how teams form and develop.

Team Development

In 1965, Bruce Tuckman, a researcher focusing on team dynamics, published his 'Forming-Storming-Norming-Performing' model. The model explains that as the team develops in maturity and ability, relationships are established; the leader changes leadership style; and the team change their inter- and intra- team interactions based on the knowledge of the task, the team and the individual-within-the-team's needs. Because the real world is dynamic, the performance of the team is dynamic in how they deal with the situation/task, but also how they evolve themselves, especially as trust is developed. However, just because you have a team of experts, it does not necessarily produce an expert team. The most effective teams emerge when their technical skills (task-work) are aligned with their teamwork skills.

The following section will describe each stage of Tuckman's model and how leaders and members develop. Understanding this progressive model will show how and why certain tensions exist, especially as personality types (discussed in the Leadership chapter – Chapter 11) can impact team development, collaboration and co-operation. As you read this, see how it applies to your own diving and/or instruction/development if you are a student.

Forming. In the forming stage, there is a high level of dependence on the leader for guidance and direction. The team often don't know each other, and they start to learn about the task at hand along with their roles to achieve this and because the individual roles and responsibilities are unclear, this introduces uncertainty and fear. There is little agreement on the aims for the team and the associated tasks other than as detailed by the leader. Due to the lack of clarity, the leader will be required to answer lots of questions about the team's purpose, objectives and external relationships. Of note, processes are often ignored e.g. gas switch protocols or the use of checklists/briefs, because their value has not been developed or understood by the members. Due to a lack of coherence and collaboration, the members of the team often push the limits and test the tolerance of both the system, the leader and the rest of the team. To facilitate communications and development, the leader needs to apply directive language.

Storming. In the storming stage, the key observation is that decisions don't come easily within group, predominately because team members are developing a hierarchy and structure in relation to other team members and the leader. In some cases, the team might challenge the validity of the person leading them. While clarity concerning the task and the team/member's roles increases, there is still a fair amount of uncertainty present which can cause problems. The team needs to be focused on its goals to avoid becoming distracted by relationships and emotional issues. It is more than likely that conflict will exist and, as a consequence, compromises may be required to enable progress. The team is coming together and rather than direct them, the leader coaches.

Norming. During this phase, there is a high level of agreement and consensus within the team. Roles and responsibilities are clear and accepted and because the goals are clear, the big decisions which need to be made are via group agreement. There is a level of trust which allows lesser decisions to be delegated to individuals or small teams within group. Again, because the role/task clarity is high, commitment and unity is also strong. The team is reflective which leads to discussion and positive-conflict when it comes to processes and working styles. Crucially, there is general respect for the leader and some of leadership is more shared by the team. Rather than coaching, the leader is now more of an enabler and facilitator.

Performing. By this stage the team is more strategically aware, and they know clearly why they are doing what they are doing. The team has a shared vision and is resilient to external factors, with a focus on over-achieving goals. The leader has developed a high-degree of autonomy within the team, because the boundaries in which the team can operate are clear. This doesn't mean that disagreements won't happen, but now they are resolved within the team positively, and necessary changes to processes and structure are made by the team. Crucially, the team members look after each other, anticipating issues and back-filling capabilities when needed. As the team develops, they expect the leader to delegate tasks and projects. Finally, because they have a high-level of technical competence, they do not need to be instructed or assisted - although if they come across a problem they can't solve individually, they will ask for assistance. The leadership role by this stage is almost transparent to an external observer during the execution phase and the leader is delegating and overseeing the activity.

You might think that this is some corporate mumbo-jumbo that doesn't relate to diving, but if we consider that the goal of every dive should be to get out of the water without injury (physical or mental), have fun and if possible, learn something which makes future dives safer and more enjoyable, then we can see the team has an implicit goal. The majority of diver training is based on the buddy system, as it provides mitigation in the event that one diver has an issue. That means we also have an implicit goal of keeping each other safe and holding each other accountable to the skills that were taught/developed.

The following two sections show how we can apply this model and where attention needs to be paid if we are to have successful teams.

Team Development: Instructional Setting

The course comes together. They might know what the course is going to entail, but in many cases they only know the outcomes; they don't know how they are going to get there. They might know the instructor and might know the other students. There will be some reticence to come forward because of the lack of psychological safety - students (and instructors) don't like to look stupid to people they've never met before. It is clear that the instructor is leading the 'instructional team', but there isn't clarity about who is leading the 'student team'. While processes/instructions are detailed, they might not necessarily be followed, because of a lack of technical competence - but also because the relevance isn't clear. Fear of failure is likely to be high at this stage. As the course progresses, the students start to understand each other's strengths and weaknesses and, if they are operating as a team, will start to help each other out, rather than looking out for themselves.

The goals for the team need to be revisited regularly, especially if they are not progressing as they'd hoped. As the team progress in technical competence, the instructor should be moving from acting as a 'teller' to coaching and facilitating the learning. The instructor should also be creating the environment such that the students are reflective on both their technical and non-technical skills development and learn to critique each other, so that when they graduate, debriefing and providing critique isn't a surprise or something new. I fully understand that time is limited on courses and therefore some of the more 'fluffy' stuff gets missed out, but the aim of a course shouldn't be to pass a course: it should be to teach the students how to dive in the real world and that means being able to learn and develop themselves, and if they are in a team, that means operating as a team.

Team Development: Project Setting

In many cases, projects come together using expertise from around the world: divers, photographers, videographers, scientists and researchers – all to achieve a common goal. For some the goal is just to dive *that* wreck or explore *that cave* system or capture *that* wildlife. Again, there is a goal which should be clear, and that also includes not having any accidents or incidents. Clear leadership in such a setting is really important, because they need to have the big picture for the team and not get involved in the minutiae. With clear leadership and direction, a team can move through the early stages of team development more quickly and because the team are motivated, the style doesn't have to be too autocratic either.

However, baseline safety procedures and rules need to be clearly defined early on because of the wide range of 'standards' in the community. If a team are to hold each other accountable for performance, they must have a standard. Richard Lundgren's example in Chapter 3 of not analysing gas is a classic example of the benefit of having standards. If goals are not being attained, then the team must identify why this isn't happening. It is easy to blame individuals, but this leads to the team becoming fractured. A high-performing team will look out for each other and go well beyond the *'that's not my job'* to ensure the team's goals are achieved. This is what makes team diving so enjoyable. You can achieve far more as a team than you can as an individual, but only if you are all working together as a team and trust each other to maintain focus on the goal.

Goal-fixation within project diving can be an issue though, especially if there have been 'promises' over what can be achieved. If you want to read an account of what goal-fixation can look like in an expedition setting, read writer and mountaineer Jon Krakauer's, *'Into Thin Air'* or watch the 2015 film *'Everest'*. In hindsight, the failures are so obvious; but in real time with massive personal, emotional and financial investments, saying, 'No', can be hard. Remember, a team of experts doesn't necessarily mean an expert team; they need to understand what teamwork is and then apply it.

Teaming vs Teamwork

Professor Amy Edmondson describes the 'Process Knowledge Spectrum' in her book *Teaming*[1] where tasks move from routine, to complex to innovative; the importance of teaming increases, because of the interdependence of team members; and their roles grows to deliver the task at hand. A car manufacturing plant, where outcomes are fairly well-known, is generally a 'Routine Operation'. In diving, this would be preparation or servicing of dive equipment. At the other extreme, in 'Innovative Operations' such as an academic research lab, or exploration of a new cave system, the outcomes are quite unknown. Although the teaming framework applies in each of these settings, the leader's specific behaviours and actions must change. Having excellent outcomes and appropriate teaming requires matching the right approach to the specific kind of operation.

A Team is Only as Strong as its Weakest Member

One of the traits of a high-performance team is the recognition that not everyone in the team has all the knowledge, skills and attitudes needed to complete the task and that if one team member is lacking, the team ethos will bring that person up to the standard of the rest of the team - because the team recognises it is only as strong as its weakest member. This is obvious when you look at Formula 1 pit teams. The pit team can only get the car out in a quick time if they are working together. Their interdependent technical skills are facilitated by effective non-technical skills. The whole team performance is impacted by the sub-team performance e.g. if the back-right wheel team are performing slower than the rest of the team, it brings the whole team's performance down in getting the car in and out of the pit lane as quickly as possible. This concept that the team is only as strong as its weakest member needs to consider not just technical skills, but also non-technical and physiological performance variability.

Case Study: Divers have individual performance variability

Gene Hobbs, the cave diver behind the Rubicon Research Foundation, recalls a dive from the early 1990s in which he learned about the variability in human physiology, specifically decompression sickness, and that how he gathered information was based on his body's physiological feedback process, a process which produced different results to that of his buddy!

My buddy and I were in our early 20s in the '90s and in great physical condition. We also leapt at any chance we could to go diving. In particular, we loved cave diving. While the fact that this dive series I am about to describe occurred in a cave, it really could have occurred anywhere and on any dive series.

In the early '90s, dive computers were just starting to be easily accessible to many, but for two poor college students, the cost of a computer was several weekends of diving with fuel to get us to the site. For 'accommodation', we used the truck seat for a bed and for gas, we obtained free air fills at a local shop for our doubled aluminium 80 tanks. For thermal protection we dived wetsuits; I am not even sure we really knew anyone with a dry suit back then. We would be cool at the end of a dive - but never freezing.

Probably hard for anyone reading this to believe, but diving was our favourite form of stress relief. Even during the stress-filled end of a semester, we were looking for any chance to get wet and it did not take much to convince us to head south. Little River, in North Florida, was our favourite system - but it was an 8-hour drive away.

If we left town following our last exam on Friday, we could drive to Little River; sleep for a couple of hours in the parking lot until sunrise; knock out two dives we had done MANY times before; and still be back in time to study a bit on Sunday before our Monday morning exams. And with that: the plan was born.

As students, we lived on junk food and caffeine. My exam the following week was later, and in those days, I drove almost all the time anyway. My buddy managed to get some restless naps between belting out songs on the radio, while I forced myself to stay awake to get there.

The first dive was amazing. The crystal-clear water was a cool 72 degree and the flow was normal, but back then it was higher than it is now. That meant that we might work a bit to get back to our turn pressure (thirds), but it was going to be the usual awesome ride on the flow back out of the spring.

Since we were in a cave, the profiles for each of us were almost identical with a few seconds of offset between dive team leader and buddy. At deco, the stops went as planned and we separated off to our usual locations on either side of the entrance at 10 feet. I finished my plan, waved, and moved to the surface where I could watch his bubbles while he cleared his deco. Once he surfaced, ten minutes later, we spent a few minutes discussing the dive standing neck deep in the water and I then climbed the steps to open the truck and start changing so we could go get more air for the second dive... Same as it ever was... (Dive time, depths? How was deco calculated and why was your deco 10 mins shorter than his?)

Our surface interval was a couple of hours and then we were back in the water. Another fun and uneventful dive... I waved goodbye after my deco and surfaced to watch and wait for my buddy to surface. 15 minutes later my buddy surfaced, and I went to the truck. Maybe an hour after that we were on our way home so we could start cramming for our exams.

Seven hours later, we merged onto the last highway for the final hour of our trip back to college. It was late and my buddy was asleep, so I tapped him to wake him up. He nearly jumped out the window, because he said it hurt that bad.

Instead of going back to college, we headed off to the emergency department and the hyperbaric treatment which followed. I had done 10 minutes less deco on the first dive and 15 minutes less on the second than my buddy. I had had less sleep, more caffeine, and yet I never had a symptom.

This event was a defining moment in my understanding that the "rules", as we knew them, were just guidelines when it came to decompression. I had heard of this concept before, but it never had any meaning as I hadn't experienced it myself.

Gene's event highlights the problem we have as divers. Even though we know the theory and the 'rules', we are all individuals and we have different strengths and weakness. It is not clear whether Gene's buddy knew that he was susceptible or that Gene had more resilience, but either way, there is a need to review activities in a manner which facilitates learning. Telling someone to be careful is unlikely to make any difference at all towards their future safety and performance, especially if they know what they are doing is something which involves risk! However, if the team work together, describing the situation, how it made sense, and what the cues/clues helped inform their decision-making processes, the individuals, and consequently the team, will make better decisions in the future and the team will improve their performance as a whole. That is what a debrief is about: reflecting on the past to improve the future.

Debriefing is the Key to Real Learning
One of the most powerful tools I deliver during my face-to-face classes is the structured debrief and, for that reason, I have included the process in the book. If you would like a standalone guide, you can download one from here www.thehumandiver.com/p/debrief.

A debrief is a simplified investigation and is an essential tool to understand what didn't work, why and how to improve. What is often forgotten though, but equally as important, is the need to understand what did work and why, so that it can be repeated.

The former is important because mistakes cost divers money: they have less fun and sometimes it can be just bloody scary (or fatal) when stuff goes wrong! The latter, because we need to understand what the effective decisions were within the process; or what communication techniques or routes worked; or what team structure and leadership was effective; and, importantly, be able to reproduce them on future dives.

In both cases, positive or negative, we have a tendency to focus on the outcome and not the process when it comes to assessing how well we did. In both positive and negative cases, it is the learning that is important, not focussing on fixing the errant activity.

When there is an adverse outcome (e.g. rapid, uncontrolled ascent; buddy separation; out-of-gas or low gas situation; one of three

H's (hyperoxia, hypoxia, hypercapnia)), we often focus on blaming individuals for not following their training or doing something 'stupid' - as opposed to understanding why it made sense for them to do what they did. A fundamental point to remember is that whatever we perceive to be the truth, is actually reality for those involved. Consequently, it is very easy to apply hindsight bias to what has happened because we know the outcome; yet those at the time didn't have that knowledge; they didn't have a crystal ball.

When looking at a positive outcome, it is easy to rest on our laurels and think we had an awesome dive because nothing went wrong. However, unless we can identify what specifically worked, how are we going to be able to reproduce it again? In some cases, the reason why something was successful was that things just fell into place, and we consider it 'luck'. We can't change how luck falls, but we can certainly influence its direction and be prepared for it when it arrives. For that to happen though, we need to analyse the situation immediately after the event whilst memories are still fresh.

An effective debrief requires a psychologically safe environment. Research states that psychological safety is the collective belief of how team members and leaders respond when another member "puts themselves on the line", by asking a question, reporting an error, or raising a difficult issue. The team member(s) will internally undertake an assessment weighing up the risk of speaking up against the interpersonal climate versus the longer-term consequences of not speaking up - in effect relating to what happened the last time I or someone else spoke up. Was it a positive response or not?

The DEBRIEF framework has been developed for use in relatively small groups of people, covering fun dives, training dives or expeditions. It is essential that everyone can relate directly to the activities which took place and provide an input. If teams are larger than this, the same broad framework can be used, but the level of detail might need to be changed when it comes to the 'I' and the second 'E'.

In addition to the DEBRIEF framework, there is a need to

understand how to deliver feedback in an effective, but non-confrontational manner; because as instructors or leaders of the dive, we have a responsibility and accountability to ensure that what we present or communicate to our students or team is correct and, most importantly, they have understood what we have said to them.

Sometimes there are different ways of presenting materials to get the point across, or that expectations of the class or the dive were perceived differently between student/team members and instructor, or intern and IT, or the leader of the dive. Given this, it is very useful to review our own behaviours. because unless we have an understanding of how others perceive us as their teacher, manager, staff member, trainee, family member, patient or clients, we are not sighted about the effect our interactions are having on others.

DEBRIEF - A Framework for Learning

I have put this framework based on the acronym DEBRIEF as a way of remembering the topics and questions which need to be covered to maximise learning after each dive or diving day:

D - Define. Define the scope of the debrief, and the aims/goals/objectives of the dive and did we achieve them? There are two parts to this definition phase. The first is to define how long the debrief will take: - 10 minutes, 30 minutes or 2 hours? This informs the team how succinct they need to be, and consequently how much detail needs to go into the debrief. It also provides a boundary which the team leader can use to provide an imperative to further focus discussions. The second part is that by defining the aims/goals/objectives of the dive from the outset, we can ensure the debrief stays on focus. Finally, describing goals and their attainment shows the benefit of having a plan to start with, because without a plan or expected output from the task, how do we know we've met it?

E - Example. Set an example as the leader. Talk about a mistake, error or violation you made during the plan or the dive. One of the easiest ways to create a psychologically-safe environment is for the leader to show humility and describe a mistake or error that they personally made during the task or activity. Maybe they didn't give enough detail in the dive brief, or the objective was unachievable - despite the team members highlighting this at the outset. Whatever the example, it needs to be meaningful and identify what led to the mistake or error being made. Fundamentally, this action sets the scene to say it is ok to talk about errors and failure and propose, in a non-judgemental way, of fixing it when the same situation is encountered.

B - Basics (pre-execution). Basics and admin for the dive (e.g. entry time, logistics and the plan itself). This covers the background and administration of the dive. Was the timing right? Was the plan clear to all involved? Was there a plan?! Were there dependencies that weren't identified as the task progressed? What about assumptions that went into the plan - had they been validated? In effect, this brief partially covers the non-operational aspects of the dive and provides the learning for the planning and assumptions element of subsequent dives.

R - Review Execution. Chronologically step through the execution, comparing it to the plan, highlighting key points. Review the execution of the dive in a chronological manner. It is important to focus on the key highlights, so that learning is managed. Depending on those involved and the time available, the level of detail can vary from top level to real detail. Don't necessarily pick up the future learning points here. Rather what happened and why. Many adverse events are down to interactions or behaviours between different parts of the system. This could be different team's understanding about what the dive was about, how certain equipment was to be used and dependencies or assumptions - this includes working with the skipper for boat dives.

I - Internal. *'One thing I did well. Why? One thing I need to improve on. How?'* When it comes to personal and team learning, the process needs to be simple. This DEBRIEF model has been developed to focus on one key learning point to reinforce a good practice and one where improvement is needed. To reinforce good practice, we need to examine the information, processes and actions that surrounded the decisions or communications. To correct behaviour, we need to do a similar activity, but this time we will also look at how to improve on the actions. Just identifying it and saying, 'We won't do that again' is not enough! This question and the next are answered by each of the team members in turn, starting with the leader.

E - External. *'One thing we did well as a team. Why? One thing we need to improve on as a team. How?'* The same as above, but this time focussing on the team aspects of the task. Both of these (Internal and External) need to describe the learning points in specifics - not generalities. If you describe 'Good communications' as something that went well, that doesn't help reinforce what specifically worked, because we all know that clear, concise and effective communications is a sign of a high-performing team. 'Your light communication was good, because you kept the light on the wall where I could see it and I immediately noticed when you weren't there. And when you had an issue and signalled, it was clear to me there was an issue', is a much better way of describing the 'What worked and why'.

F - Follow-up. Reinforce what needs to be done following the debrief – for example, maybe file an incident report or fix/modify a process or equipment. Learning does not always happen with what was discussed in the debrief - it nearly always requires application afterwards. This could be some modification to equipment, a revision to a planning assumption or to post a report within the local and/or global incident reporting system or forum. Given the similarities across the different diving communities, plus the fact that humans are roughly the same when it comes to decision-making, then sharing the learning helps more than just those involved in that specific dive to improve. However, for this to happen, there needs to be a culture in which divers look for those 'lessons learned' and understand why it made sense for the divers to operate in the way they did - and not immediately judge them.

DEBRIEF Summary

The DEBRIEF framework provides a simple and memorable structure which can be used for simple, fun dives, or complex expeditions with many competing goals. It looks to build and develop individuals and teams, by focussing on the positive and the improvements possible with a way forward identified - and not on the negative aspects of what went wrong, and the subsequent natural tendency to blame individuals.

Fundamentally, a debrief is about learning - not blaming. To learn, we need to understand the stories which were relevant and important to those involved. That relevance is shaped by experience, goals, objectives and the social environment in which we reside. However, to allow those stories to be told honestly and with candour, we need to have a psychologically-safe environment where it is okay (or even encouraged) to tell the instructor, expedition leader or just a friend the bad news and how to potentially fix it. Without such an environment, systemic issues will not be resolved.

This framework can be further enhanced by asking two more questions during the follow-up section:

- *"What was the greatest risk we took and got away with?"* This will inform and calibrate the level (s) of risk-taking within the team. If it didn't end up in a failure, why didn't it? What measures were put in place to prevent it? Or was it luck?
- *"If we had a bottomless pot of money, what would we do differently?"* Not because there is a bottomless pot available, but because it frees the mind of a restriction and thereby encourages creativity. It is the need to understand what that expensive capability can provide; and the discussion that follows looks at how else that same capability can be achieved.

A key trait of a high-performing team is the continual development which comes from learning about the system, the people within it, and the poor or good decisions which were made. Such a process is informed by an effective debrief; but that debrief requires honesty and strong leadership. A debrief is a tool, but just like any tool, it is only as good as the operator who is using it and for that operator to be effective, they need to practice using the tool.

Case Study: Teams work together to resolve issues

Alex Adolfi and Jim Dixon are active technical and CCR divers in the Pacific North West, based in Seattle and Vancouver respectively. A number of their community, including Jim and Alex, have taken human factors classes with me and recognised the value in learning from others by writing context-rich incident reports. This event was posted in their closed group on Facebook and it shows that when communication and situational awareness fail, teamwork can recover the situation. This narrative is told from two perspectives with the commentator identified.

The day saw us heading out to dive a wreck that is at Tech 1 (50m/165') depths and does not have mooring lines, so a shot-line was placed which was used to guide us down to the vicinity of the wreck. We had four divers on JJ-CCRs and three divers on open circuit. The plan was to have the open circuit team drop first and although the 4 JJ divers had broken into 2 teams, we would try to dive this as a team of four.

Once the boat crew had placed the shot-line, it was time for team 1 to enter. As they entered, we saw there was a strong surface current and the first diver in was having issues staying on the line even with his scooter on full throttle. His buddies joined him and, after some excitement, they managed to drop down the line. This revelation altered our plan for teams 2 and 3 somewhat, so Alex and I (team 2) were going to drop in first and meet team 3 down on the wreck in order to avoid fighting the surface current together. Alex was leading the dive and we dropped down and arrived on the wreck to await team 3. After waiting a period of time, Alex indicated that we should continue on with our dive as we had only planned for 30-minute bottom time, so away we went. This was a good call as team 3 had some issues and aborted their dive! The bottom portion of the dive was enjoyable and passed without issue.

Prior to the dive, our plan was to come up the shot-line, unless the current was too strong. When Alex thumbed the dive at our allotted bottom time, we decided not to attempt to come up the shot-line, but go to plan B and deploy a dSMB for the boat to follow. Once we started to ascend, Alex decided to deploy the SMB at around 36 metres. This was slightly deeper than the normal 21m, but given the current, we didn't want to be too far from the wreck.

Jim: I noticed that once Alex pulled the dSMB out of his pocket, the line had come loose and quickly became quite a mess. I moved over to Alex to help clean up the line as it had become entangled. At this point, Alex signalled me to deploy my dSMB. Where I normally dive, it is unusual to deploy SMBs shallower than 21 meters, and after the first gas switch. I hadn't dived with Alex before, so wasn't sure how to communicate that I wanted to wait to deploy dSMB. At this point, Alex looked concerned (at least I imagined) that I wasn't deploying my dSMB and signalled to me again to deploy my dSMB. I decided it would be fine that once deployed, we could sort Alex's entanglement, so I deployed my dSMB.

Alex: Knowing the current was moving us quickly away from the wreck, I wanted to let the boat know our location as soon as possible. So, I started to pull my SMB out almost as soon as we left the wreck. I pulled the dSMB out of my pocket and felt the spool come off almost immediately! Before I could reach down it was well out of reach and dropping fast and I still had the dSMB and double-ender in my hand with the line from the spool attached. My thought at this point was that I would hold on to it, while Jim sent up his dSMB and then we would reel up my spool once we started our deco. I didn't realise at this point the spool had gone through the shroud of my scooter. I signalled Jim to shoot his dSMB. Jim looked a little confused by this (I now know why as he was accustomed to doing this at 21m), so I signalled again, and he then began the process of sending up his own dSMB.

Jim: As my dSMB was spooling out line, on its way to the surface, the finger spool got stuck on my gloves, pulling me up about 60 centimetres (2 feet) above Alex, where I am sure he couldn't see me. I got my glove free by letting go of the finger spool knowing/hoping that it would come down to me as the dSMB continued towards the surface. It did come down to me, but I missed grabbing it as it passed by me - so I reached for it as I swam in close to the line. Oops, it became tangled on my deco bottles and quickly became tight, again pulling me toward the surface. I started swimming down while attempting to untangle it.

Alex: I noticed Jim appeared to have a loss of buoyancy while deploying the dSMB. I signalled once and was about to move up to see what was going on, when I felt a tug from underneath me. It was at this point, I discovered the entanglement in my scooter and that the spool or line somewhere beyond where I could see, was tangled in the wreck/bottom and preventing me from ascending. I looked up to see Jim rising away from me, while his spool descended towards me. Not wanting to lose all contact with Jim, I reached for his descending spool, but I missed it. I managed to grab the line just as it passed and held on to that with my right hand. I looked up and could no longer see Jim.

Jim: Unfortunately, my movement of swimming down and attempting to vent gas caused the line to become further entangled. I realised Alex couldn't see me as this happened as I was about 3 meters (10 feet) above him by now. I reached for my scooter and quickly came to the second realisation that it was part of the entanglement and could not be accessed. I decided to attempt again to swim back down to Alex, but couldn't dump enough gas as the dSMB was pulling me to the surface. My next thought was to let go of the finger spool in the hope that Alex would see it and potentially help me by assisting me in getting negative. I saw the finger spool pass by Alex and got concerned that I was working way too hard and might end up over breathing my CCR. So, I decided to let myself get a little shallower with the hope the dSMB would reach the surface and I could work at untangling myself while deciding next steps (I must admit I was a little excited by this time!)

Once I reached 21 meters (70 feet), I tried to stop my ascent by swimming down again, but still no relief. After a short time, I decided to head up further - despite our plan for approximately 40 minutes of deco. This strategy was continued every three meters until I hit six meters (20 feet) with no relief from the strain of the line. I rationalised that the dSMB had to be on the surface, yet it was still pulling me up. The only thing I could think of at the time was get to the surface to untangle or cut the line. So up I went! I recalled what I was told by my Tech 2 instructor after one of the students had an issue that almost caused him to surface on our ascent from 75 meters. The instructor had told me to follow your buddy up and at that point you have about 6 minutes before you will be in a lot of trouble from missed decompression stops. Once on the surface, I managed to get some slack, but couldn't get it untangled. I didn't want to cut it unless absolutely necessary as we needed a dSMB to let the boat know where we were, as I knew Alex's dSMB was out of commission.

Alex: While holding the line from Jim's dSMB with my right hand, I used my left hand to eventually untangle my own dSMB line from my scooter - after quite a bit of fussing. I then abandoned my own dSMB (uninflated but still attached to a spool somewhere below me) and began to pull in the slack on the portion of Jim's dSMB line that went towards the surface. I could not see Jim at all and hadn't for several minutes. I was becoming extremely concerned! My first thought was that I needed to get up to Jim to help him out; however, I had no idea if he was still with the dSMB line or not. I decided to try and signal him by tugging urgently on the line. I figured if I felt him signal back, I would be able to at least get to him to help...

Jim: Just then I felt Alex tug on the line, so I knew he was down there somewhere. I tugged back to let him know I was okay. I decided I get as negative as I could and managed some slack, so decided to attempt to swim down. I got down to Alex who was at 21 meters (70 feet). Once down, he noticed that I was still entangled and that I was quite excited. He helped me relax and stabilise by signalling to me just to breath and get settled - before we did anything else. Once things slowed down, Alex spent about 4 minutes untangling me as we hung out at 21 meters (70 feet).

Alex: Having felt Jim tug back I was preparing to ascend, to assist him with whatever problem he might be having, when he swam down the line into sight. I breathed an initial sigh of relief that we were reunited, but quickly realised that our problems were not over yet. The reason he had lost buoyancy was a significant amount of entanglement. We were stable at this point, so we just sat there for a few moments and regained our composure. I then signalled to Jim to monitor our depth while I began the task of untangling him. This involved the removal of both the tow cord and nose clip of his scooter from his crotch strap D-ring; removing the bottom bolt snaps from both his deco bottles; and removing his SPG bolt snap from the D-ring. Once those were cleaned up and replaced, I had to then remove the top bolt snaps from both deco cylinders from the chest D-ring and replace them. Finally, I had to untangle the remainder of the line that was wrapped around the left post LOLA valve on the JJ.

Jim: We then decided to add additional deco and spent more time at 21 meters and added additional time at 9 meters (30 feet) and quite a bit at 6 meters (20 feet). I can tell you I was very aware of how my body felt as we ascended during our deco and was waiting for some ill-effects. Luckily, I felt good at each stop so we continued on. I continued to be very aware of how I felt for the next few hours, but I am happy to report I dodged this bullet.

Alex: We extended deco as Jim mentioned and I don't think I took my eyes off of him for a second. I was sure that at any time he was going to signal me that something was wrong. Luckily that moment never came. We did have plenty of time to use a trick that Guy taught me several years ago where a double-ender is used to weight down the line and keep it away from the team, while the dropped spool is recovered. Once we had the spool back in hand, we reeled the excess line back in and replaced the double-ender. The rest of the deco was, thankfully, uneventful.

There were a number of events on this dive which were caused by changes and changes create uncertainty. However, having standards, expectations and trust within a team means that is easier to deal with such uncertainty. In hindsight, it is easy to look at this event and say, "They shouldn't have done that" or "I would have done this differently" and now armed with this information, you probably would. What is more important to recognise is that the team worked together to deal with the first changes (increased tidal current on entry and then amended the plan); they deviated from a plan (waited at the bottom), but should have had a contingency for that (expectation is that team #3 will make it to the bottom; what if they don't?); and when the ascent problems started, they resolved them based on contingency plans which had been developed in training through the telling of stories; and always trying to work out what the other team member was doing to help the situation. There was a high level of trust within the team and that helped keep the anxiety from rising. That doesn't mean that every team dive is a 'trust-me dive', but rather team members will work to help each other out with the common goal of getting everyone out and not just looking out for themselves. Mutual accountability with a common goal is what teamwork is about, and that takes time to develop.

From my perspective, one of the most important things this team did was post the account to their local dive team Facebook group so that others within their community could learn from it. They have created a culture within their dive community that allows such incidents to be shared. The genesis of that attitude came from the courses which a number of the GUE community in the Pacific Northwest have taken with me - the realisation that 'team' isn't just a 2 or 3-person dive team; it is much wider and that they can help each other develop by sharing such stories.

Teams are about relationships and instructors can create their own 'team' of previous graduates with the common goal of improving their safety and performance. An example of how to do this came to light when I spoke with Becky Kagan Schott at a recent diving conference. She said that she has also created a closed Facebook group and only previous course graduates are invited. She uses the group to share product notices, tips and tricks which she has learned over time and recounting learning events, like her narrative which is in the next chapter. This event involved a total electronics failure of her rebreather at 75m with 75-80mins of decompression to complete!

Summary of Key Points
- A team is most effective when their technical skills (task-work) are aligned with their teamwork skills. The reverse also holds true. A team of experts (high technical skill competence) does not necessarily produce an expert team.
- Teams don't just happen. They take time to develop the trust which allows greater risks to be taken.

Questions to consider
- What stops your dive team developing from a group of divers in the water together to a real team who trust each other? What can you do about that?
- What has been the best success you've had when diving within a team? What was the cause of success?
- What has been the biggest failure when diving as a team and why do you think it happened in the way it did?
- What barriers can you see to implementing a DEBRIEF structure in your dive team?

References
(1) Edmondson, A. C. (2010) *Teaming: How Organizations Learn, Innovate, and Compete in the Knowledge Economy* (Kindle Location 740). Wiley. Kindle Edition.

Additional Reading
Edmondson, A C. (2010) *Teaming: How Organizations Learn, Innovate, and Compete in the Knowledge Economy*. Wiley.

Lencioni, P. (2002). *The Five Dysfunctions of a Team: A Leadership Fable*. San Francisco, Calif: Jossey-Bass.

McChrystal, S. A., Collins, T., Silverman, D., & Fussell, C. (2015). *Team of Teams: New rules of engagement for a complex world*. New York: Portfolio/Penguin.

Scott, K. (2018). *Radical Candor: Be a kick-ass boss without losing your humanity*. Griffin.

Teschner, R. C. (2018). *Debrief to Win*. St. Louis, MO: RTI Press.

Chapter 10

Leadership and Followership in Diving: The need for it is far more common than you'd think!

"Leadership consists of guiding, encouraging and facilitating the pursuit by others of ends using means, both of which they have either selected, or the selection of which they approve. In this formulation, leadership requires an ability to bring the will of followers into consonance with that of the leader so they follow him or her voluntarily, with enthusiasm and dedication. Such voluntarism, enthusiasm, and dedication are not necessarily involved in either management or administration."

Russell Ackoff.

Case Study: The standard you walk past is the standard you accept. Leadership is in everyone

This is an account by Lanny Vogel, a close friend of mine and owner of Underworld Tulum, Mexico of a near-miss that happened in the summer of 2018. Although Lanny was not one of the divers most directly involved, there are some excellent lessons to be taken from it, particularly in terms of judgement and responsibility for dive professionals. Unfortunately, as you will see, the majority of the divers involved were completely unaware of the situation they were in.

The incident happened whilst I was teaching a Full Cave Class in a busy training site in Mexico. Cenote Ponderosa has some great training cave, but as it has a large and picturesque open water area, it is also used for Open Water Training, Guided Cavern Tours and for Discover Scuba

Diving/Try Dive programmes. For this reason, all the cave lines and even the permanent cavern line all start well inside the overhead environment to prevent untrained divers from straying into the cave. At least in theory.

I was conducting a zero visibility exit drill, with my student divers in blackout masks. They had just negotiated a 'jump-in-touch-contact' and were reading their markers on the River Run line, before heading out towards their primary reel. I was intending to run the drill all the way to the surface, so the team surfaced in simulated zero visibility – something that is a good confidence-builder and that I try and do at least once on each course. As I looked over towards the exit, I noticed a large group of over a dozen divers swimming around the fairly unambiguous "grim reaper" cave sign, which although in the light zone, is around 20m inside the overhead environment. Every one of them was in a single tank, none of them had lights and most had snorkels. The majority were clearly not especially comfortable or skilled underwater, with a lot of hand-swimming and completely upright trim, which meant that a fair amount of silt was being stirred up.

To provide some context, guided cavern dives are a big part of the dive industry in Mexico. Hundreds of cavern dives are conducted for open water divers every day, but there are rules governing ratios, lights, guide qualifications and strictly staying on the line. Exploring whether these rules are wholly sufficient would be the subject of a whole other book, but the fact remains that there is a well-established procedure for taking certified open water divers into the cavern zone in a controlled manner. These rules and procedures had been completely flouted in this instance.

Seeing such a large number of clearly non-overhead qualified divers that far into the cave was something of a surprise, to put it mildly. My priority was the safety of my own students, so I stopped the drill and indicated that we should exit. Fortunately, the procession of potential accident statistics also managed to safely make their way out just ahead of us, aided by our lights. As they did so I made a mental note of the divers' general appearance, including brands of wetsuits and BCDs in order to identify them later on.

Having exited the water, I chatted to some of the divers that I had observed, and it transpired that there were a total of 15 divers in the group, which came from one of the big Hotel-based dive operations with multiple locations in the Riviera Maya. There were 3 instructors, 'leading' the dive, only one of whom was cave trained, and amazingly the majority of the clients being guided were on a Discover Scuba Diving programme. Given that the majority of divers were uncertified as open water divers, let alone cavern or cave divers, this could have ended very badly. A non-cave certified instructor/guide supervising 4 non-certified divers in a dark, silty environment with no lights, could have easily had the worst possible outcome.

I identified the lead instructor and pulled him to one side away from his customers to ask him what he was thinking taking unqualified divers into the cave environment. He was pretty unrepentant, maintaining it was fine as there were instructors present and that they could see the light. This was quite a disappointing attitude from a dive professional. I politely outlined that the dive could have gone badly wrong given the ratios, lack of a line, lack of lights and lack of training. The thought did occur that if there was such a thing as Cave Accident Analysis Bingo, I would have had a full house of all the factors that have been historically identified as causing fatalities in caves. I informed him that I would submit a Quality Assurance report to his Dive Agency, and I understand that he subsequently received a sanction and was fired from the dive centre.

As I reflected on what was a fairly spectacular near-miss, I considered what lesson I had learned from the incident and whether I could or should have done anything differently. I was reminded of some excellent advice given to me in my previous life as a Royal Navy submariner - "If you walk past it, you condone it, whether it is a set of firefighting breathing apparatus not fully charged or a serious breach of discipline". Divers, and especially dive professionals, should not be afraid to challenge behaviour that appears to put people at risk. The downside of an embarrassing conversation, or bruising someone's fragile ego, is hugely outweighed by the benefits of preventing an incident or giving someone the opportunity to consider their actions.

Leadership doesn't just exist in a title or experience: it is about having an ability to get the most out of the people or team involved in the task or situation. In this case, Lanny displayed effective leadership by trying to improve diving for all, and not just those in the water at the time; and while the instructor was fired from the dive centre, I very much doubt the instructor did what he did without sanction from his dive centre manager/owner. Without addressing the wider, systemic issues, such events will continue to happen because human behaviour is a function of the person and the environment in which they reside. The research indicates that replacing that instructor with another one, without changing the situation, means that it will happen again.

The need for effective leadership in diving is far more prevalent than many would think. It applies to:

- Those at the top of the training organisations who know what goes on at local dive centres, where standards are being broken, but because these do not end in fatalities they are ignored. Author and presenter, Margaret Heffernan describes this term of knowing about a problem and ignoring it as 'wilful blindness'[1]. Another way of looking at this is that the lack of evidence of a problem does not necessarily mean that the problem does not exist; it just means no-one has collected the data or completed the analysis.
- Those involved in ecology and conservation operations, such as 'Ghost Fishing', who are leading the way showing governments how conservation and citizen science can improve the eco-system by providing tangible evidence which can lead to policy changes.
- Those who make a stand and adhere to or exceed the standards of their organisation, even if this means they are not as commercially competitive as other instructors, instructor trainers or dive centres.
- Those who lead expeditions and sacrifice their own diving experiences to ensure that safety is managed effectively and adverse events do not occur.
- Those who show a complete novice diver the wonders of the subaquatic environment, keep them safe and create a spark of

enthusiasm to stay within the sport for life.
- Those who will compromise on their aims and objectives of a dive to ensure that others within the team remain safe by stepping back from the task at hand and maintaining the big picture.
- Those who develop themselves, recognising that continual improvement is essential, because the world does not stand still.

Those who do the above, are all leaders. Not necessarily leading others in a direct task, but showing them, guiding them and coaching them in ways which to improve diving safety, enjoyment and performance and reduce the ecological impact we are having on the world. Crucially, they all require leadership skills. In addition, to first be able to lead others, you also need to be able to lead yourself and sometimes this is the hardest skill to develop.

What is Leadership?
Unfortunately, leadership is often portrayed as being autocratic and directive, operating from a position of power, and yet there are many great leaders who have create change by being recognised for their vision - a vision which became a reality. The following two examples show that effective leadership can overcome incredibly harsh conditions, both environmentally but also socially. Firstly, Shackleton's epic expedition in which he led his team to reach the South Pole, but before they got there they had to abandon their ship, the *Endurance,* which was trapped in the ice and evacuate across the Southern Ocean via Elephant Island and South Georgia in small whaling boats. The odds of survival were minimal, but through effective leadership, and their team believing in him, most of those who initially set out, survived. Tragically, despite surviving the harsh weather and conditions of Southern Ocean, most of those who made it back to the UK were then killed in the trenches of the First World War. Secondly, Martin Luther King Jr., whose *'I have a dream'* speech brought together millions of people together with the same goal: to improve the lives of black citizens in the United States of America through extending their participation in civic life through the vote.

No matter what space you are in, leadership is about building an effective team by ensuring that physical and psychological safety is present in order to maximise the team's and task performance. While leadership is often assumed to be an innate quality, training and coaching systems can help develop all but the most incompetent. The tipping point for effective leadership is based on how much you want to invest in yourself and how much the organisation you are part of wants to invest in you. This can be a challenge in a sport where the majority of the activity takes place outside a formal organisational structure.

A leader has been defined as the *'person who is appointed, elected, or informally chosen to direct and co-ordinate the work of others in a group'*[2]. Teamwork and leadership academics have defined team leadership as: *'directing and co-ordinating the activities of team members; encouraging them to work together; assessing performance; assigning tasks; developing team knowledge, skills and attitudes; motivating; planning and organising; and establishing a positive team atmosphere'*[3]. The UK Civil Aviation Authority (CAP 737[4]) has defined an airborne leader as, *'a person whose ideas and actions influence the thought and the behaviour of others. Through the use of example and persuasion, and an understanding of the goals and desires of the group, the leader becomes a person or change and influence.'*

Leadership in the traditional sense isn't easy in a recreational activity. Part of this is because the social framework is in conflict with the traditional or stereotypical view of leadership of being autocratic. However, leadership styles and needs vary from person to person (as leader and as follower) and situation to situation. In effect there is a spectrum of leadership styles which go from autocracy where directive language is the norm, through to delegation which has a very relaxed environment or laissez-faire (French word translated as 'leave alone') attitude associated with it. Furthermore, this variance isn't just situational to environment (training/fun dives/expedition) or task at hand, each leader and follower will have a preferred style when they engage with others or others engage with them and this difference can cause negative conflict in the team.

Leadership Styles

In 2016, I was certified to teach the Process Communication Model™. This is a communication, behavioural and teamwork tool that is based on the principle that our interactions with the world and others are based on our perceptions. For nearly 20 years it was used by NASA as part of their astronaut selection programme and is now used by major corporates to improve relationships, collaboration and teamwork. It was one of the most powerful and influential courses I have undertaken, changing my perspective on how to communicate with others and how I view stress and discourse. I originally took the training programme so I could engage with my students during classes more effectively. It certainly facilitated that, and much more. However, I have also found that by explaining the concepts behind PCM to dive instructors, they are able to relate to *their* students more effectively, with improved outcomes in terms of learning and reduced stress.

The model details that we have six personality types which reside within us all, and that one or two of those are our preferred type for interactions. Each personality type has a preferred interaction style (both for communicating with others and for others to communicate with us). These styles are known as the Autocratic, Democratic, Benevolent and Laissez-Faire. The words, tones and gestures associated with each style are specific. By using the correct verbal and non-verbal language, it means we will get the effect we want in the other person or team member. However, if applied incorrectly i.e. using a style and vocabulary not suited for the other person, it is easy to create distress and miscommunication. For example, *telling* someone who is motivated by thoughts, logic and data to do something is unlikely to be effective, because they would prefer to be *requested* to do something and have their knowledge to be taken into account. e.g. *"Take those cylinders over there."* (Directive - Autocratic) will likely be less successful than *"Will you take those cylinders over there?"* (Requestive - Democratic). Another example would be for someone who prefers a benevolent style to be asked, *"I appreciate you *being part of the team. Will you help us with this problem?"* (Nurturative - Benevolent) would be more effective that saying in energetic way, *"Let's get going with this! "(*Emotive - Laissez-Faire).

If a person is stressed (for whatever reason), their ability to speak the 'language' of another person is limited, and so they only 'hear' what works for them. It is possible, through relatively simple training, to understand the signs and behaviours of the different types of personality, without the use a profiling tool - by just listening to the language that individuals use during normal discussion and when they are in distress.

Another leadership model comes from the work by Hersey and Blanchard who developed the situational theory of leadership which considers four styles based on a continuum from autocratic, persuasive, consultative and democratic.

- Autocratic: The leader takes the decisions and announces them, expecting subordinates to carry them out without question (the *Telling* style).
- Persuasive: At this point on the scale, the leader also takes all the decisions for the group without discussion or consultation, but believes that people will be better motivated if they are persuaded that the decisions are good ones. The leader does a lot of explaining and 'selling' in order to overcome any possible resistance to what he or she wants to do. The leader also puts a lot of energy into creating enthusiasm for the goals he or she has set for the group (the *Selling* style).
- Consultative: In this style the leader confers with the group members, before taking decisions and, in fact, considers their advice and their feelings when framing decisions. They may, of course, not always accept the team members' advice, but they are likely to feel that they can have some influence. Under this leadership style the decision and the full responsibility for it remain with the leader, but the degree of involvement by team members in decision taking is very much greater than telling or selling styles (the *Consulting* style).

- Democratic: Using this style the leader would characteristically lay the problem before the team and invite discussion. The leader's role is that of a facilitator rather than that of the decision-taker. They will allow the decision to emerge out of the process of group discussion, instead of imposing it on the group as its boss (the *Joining* style).

Researchers have shown how these different styles can be matched against a 2 x 2 grid with 'Tasks' (concerning roles, actions and activities) and 'Relationships' (welfare in the team, friendliness and approachability) and high/low importance attributed to each style[5].
- Telling (high task, low relationship). The leader is focused on defining goals and roles. When inexperienced, but committed members are present, the leader provides clarity in direction. The telling style is applicable to simple or repetitive tasks or when there is limited time available to complete the task. Very much applicable to high-stress, emergency situations. In diving, this could be normal operations in a dive centre or a skipper telling the divers what is happening next or when an emergency e.g. a rescue needs to be executed.
- Selling (high task, high relationship). The leader provides most of the direction. However, as the team develop their technical competency, they are encouraged to take ownership of the task.
- Participating (high relationship/ low task). The leader and followers share the decision-making process with the main task of the leader to communicate intent and facilitate discussion. Again, this style is useful when there is a level of competence within the team, but commitment is not consistent.
- Delegating (low relationship/ low task): When the team have high levels of competence and commitment to the task, the responsibility for completing the task is delegated to the team. Requires that the leader trusts the team to complete and also the team trust the leader not to give them something beyond their skillset.

Developing Teams

Effective leadership can quickly develop a team, moving them through the early stages of Tuckman's model, by creating trust and allowing failure and, hence, create a positive, learning environment. However, poor leadership can prevent effective teams from forming or destroying established teams. Sometimes it takes a number of iterations of a task or a project before the leadership realise they are not suitable for the role or that the team lose confidence in them and the team dissolves. One of the problems I see in the diving world is that because leadership, especially situational leadership, is not taught, instructors may not respond to the cue/clues presented to them as they don't have effective reflective skills. The kudos associated with being a 'name' in the industry can severely impact leadership performance. The following quote from the corporate environment is equally applicable to diving, *"People don't leave their jobs, they leave their manager."*

Leadership is about 'walking the talk'. It is about being authentic. Lanny's narrative describes this perfectly. It would be easy to walk past that situation and not say anything, but then nothing changes. In fact, the situation gets worse - because there is a natural human tendency to drift towards more risk behaviours.

Leaders need to be confident in their abilities; but at the same time, many people are naturally cynical which means that when leadership figures are not authentic, then they lose the trust of the community. This confidence has major benefits, not just in passing on technical information, but also because research has shown, *'that the most effective leaders of multi-disciplinary teams, whose team members must co-ordinate action in risk[y], uncertain, dynamic situations, are those who communicate a motivating rationale for change and minimise concerns about status differences.'*[6]

The most effective leaders in diving are those who can see a gap in a team or individual and then develop and coach them towards excellence - be that a technical skill, a non-technical skill or to achieve a goal like a wreck or cave exploration, which requires multiple technical and non-technical skills to be at a high-level if the goal is to be succeeded. They do this by sharing their knowledge, problem-solving and critical thinking and when they are unable to solve the problem themselves, they admit it and seek help from another expert. They recognise that for a team to be effective there needs to be a level of alignment between the task at hand; the skills, knowledge and attitude of the individual; and the skills associated with operating as an effective team.

Academic and theorist John Adair developed the Action-Centred Leadership[7] model which explains this topic in great detail, but in summary there is a need to understand:

- The task. The ability to set objectives with associated timescales and plan these to take into the skills, knowledge and experience of the team, along with determining performance metrics - what is considered success.
- The individual. The ability to coach, mentor, develop and motivate the individuals within the team to achieve their own objectives.
- The team. The ability to communicate with the team, to build and train them, to motivate them at a team level and an individual one, as well as instil a level of discipline and define acceptable standards within the team.

Interdependent teamwork is about achieving a goal which is greater than the sum of the parts. To achieve this, all three aspects (task, individual and team) need to be taken into account. If you don't develop the individuals and motivate them, they aren't going to operate as a team and without a team, the task cannot be achieved. Multiple examples in this book demonstrate the lack of effective leadership but one which is very clear is from chapter one where John took the reins of leadership, even though he wasn't the 'dive leader' to ensure that the two novice divers were able to dive safely, taking into account task, team and individual. Furthermore, the individuals involved weren't just the two novices, but also Graham, the coxswain, whose needs were addressed.

Leading Yourself

There is an adage in professional development that you can't lead others if you don't lead yourself first. In this context, leadership is about ensuring you have integrity, that you maintain compassion towards yourself, that you are clear in your purpose and that you have a goal that you believe in and will continue to progress towards it. It also means the ability to walk the talk, to do what you say should be done. There is nothing like watching a senior diving instructor, instructor trainer or agency representative say one thing and then do another, because *'they are more experienced'*. Either a standard should be followed, or it isn't a standard. Integrity is about doing the right thing, when no-one is watching. However, I would personally go further and say, it is doing the right thing, especially when no-one is watching.

Leadership specialist and published author Chris Avery has written an excellent book called, *'The Responsibility Process'* and in it he describes the process to take responsibility for the situation and your own development. The word 'responsibility' can be broken down into the ability to respond and Avery outlines the process where those taking responsibility move from denial; to laying blame; to justifying our practices; to shaming ourselves; to feeling an obligation to do something before we actually move into responsibility; and provides plenty of activities whereby we can develop a high level of personal responsibility. By understanding what goes into each step and then how to progress to the next one, we can develop ourselves as being responsible leaders.

The Greek philosopher, Epictetus is widely quoted as saying, *"It's not what happens to you, but how you react to it that matters."* In, *'The Responsibility Process'*, Avery references the motivational speaker Zig Ziglar and others who have changed Epictetus' word *react* to read, *"it's how you respond that matters."*[8] This is a really important concept to remember when leading and following. If you remember, in the communication chapter I referred to the four myths of making others feel good or bad: - no-one can make us feel good or bad; nor can we make them feel good or bad. No matter what someone says or does to us, we generate the feelings associated with our response - they don't do that. Fundamentally, we may not always be in charge of what happens to us, but we can always choose our response to what is said or done. So, if you are teaching a student and they aren't doing what you expect and you are getting frustrated with this as a consequence... that frustration is generated by you, not them. The same goes if you are diving with a buddy or team member who frustrates you or makes you angry, the myths are at play. You are generating those feelings, not them.

Responsibility and Attribution

Responsibility is often used as a way about finding someone or something to blame based on a cause and effect process - *'the pilot was responsible for the failed approach'* or *'the instructor should have taken responsibility of the situation and not completed the dive in that manner'*.

In psychology, attribution is the term used to describe how we 'attribute' an effect to a cause after the event has happened. The terms Internal (or dispositional) and External (situational) attribution describe where the 'cause' lies. Most of the time we attribute failures in others as an individual failure (internal); but when we fail ourselves, we attribute the causes to external influences like, *'How was I supposed to know that was going to happen?'* Conversely, when others succeed, we often make an 'attribution' to the wider 'system' or luck and not necessarily down to the hard work, concentration, focus and values which were required to produce the results. Ironically, these same traits are how we attribute the affect to ourselves when we are successful! Figure 11 shows the hypocrisy of attribution when it comes to why something has happened, good or bad, or how easy it is to 'blame' the wrong thing. Self-leadership is about owning the problem and solving it by understanding the true cause and not what we 'think' the cause is.

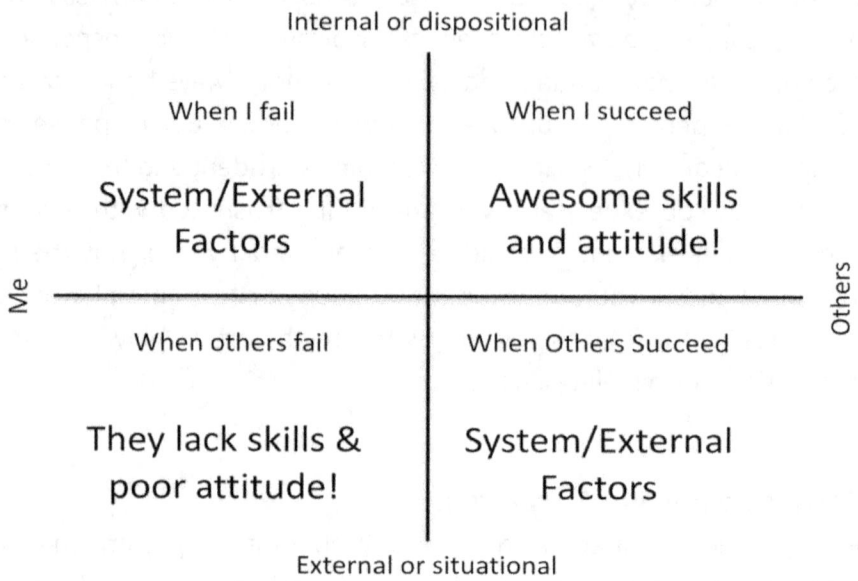

Figure 11: Internal and External Attribution versus My Own/Others' Success and Failures

Efficacy is about causing an effect e.g. pharmaceutical companies run trials to determine the efficacy of their drugs against certain criteria. Self-efficacy or *"perceived self-efficacy is the people's beliefs about their capabilities to produce effects"* according to the leading psychologist Albert Bandura in this area.[9] In effect, if we have high self-efficacy, we believe we can produce the results we want.

Bandrua's research shows that self-efficacy affects our perspective towards goals, tasks and the problems we face. Those with high self-efficacy see challenges as opportunities to gain new mastery rather than something to shirk away from: they set themselves challenging goals and remain committed to them; they treat failure as a learning opportunity, rather than a loss and recover quickly when failures happen; and most importantly, they attribute failure to insufficient effort or a lack of skills and knowledge (internal attribution) rather than external factors. High self-efficacy reduces stress because we perceive that we are in control.

Compare this to those with low self-efficacy. They have low aspirations; weak commitment to goals; they slacken their efforts and give up quickly when adversity strikes; and when failures do happen, they are slow to recover. These individuals perceive incompetence as the lack of aptitude and as such, it is easy for them to lose faith in their abilities to complete the task at hand. They are more susceptible to stress and depression.

Ultimately, when it comes to self-leadership, we need to be proactive in the decisions we make now for the future, and reflective on the decisions we made in the past, be those right or wrong. Hindsight can inform that learning process, but only if we are honest in our own abilities and limitations; and once we've made an assessment, we follow through with the 'correct' decision. Such an example comes from Becky Kagan Schott who was on a media dive to document a newly-discovered wreck. Becky is an experienced photographer and videographer who has won numerous awards for her work topside and underwater. She is also a CCR trimix instructor and has been diving rebreathers for 12 years.

Case Study: Total electronics failure at 70m and I've got 75 mins of deco to do. Great!

We had been notified that a wreck had been recently discovered and a TV production company wanted to make a documentary of it. The wreck lay in approximately 80m, a depth I am more than comfortable diving in; so I said yes to the offer. The challenge was that we only had two days to complete the shoot: the expected visibility was in the order of 1-2m and we had dived with the divers who would be the subject of the video. As with many media shoots, there are many moving parts which adds significant pressures to complete the shoot, because time is nearly always the critical factor.

We flew out to the location and met the dive team the day before the dive. The dive was to be completed as a team of 3 (2 x subject divers and 1 x cameraman) and a team of 2 (1 x subject diver and me). The production company wanted 45 mins of bottom time per dive, but as I went through the dive plans, I decided that with the bailout cylinders and gases I had, I was going to limit my bottom time to 25 mins. My subject diver was in total agreement with this. However, the other team decided on a 45 mins bottom time even though they had the same gases as we did.

The following morning we met at the quayside, loaded the boats and set off. Unfortunately, because this was supposed to be a 'first discovery' dive, we were not to be on the same boat as the subject divers so we boarded a smaller vessel which would stand off and remain 'out of sight'. The plan was for the main dive boat to hook into the wreck with the subject divers entering the water, swimming over to the shot-line and starting their descent. At this point we, as the videographers, would be dropped onto the same shot-line and would join up with our subject divers at 6m to conduct a bubble check before descending the remaining 70+m to the wreck. This meant that the only time we managed to speak to our subjects was the night before and on the quayside - and this was a 80m deep wreck in extremely limited visibility; a wreck I had never been on before and with divers I had never dived with before!

The first team's entry and descent went well. I waited for my subject diver to enter the water, swim to the shot-line and start their descent. We motored over and I entered the water, joining up as planned at 6m. All systems ok and we started our descent. The visibility was indeed 1-2m!

The location for our team's video shoot was the debris field which was approximately 30m off the wreck. After 25 mins of bottom time, we thumbed the dive and started our ascent. Almost immediately my HUD started to go crazy and then quit. I looked down at my handset and there was no pO2 information displayed! Great, a total electronics failure! This hasn't happened before! As an instructor I am used to running this scenario on classes, but this is the first time in 12 years of rebreather diving that I have needed to bailout for real. So, I bailed out to OC, switched the backup computer over to OC and showed my CCR handset to my buddy. Even though he was on a different rebreather to me, the meaning behind a handset with no pO2 information is universal! My first 'for real' bailout and I am with an 'unknown' diver and we have more than 75 mins of decompression to do! However, because I have taught at least two CCR trimix classes per year, the drills are normal as I practice them with my students, and so the 'muscle memory' was there to do what needed to be done without panic or fear.

Task-loading can be an issue when dealing with contingencies, so I permanently have a line on my camera which is slightly longer than my reach and the video rig is slightly negative. This means that I can drop it and it won't go too far, hanging directly below me. This is what I did on this occasion and therefore didn't need to hand it to the subject diver.

The ascent wasn't difficult, just annoying breathing the OC gas. The electronics continued to be erratic during our journey to the surface and at 6m they started to come back, providing me with some pO2 information. At this point, I went back onto the breathing loop and manually injected pure O2 for the remainder of the deco.

So what happened? In the previous months I had some signs that something wasn't quite right. However, I never dreamed it would end up with a complete electronics failure as the unit I dive has a reputation for being very reliable and robust. I had been having intermittent problems all summer with solenoid. I tried changing out the batteries, battery unit, electronics unit, pretty much everything I could change, I tried to change. Each time I would do that, I would go diving. In the majority of cases it appeared to clear the issue, then a number of dives later it would come back.

I now know what the problem was. It was the primary network on the canBUS system that failed. Both the solenoid and the HUD are on the primary network, and the solenoid issues were indications there was a bigger issue brewing.

The reader might wonder, 'Why didn't I just send the unit back?' and this is a fair comment. However, I am a professional cameraman which means not having a unit means lost revenue, and potentially more importantly, lost clients if I can't respond at short notice. The first rebreather I had broke several times in the first year and I sent it back to the manufacturer twice. At the end of that year, I then bought a different rebreather because I couldn't afford to lose a shoot or a client because of a failed rebreather. The rebreathers I have had for the last 11 years have not failed once while on a dive.

On surfacing, and that evening I had a huge dilemma. 'Do I do the shoot tomorrow?' I wasn't sure I was going to be able to dive with this unit. I spent the next five hours problem-solving and fault-finding, trying to work out where the failure had happened. I was confident that it was the HUD that was the problem, but I didn't have a spare HUD with me. I normally bring along a full rebreather 'save the dive' kit which has a spare HUD, handset and other electronics/spares that I need. However, I decided that as it was only a two-day shoot, I would leave the spare HUD behind, even though it only takes up little space! So, because the canBUS system allows you to swap components out, I swapped the HUD for another handset and retested the unit. All was working ok.

The following day I went diving. Everything regarding the unit worked as planned. However, now I was working much harder on the dive. In 1-2m visibility at 80m it was pretty dark. Whereas before I could use the HUD to let me know my pO2, I now needed to move my hands to read the handsets which impacted my flow and creativity as a videographer.

Becky's account highlights a number of important factors which all divers, but especially those who are in high-pressure situations: external pressures will likely lead you to drift towards unsafe situations e.g. in this case, the production company wanted a 45 minute bottom time, but there was only really enough bailout for a 25 minute bottom time. If Becky had done the longer bottom time and the electronics had failed, she would have to have used her buddy's gas compromising the safety of the team. The uncertainty caused by not being able to track down the real issue and the intermittent nature of the problem, leads us to push the margin of safety further and further out (see Chapter 4 on Risk & Uncertainty for more on this topic), especially when trading the small probability for a minor loss (in this case, the failure of the rebreather, bailout and ascend) - compared to a guaranteed loss (not completing the shoot and losing money plus reputation as a consequence).

When you are running your own business in diving, such pressures are very real. In February 2013, an Australian rebreather instructor died after a double cell failure happened on his rebreather. The cells were current limited and the controller kept on injecting oxygen into the loop based on the flawed outputs from those cells and the voting logic operating correctly. This wasn't the first time such a failure had happened on his unit, but reliable replacement cells were not easy to source at the time and it is believed he kept pushing the limits of his cells so that he could keep teaching. Unfortunately, it cost him his life[10].

What is also interesting reading Becky's account is the number of warning signals that were presented over a period of time, but because 'stuff' is happening inside the black box of tricks, it is often hard to join the dots until after the event - when it becomes 'obvious' what the issue was. High-reliability organisations (HROs) call this behaviour 'looking for weak signals' - where the clues are present, but they are often lost in the noise of the situation. Therefore, if we are getting a number of potentially-related issues but the outcomes aren't obvious, it is worth biting the bullet and getting the equipment examined by the manufacturer and then asking them for a loan head or similar if work is a priority. Normalisation of deviance, a totally normal human behaviour, means that as we deviate from 'safe practices' due to external pressures like resource, workload and time, then the acceptable 'safe limit' changes and we set a new baseline. Unfortunately, this means that we get closer to the failure line but we still don't know where it is, and as we saw in the risk chapter with the turkey illusion, the longer something doesn't happen (or the risk is accepted if the problem is known), the more likely you think it will never happen to you.

Leading Teams

The following narrative from Joel Silverstein, one of the pioneers in technical diving, recounts an incident which happened in 2004. At that time, deep shipwreck exploration and research operations were routinely being completed by free-swimming divers using open-circuit mixed gas scuba systems. (Of note, 'deep' in this context covered depths down to 100m.) While rebreathers in the civilian market were available, few divers in the United States were using them on a regular basis. The mode of diving mentioned is important, because it is helpful for readers to put themselves in the context of the knowledge and procedures available and known of the time. Despite the best of plans, accidents can and will happen when least expected. Consequently, the role and actions of the leader are critical when things do pear-shaped.

Case Study: SOPs helps teams perform and help leaders make decisions

In 2004, the National Oceanographic and Atmospheric Association (NOAA) granted our company a civilian research permit to visit the USS Monitor. NOAA had stopped issuing civilian permits in 1997 when they began working with US Navy to salvage certain parts of this historically-significant wreck. With the use of US Navy mixed gas salvage divers, they removed the propeller shaft, engine, and the gun turret between 1998 and 2002. These landmark recoveries cost taxpayers millions of dollars while utilising some of the most advanced salvage technologies. Our visit, however, would be the first civilian view of the site in more than seven years. The USS Monitor rests in 71 metres (235 feet) of seawater 18 miles out from Cape Hatteras, North Carolina. At that depth, our divers would be breathing multiple gas mixes to document the changes to the site since major portions of the Monitor had been removed. In addition to shipwreck documentation, we were gathering decompression and functionality data for a new mixed gas dive computer for Cochran Undersea Technology.

The work we were doing on the USS Monitor fell under the concept of Citizen Scientist. Everyone on the team was a volunteer and had paid a portion of the overall expedition costs. Every diver on the team was known to me, the expedition leader and principal investigator. Each participant had many years and hundreds, if not thousands, of shipwreck dives in deep waters. In addition to vetting experience, each diver had a "clean" medical history.

Two days into the second week of our project, we had a rare incident occur. One of our photographers, a 51-year-old male with five years of technical experience and more than thirty years of overall diving experience, suffered an oxygen toxicity convulsion underwater. Because we were rotating dive teams in and out of the water, it was not uncommon for a single diver to make a short exposure for a specific task. [Note all of our team had experience doing solo dives, so at the time we did not think this activity to be overtly risky.] This dive was to be no more than 20 minutes on the bottom (~70m) with a total runtime of 60 minutes. The diver used twin tanks filled with 17/40 trimix and decompression cylinders of 50% nitrox and 100% oxygen respectively.

I had been in the water finishing my last few minutes of decompression when our photographer passed me on down the line. We exchanged acknowledgments and an OK signal. I had looked over his kit and confirmed he had appropriate deco gas. He was running lean left, rich right set up with oxygen on the right and 50% on the left. I also noticed he had not heeded my suggestion earlier to put a tether on his camera; the camera was draped on his arm. I completed my last few minutes of decompression and returned to the deck.

After 14 minutes run time, the diver had completed his photographic task and was on the way up. [In 2004 film cameras were the primary tool; deep water digital camera housings were limited in availability.] On the way up, the diver passed other divers on the way down. At 70 feet (21 meters) the diver was to make his gas switch to his 50% decompression gas. However, while managing a large camera without a tether, the diver made the gas switch to 100% oxygen instead. This put his pO2 at 3.12 atm, more than twice the considered maximum safe oxygen level for a working diver (pO2 1.4). The photographer continued breathing the oxygen for the next nine minutes while making the ascent. At 38 feet (11 meters) the diver came face-to-face with another diver [diver two] who was on his shallow decompression stops. With a wide-eyed stare, a full-blown convulsion begins, and he drops the untethered camera to the seafloor. The other decompression diver grabs hold of the photographer and the up line. Life just got complicated— survival instincts and great training skills took over.

Unable to break his own decompression, diver two continued to hold the photographer while the convulsion continued. With the diver's entire body shaking diver two, managed to deploy a dSMB to get some attention. Two new divers had just entered the water met up with diver two and the photographer as part of the dive plan. Diver two was able to hand off the photographer to diver three and four, who then took him to the surface. We heard a yell for help.

We were working from a small vessel, sufficient for working with about 12 people on board. It was a classic open deck fishing vessel converted to a dive boat, and it was easy to see the water all around the boat without much effort. We had just put a team of divers in the water and were expecting another set out momentarily. Back on board, I resumed my role of managing the deck. My co-leader had also dived earlier, and she was on deck sitting on the starboard gunnel. She glanced over into the water and shouted "MARKER UP" as it was sliding along the side of the boat. There was no reason for a marker to be up to other than an emergency. Within the same breath as her announcement, we heard a yell for help. This sound came from divers #3 and #4 who had just rolled in. At that moment everything changed, and our operations went from a happy day diving into something we did not yet know. I immediately called a halt to operations and shouted, "start the timeline" and relinquished control to one of our second captains.

We went into rescue mode. A safety swimmer and I rolled into the water with mask and fins to get the photographer up and on the deck where we stripped him of all gear. He had a weak pulse and had laboured breathing with clear froth coming from the nose and mouth. First aid was initiated with oxygen administration. I informed the Captain to radio the Coast Guard and issue a May-Day call requesting a helicopter. The Coast Guard responded with a 40 minute ETA (expected time of arrival).

This was not my first incident at sea. I had crewed a major dive vessel in NY for many years; had run other expeditions; and had seen my share of dive incidents. I had also done training with the US Coastguard (USCG) and our dive boat association in how to conduct and manage rescues at sea. As the senior person on deck [other than the Captain], my job was to manage the incident; secure the safety of the other divers and passengers; and help the Captain prepare for his first air-lift. All of our expedition personnel were experienced in some level to handle different aspects of a situation. Each had been familiarised with our Diving Operations and Emergency Procedures Manual. We had discussed how to handle emergencies in our operations meeting during the first day before diving operations commenced. Everyone had a job to do. There was no chaos.

Our Diving Medical Officer and one of our divers worked on the victim for almost 30 minutes when, without any notice, he regained consciousness and sat up. There were still two divers we needed to get out of the water before we could move the boat. We prepared the boat for an airlift which requires every item on deck to be tied down and secured so nothing can accidentally fly up into the rotors. Within minutes, the high-pitched squeal of the famous USCG Dauphin helicopter came swooping in while we were underway. In under 20 minutes from when the helicopter was spotted, the Para jumper was on the deck, got the vital information, and extracted our stricken diver. The helicopter flew to Virginia Beach where they had a Level 1 Trauma Centre and a hyperbaric unit. Total time from diver on the surface to extraction was 72 minutes. Not bad for being more than 150 miles from the nearest helicopter station.

At the hospital, the victim was examined, found to have no barotrauma, was treated with a USN Table 6 (TT6) recompression treatment as a precaution and was observed overnight for near drowning. The diver was released the next day with the recommendation to get checked by a pulmonologist in a few weeks. After an interview with the USCG, our dive operations resumed the next day.

The Decision-Making Process

The outcome of this accident was positive, but could have quickly become a fatality. Fortunately, we had a management plan and personnel in place to effect this rescue and have the victim airlifted within 60 minutes of the incident occurring. Much of the readiness factor is due to prior experience with management of expeditions. In addition to all participants receiving a Dive Operations Manual and an Emergency Management Plan, a dive operations meeting occurred for a half day before any diving activities beginning. In addition, participants understood that incidents happen and to be vigilant and aggressive in minimising risk as best as possible. Added to this good management, was the careful selection of the team. Even with a well-trained team and almost every aspect of an operation planned, some things get overlooked.

Decisions as to how the incident was managed were done in real time with input from different people providing critical information; yet all persons involved understood and accepted who would make the final decisions. For the vessel, it would always be the Captain. For emergency management and dive operations protocol, it would be the expedition leader. By knowing where the final say would rest removed all ambiguity when an incident occurred.

From a dive leader's perspective removing all emotion from a situation allows for keener ability to manage a situation. The stricken diver was a close friend; his possible death would have been difficult to accept. To that end seeking a positive and direct approach to the incident was best. Working with real-time information and trusting the information coming in was critical. There was never a wonder as to why the incident happened until after the victim was removed to higher medical authority and all reports and documentation would be completed. This approach allowed for a much clearer decision-making process than if emotion clouded the situation.

Once the victim had received care and was released, the team needed to resume diving operations. A critical analysis revealed a need for improvement in the protocol. The specific cause of the incident was the diver was more concerned about the camera than the gas management. Also, the diver refused to use a tether on the camera - despite being warned of its potential problem. Another problem included solo diving with the assumption that with enough people on site, it would be low risk. It was in fact a higher risk, because all on the site thought someone else was watching out for them thereby creating a false sense of security. To that end, the following protocols were initiated for all remaining diving and all future dive expeditions:

- Divers require at least one dive buddy.
- Divers make gas switches only while buddy is watching and confirming.
- Divers descending and ascending verify other divers for proper gas in

the mouth.
- *Cameras and tools must be on tethers; all hands must be available for ascent and descent.*

Technical diving operations require a support crew, not only to run the diving operations, but to manage the accidents when you least expect them. Oxygen toxicity rarely happens; this incident illustrates how easily an incident can occur when divers become complacent and tasked with other activities.

This is an excellent case study from Joel highlighting the benefit of training, screening and the continual practice of both technical skills and non-technical skills. It also demonstrates the power of role clarity to improve performance when things start to go wrong. This clarity means that decision-making processes are simplified as the Captain sorts the vessel out and the expedition leader sorts the diving out. Unfortunately, it is easy to get sucked into being part of the expedition and miss the key role of the leader: keep the big picture and make sure the critical goal is maintained - get everyone back on the surface alive and well. Using protocols, procedures and ensuring everyone is on the same song sheet, can help achieve that goal. Another example of this is Richard Lundgren's expedition in Chapter 3, where he ensured that the gas was analysed which then prevented a fatality.

Focusing on the maintenance of the goal is a crucial skill for an effective leader. That doesn't mean total fixation on the goal to the exclusion of safety, as in the case of Guy Garman (Doc Deep) who died while trying to break a world record in deep diving in the Caribbean, or the Everest teams in 1996 who lost eight climbers including two of the world's best guides; but recognising that in a high-risk activity, the goal should be to have safety as a very high priority ensuring that everyone makes it home. However, leaders don't operate in isolation: they often have many other tasks at hand and this means that Standard Operating Procedures (SOPs) and the ability to delegate within the team, become extremely important. Failing to do this often means that mental capacity is exceeded and important or critical items get missed.

Such an example of this happened in 2009 on the multi-national Britannic Expedition, when Carl Spencer lost his life through a seizure caused by oxygen toxicity as he ascended from filming on the HMHS Britannic. Carl was the expedition leader and as such was heavily involved in all of the administration activities needed to make the expedition run smoothly. In addition to arranging and managing the core team and his own tasks as lead videographer, there was also the liaison with local authorities and National Geographic, the media company who they were working with. Unfortunately, this meant that Carl did not complete any work-up dives prior to the day of the accident, something not realised by the team. The stresses involved in running an expedition like this are massive and also likely contributed to an addition to the contingency gas plan, which meant that Carl placed a cylinder marked with 'air' on the shot-line for the wreck, a change which was not part of the plan and not noticed by anyone else in the team prior to the fateful dive. It was found out afterwards that the cylinder contained 50%.

Due to a number reasons, likely down to his lack of currency on the rebreather (having not dived for 11 months) and because of the large, cumbersome camera rig he was operating on behalf of National Geographic, he bailed out at depth and made a fast ascent. He was met by other divers on the shot-line who helped him with more spare gas. At around 40m, still with a significant amount of decompression to do, he changed to this unknown cylinder on the shot-line and had a seizure very shortly afterwards. The pO2 at this stage was 2.5. The divers around him did what they could to bring him to the surface safely, but unfortunately, he died.

It is not clear why the cylinder was part of Carl's plan, the rest of the team didn't know about it and they had analysed all the other gas on the boat on the day prior. However, this was an incredibly important trip and so the pressure was likely to be high to produce the video for an influential client - even though Carl hadn't dived for 11 months prior to the expedition. Given this context, how easy would it be for Carl to say, *"I can't do this dive"*?

What is Followership?

"Leadership is not something a leader possesses, so much as a process involving followership. Without followers, there are no leaders or leadership."[11]. At its most base level, teams are made up of leaders and followers. However, that doesn't mean that the followers are 'sheep', but rather the leader influences the behaviour of the team towards them to be supportive and generative. The skills to be an effective follower can also be developed in the same way that leadership skills are developed. The best way to develop followers is to get them to lead - as they then understand what it is needed for their team to support them and they can transfer these skills and knowledge when following or supporting their leader.

Good followers will have found congruence or a level of agreement between the team's needs and their own. As nothing is perfect, there is usually a discrepancy but where this exists, followers have to accept that their own needs will take second place to ensure that the team's needs and goals are met. However, leaders should be aware that when followers provide resources and goodwill, this only lasts for a small period of time before the acceptable level of compromises reaches a stage where the team break away from the goals and look after themselves. In diving, this can be a major problem with the voluntary nature of many clubs and organisations. As such, the leadership need to ensure that the motivational needs of the individuals are met in an authentic manner.

Developing Leaders and Followers

There is a difference between being a 'be-er' and a 'do-er' when it comes to leadership. A 'be-er' is someone who has a title and is proud of that title; the latter, a 'do-er', is someone who takes the knowledge associated with the title and does something with it. 'Do-ers' achieve more than 'be-ers' and they are more respected too! However, developing leadership skills in a recreational activity is not easy, especially as there are few programmes aimed at achieving this outcome.

Flin et al in, *'Safety at the Sharp End'*[12] describe a number of ways to develop leaders in high-risk environments using evidence from management, military and aviation training programmes. Three of these are briefly described below.

- Behavioural role-modelling, whereby exemplar behaviours are demonstrated and then practiced by the student, with critique provided by the trainer/leader. In the case of diving, this could be briefing/debriefing or explicit; closed-loop questioning techniques; or creating a psychologically-safe environment by demonstrating their own vulnerability through the discussion of mistakes, errors or violations they have made and why they happen. (See DEBRIEF model in Chapter 9 on Teamwork)

- The use of case studies to look at historical examples of where things have gone wrong or gone well. The important part when conducting case study examination is not to focus on the outcome; this is the uninteresting part. Rather, there is a need to look at how the situation developed; the cues and clues which were present and why they were missed/observed; and then how the situation was developed and resolved. For a leader to develop, they must apply critical thinking skills - the ability to 'think about thinking' - in effect to reflect and develop our own thinking processes, especially when it comes to our and others' memories of the event, our comprehension of the situation and our own performance. This reflection and developmental process includes explicit facts and knowledge, as well as implied, unconscious knowledge and beliefs.

- Simulation exercises whereby technical and non-technical skills are exercised and developed through robust and honest debriefs. Simulations are not prevalent in the diving environment. I believe this is because most training courses are there to develop technical skills rather than non-technical skills. I have personally developed a training programme which uses a computer-based simulation called GemaSim (http://www.gemasim.com), software specially designed to develop and test the application of non-technical skills. It is immersive and provides a brilliant platform to train divers in non-technical skills and I have also used it with surgeons, Intensive Care Unit teams and software development teams to great success.

Summary of Key Points

- Leadership is not about being in charge. It is about taking care of those in your charge, developing and motivating them in a manner which is aligned with the team members' needs to achieve the team's goals.
- Every diver, irrespective of title or role, can be a leader. However, every diver who is in a supervisory position e.g. divemaster, instructor, instructor trainer or agency staff must seriously consider their role as a leader in the diving community. Your actions and behaviours shape and influence how others behave.
- We are conditioned to follow and mimic others because of social conformance. If you are in a leadership position, others will look to you as an example of 'good enough'. If you don't do checks properly, if you don't analyse your gas every time, if you don't run briefs/debriefs, you will be copied.
- Leadership style is situational, not one size fits all. Therefore, understanding how teams develop (forming, storming, norming and performing) and the context of task/team/individual means you can have a better idea of the leadership style needed for the situation at hand.
- Leadership is having the courage to speak up when needed, to prevent drift and improve performance and safety. In a sport which is based around personal risk management, speaking up can be hard. Much better than looking back and wishing you'd said something.

Questions to consider

- What are your greatest leadership challenges if you are an instructor or instructor trainer and have to balance standards with commercial pressures?

- What are the times you wished you'd said something but were unable to? What would you do differently the next time?
- How would you like your instructor trainer or agency staff to behave, to show greater leadership in the community?
- When was the last time you tried to challenge your leader on a dive? If it was successful, why do you think that happened? If not, what were the barriers to getting the challenge heard or accepted?

References

(1) Heffernan, Margaret. *Wilful Blindness: Why We Ignore the Obvious* (Kindle Locations 64-66). Simon & Schuster UK. Kindle Edition.

(2) Fiedler, F. (1967) A Theory of Leadership Effectiveness. New York: McGraw-Hill. Fiedler, F.E. (1995) Cognitive resources and leadership performance. Applied Psychology: An International Review, 44, 5– 28.

(3) Salas, E., Burke, C.S. and Stagl, K.C. (2004) Developing teams and team leaders: Strategies and principles. In D. Day, S. Zaccaro and S.M. Halpin (eds.) Leader Development for Transforming Organizations. Growing Leaders for Tomorrow. Mahwah, NJ: Lawrence Erlbaum.

(4) CAA (2006) Crew Resource Management (CRM) Training. CAP737. Guidance for Flight Crew, CRM Instructors (CRMIs) and CRM Instructor-Examiners (CRMIEs). Hounslow, Middlesex: Civil Aviation Authority.

(5) Flin, Rhona. *Safety at the Sharp End* (Kindle Locations 2899-2909). Ashgate. Kindle Edition.

(6) Flin, Rhona. *Safety at the Sharp End* (Kindle Locations 2775-2776). Ashgate. Kindle Edition.

(7) Adair, J. (1973). *Action Centred Leadership*. London: McGraw-Hill.

(8) Avery, Christopher. *The Responsibility Process: Unlocking Your Natural Ability to Live and Lead with Power* (p. 28). Partnerwerks, Incorporated.

(9) Bandura, A. (1994). Self-efficacy. In V. S. Ramachaudran (Ed.), Encyclopedia of human behavior (Vol. 4, pp. 71-81). New York: Academic Press. (Reprinted in H. Friedman [Ed.], Encyclopedia of mental health. San Diego: Academic Press, 1998).

(10) Dillon, HCB. Inquest into the death of Philip Andrew Gray. 1 May 2015. Retrieved from https://cognitasresearch.files.wordpress.com/2015/05/dillon-2015-findings-in-the-inquest-into-the-death-of-philip-gray.pdf on 8 Dec 2018.

(11) Hollander, E. (1993) Legitimacy, power, and influence: A perspective on relational features of leadership. In M. Chemers and R. Ayman (eds.) Leadership Theory and Research. Perspectives and Directions (pp. 29– 47). San Diego: Academic Press.

(12) Flin, R., O'Connor, P. and Crichton, M. (2018). *Safety at the sharp end*. Johanneshov: MTM. (Kindle Location 3118). Ashgate. Kindle Edition.

Additional Reading

Adair, J. (2009). *Effective leadership: How to be a successful leader.* London: Pan Books.

Avery, C. M., & Kimsey-House, H. (2016). *The responsibility process: Unlocking your natural ability to live and lead with power.* Pflugerville, TX : Partnerwerks Incorporated.

Bolden, R., Gosling, J., Marturano, A. and Dennison, P. (2003) A Review of Leadership Theory and Competency Frameworks. Exeter, UK. https://ore.exeter.ac.uk/repository/bitstream/handle/10036/17494/mgmt_standards.pdf

Feuersenger, E., & Naef, A. (2012). *If you want them to listen, talk their language: Communication, motivation and success in business and personal relationships using the process communication model.* Waikanae, N.Z: Kahler Communications Oceania.

Heffernan, M (2015). *Wilful Blindness: Why we ignore the obvious.* READHOWYOUWANT COM LTD.

Marquet, L. D. (2015). *Turn The Ship Around!: A True Story of Turning Followers Into Leaders.* London: Portfolio Penguin.

Chapter 11

Performance Shaping Factors

"Astronauts are taught that the best way to reduce stress is to sweat the small stuff. We're trained to look on the dark side and to imagine the worst things that could possibly happen. In fact, in simulators, one of the most common questions we learn to ask ourselves is, 'Okay, what's the next thing that will kill me?'"

Cdr Chris Hadfield

Stress and fatigue, and other performance shaping factors, can reduce high-performing teams and individuals into dysfunctional wrecks who are incapable of making 'logical' decisions which can lead to their demise. At the same time, stress can be used as a tool by which performance can be developed so that excellence is the norm by continually stretching people, but not to breaking point. However, as we'll see in this chapter, the tipping point between eustress (good stress) and distress (negative stress) is both individual and contextual. This means that positive (or negative) results from one situation might not be applicable to the same person in a different time and space, or with a different person and the same situation leading to the same outcomes as they have a different outlook and are subject to different personal pressures and drivers. We also need to recognise that it isn't just internal issues like stress and fatigue which can cause problems with human performance, there are many external factors which reduce the effectiveness and efficiency of teams and individuals.

Jon Kieren is an experienced CCR instructor and cave instructor. His account below highlights that it isn't just tangible task loading during a dive, or the preparation for it, which can impact human performance, it can be external factors which reduce the space available in the working memory to process critically important information. What made this event worse was confirmation bias - finding what he believed to be the source of the 'mental niggles' while there was still a 300lb gorilla sitting in the corner waiting to catch him out. Frustratingly, if the incident had ended up as a fatality, I could easily see the armchair pundits shouting out, *'How could he have been so stupid as to miss that?'*

Case Study: The mind plays funny tricks when you're stressed

I have been going through some pretty rough times in my personal life and I found a great friend in one of my dive buddies. We'll call him "John" for the sake of this narrative. Over the course of several months, we have spent many hours in the water together conducting some fairly large and complex dives. However, it was the pre- and post-dive chats that were really the most meaningful. His friendship and support meant a lot to me. He was getting ready to move away, so we decided to plan one more last-minute big dive to a far-away section of one of his favourite caves. A section I had been to before, but he hadn't. We had tried to make the dive once before, but didn't quite make it to the section we were aiming for. So the day before he was to leave, we met at the dive site at the crack of dawn, got dressed, and entered the water.

In the days prior to this dive, I had just finished teaching a class where I was on my rebreather every day for a week. I have a very specific rhythm when it comes to setting up and breaking down my gear when I am teaching, which ensures my gear is always fully assembled and checked before I meet my students. Also, over the course of that week, I had dealt with some major life issues that I was looking forward to escaping from underground with my good friend for a while.

Because I knew I was diving with John the next day, I broke my rebreather down how I had been doing all week during class, and then finished re-assembling it very early the morning of the dive. I hadn't slept well the night before, and woke up late. But I knew I had everything prepared properly the night before, so I quickly organised my stuff, finished building my rebreather with the checklist sitting on the bench next to me. All checked out perfectly, and I loaded it up into the truck and headed over to the site while I drank my first cup of coffee for the day.

Upon arriving on site, John had already brought all of his bailout bottles and scooters down to the water, and was chatting with another team while waiting for me to arrive. Knowing that we were on a pretty tight schedule (John still had to get home to finish packing for his move the following day), I rushed to get organised as quickly as I could. Having geared up for this type of dive hundreds of times in the past, I readied myself smoothly and without issue.

I did my pre-dive checks on the rebreather, did a quick pre-breathe to verify the unit was adding O2 and maintaining set-point, and walked down to the water (still breathing from the rebreather). As I entered the water, I could not help thinking that I was forgetting something major. I did a quick head to toe inventory, and realised I had left one of my backup lights on my other harness in the garage. Whoops, that must have been it. John had 3 backups on him, so we were still good to go.

While in the water, I started to don my bailout bottles (total of 5), while still breathing from the loop. As I was donning equipment, John asked me "hey man, are the red dots on your lid and can supposed to be lined up?" "Shit, yes, can you close it for me?" THAT must have been what I was forgetting! Finished clipping everything off, did a quick verbal and visual pre-dive check and bubble checks with John, and started to descend. As soon as I started to drop down, I felt I was lighter than normal. That's a bit odd, I've been diving this exact configuration all week. Hmmm, oh well, last big dive with John before he takes off, I'm sure it's just because I feel a bit rushed and stressed about the backup light and lid. I hit the trigger and down the spring run towards the cave entrance we went.

About 50 yards down the run, things started to feel really off. Which was strange, because my kit felt fantastic, I felt balanced and trimmed, and I wasn't fighting anything on the scooter. But my breathing started getting shallower and more rapid, my heart racing, and my pulse pounding in my ears. I started to run through my unit assembly in my head, checking all the boxes as I went. I was convincing myself that I was just rattled by the red dots situation. I have heard of people forgetting it in the past, but I had never done it myself. I tried to calm myself down and just settle in for the dive, but by the end of the run, I had to make a decision. Drop into the cave and see if this thing sorts itself out (which I strongly considered, knowing it was John's last chance to do this dive, and my last chance to dive with him for a while), or pull out the thumb. Thankfully, I made the decision to call it. We popped up, I apologised and said I needed to check my unit. I pulled all my bottles off and climbed out.

I set my unit down on a picnic table and pulled the lid off. Looked inside, and said to myself "yup, there's the scrubber basket, we're all good here" and started to close the lid back up. Just before doing so, I thought "I'm here, I should really just check just so it's not in the back of my mind". I grabbed the scrubber basket and started pulling it out of the can. Empty. No Sorb. "Shit". I knew exactly what happened, I just couldn't believe I was that stupid. I walked back to the water with my head hanging low. John asked jokingly "let me guess, no scrubber"?

"Nope, it's there" I responded. "There's just no sorb in it".

"Shit"

"Yeah, shit".

We discussed a few potential options for getting some sorb and packing my scrubber quick and still getting the dive in. Eventually we just agreed "you know what, today just is not the day", and we packed up.

I'm glad I was with John that day. Not only did I know he would understand the crappy situation and be at peace with the result, but because he is a good friend, I was able to explain to him why we ended up in this situation to begin with. We talked for a couple of hours while we slowly loaded up our vehicles. Discussing normal life problems, relationships, illness, and of course, diving. We both learned a lot that day. Literally anyone can make these simple, stupid, and nearly fatal mistakes.

So what happened? Where did I mess up? I used my checklist, but only halfway. When I had broken my unit down the day before, I had intended on filling my scrubber right back up. However, I got caught up in chatting with my student, and ended up just tossing the basket back in the canister unfilled. I never do this. The basket never goes in the can unless it's full.

So when I went to build the unit and review my checklist, I saw "check remaining scrubber duration, and reset stack timer on handset", I peeked in the can to see my basket sitting inside, remembering that I had dumped the sorb the previous day which must mean it's a fresh pack, and went about resetting the stack timer. Never thought twice about it.

Of note, the rebreather I was using did not have a CO2 detector/alarm. If it had had an alarm fitted, I may have just dismissed that as something else just 'going wrong' given the reputation of some units when it comes to false alarms. A temperature stick, on the other hand, would have shown that there was no sorb in the canister, but these do not provide a capability to detect in-loop CO2.

In hindsight, it was obvious that I had put so much pressure on myself to do the dive, I ignored several serious warning signs and wrote them off as just a bit of stress.

- As I was breathing my unit walking to the water, I started to feel concerned and stressed almost immediately. I wrote this off as the missing backup light "must have been" what was causing that physiological response. Then when John noticed the red dots on my scrubber lid, "ah, duh, that's what it was". I then breathed from the unit for roughly 5 more minutes getting bottles clipped off and doing pre-dive checks, all the while becoming more stressed and anxious.
- As I tried to descend, I noticed I felt light. This should have been an immediate and clear sign that I was missing 8lbs of scrubber material. I thought to myself, "nope I know I saw the scrubber in there, it's all good" and headed off.
- As I continued down the run, the symptoms of hypercapnia were clearly setting in. All the while I continued to convince myself that this was normal stress, until I realised I simply could not catch my breath or focus on anything other than the nose of the scooter.
- Even after all of that, I was still sure of myself when I pulled the lid off the canister. Picking up the scrubber basket was just an attempt to justify my original diagnosis, that it was just a bit of stress.

So WHY? I am a pretty experienced diver. Over 3000 dives, 500+ rebreather dives, 500+ cave dives, CCR Instructor, and Cave Instructor, and never had a mindless moment as significant as this. But my head was on another planet that day. I put a lot of pressure on myself to make the dive, was dealing with outside stress, was in autopilot mode, didn't double check my actions, and made a lot of assumptions while getting in the water. Because I have a lot of experience to fall back on, I was able to relate my current situation to experiences I've had in the past, none of which included an empty scrubber basket. So even though it was the most obvious, it was the first scenario to be dismissed. It's just not possible that I would do that.

Now what? This is a hard one to shake off, and the gut wrenching feeling of picking up that scrubber basket will haunt me for a long time. It's important to remember that these are stories that we all hear time and time again, and being experienced does not in any way protect us from making the simplest and stupidest mistakes. I've found it to be the exact opposite. The more experience we get, the less likely we are to accept a real problem when it presents itself. We will notice it, but can easily talk ourselves into something far less severe in order to not miss the dive.

Jon's self-reflection is great to see. The ability to look at the multiple contributory factors and the biases involved is a critical skill to self-development, team development and consequently, improved performance and safety. As I highlighted immediately prior to the account, it would be easy with hindsight to pick out the obvious mistake (missing the scrubber) but we would not be able to look at the cognitive biases at play and the impact that the external factors were having on his decision-making. I remember when I was a junior staff officer in the RAF and I was dealing with a £100k IT project which had just been delayed by one month when the training sessions were due to start the following week. I drove home from the contractor's offices wondering what I was going to tell my Group Captain (3 ranks above me). My mind was so distracted that I nearly crashed twice. When I went in the following day, he said "Oh, okay. Don't worry about the delay, these things happen." If we see that we are succumbing to the internal and external pressures which are being generated, it is essential that we take a pause and gather our thoughts, focusing on disconfirmatory evidence (why is this wrong) to limit our susceptibility to confirmation bias which works on the 'that is right because it was what I was expecting'.

Such 'obvious' pressures aren't the whole picture though. We, or the physical and social environments we operate in, can create error-producing conditions which increase the likelihood that we will make a mistake. Research following nuclear power plant accidents and incidents highlighted four domains in which these stressors/problems could originate from. These were grouped under the headings:

- Work, the physical work environment including social pressures,
- Individual, the individual worker's traits/behaviours/limitations,
- Task, the complexity of the task and processes/rules associated with it, and,
- Human, normal human performance variability and cognitive biases,
- which led to the WITH model (or TWIN - Task, Work, Individual, human Nature) being created. Some of the topics within each of the categories are shown in the table below.

Work Environment	Individual Capabilities
Distractions / Interruptions	Unfamiliarity with task (first time)
Changes / Departure from routine	Lack of knowledge (faulty mental model)
Confusing displays / control	Imprecise communication habits
Workarounds	Lack of proficiency; inexperience
Unexpected equipment conditions	Over-keen for safety critical task
Back shift or recent shift change (circadian rhythm issues)	Illness or fatigue – Fitness for duty
Complex / High information flow	Lack of big picture

Task Demands	Human Nature
Time pressure (in a hurry)	Stress
High workload (memory requirements)	Habit patterns
Simultaneous, Multiple tasks	Assumptions
Repetitive actions (monotony)	Complacency / over confidence
Unclear goals, roles or responsibilities	Inaccurate risk perception
Lack of or unclear standards	Communication shortcuts
Irrecoverable actions	Mindset (intentions)

One of the reasons behind the initial development of non-technical skills/crew resource management programmes was to prevent or reduce the impact of these performance shaping factors on human performance and thereby creating a more accurate, shared, mental model of the situation. Some of these factors require 'work' to be changed so that the 'work' environment is more aligned with the limitations of human performance e.g. shift patterns or multiple tasks or confusing display systems. However, a large percentage of diving is a recreational activity i.e. fun and is therefore conducted in our own spare time so the concept of 'work' might appear odd. Notwithstanding this, consider how many of these factors are applicable to dive centre operations, diving instructors or guides and how prevalent they might be. Now consider how many of these are under your direct control as a diver?

Outside of the designing hardware and tasks to be more accepting of human limitations, two of the major areas in which the research and practitioner communities within high-risk industries have looked into are the impacts of stress and fatigue on performance and safety.

Fatigue

We know that when we are tired we make mistakes, we forget things, our communication suffers and we lose track of what is going on. For the majority of our terrestrial lives it doesn't matter if we make an error like putting milk into a black coffee or picking up the wrong keys and walking out of the house closing the door behind us with the correct ones inside, or jumbling up the numbers in a cash purchase so we hand over the wrong money. The reason being that most of the time we get feedback immediately and the outcomes aren't normally that serious. However, reading the wrong figures on an SPG or an incorrect pO2 can have fatal consequences if they aren't picked up in time. The same criticality exists if details are missed in a dive brief because you were unable to concentrate, details which outlined the turn-pressure or the navigation sequence in a cave system.

Fatigue can have severe consequences, potentially none more serious than in aviation given numbers of people involved if the fatigue risk management is handled poorly. The International Civil Aviation Organisation (ICAO) have produced a 204-page guide to the Manual for the Oversight of Fatigue Management Approaches[1] and within it they have defined fatigue as *"A physiological state of reduced mental or physical performance capability resulting from sleep loss or extended wakefulness, circadian phase, or workload (mental and/or physical activity) that can impair their alertness and ability to safely operate an aircraft or perform safely related duties."* This definition takes into account not just sleep loss but also workload and circadian rhythms (the natural body-clock which can be disrupted with travel or day/night shift swaps).

The problem with fatigue is that it is such a personally-specific issue with both the factors which contribute to fatigue and the effects seen by themselves and others being very particular to that person. For example, one person might manage on 5-6 hours sleep per night and not have any perceivable issues, whereas others might need 8-9 hours otherwise they get cranky and are more prone to errors. An added complication in diving is that because diving is a social activity and we have limited time to go diving, we want to make the most of the time we have away from work to have fun and are happy to accept increased levels of risk to maximise the reward. Examples of

this are:
- Partying all night at a resort and taking students diving the following day because *'it is what everyone else is doing.'*
- Driving long-distances to the dive site on a Friday evening after work, having a few (too many?) beers and getting up tired for the long boat trip to the dive site.
- A liveaboard in a location which takes 30 hours of travel to get there and involves a 10-hour time-zone change.
- A two-week expedition where long hours are needed for gas fills, equipment preparation and post-dive review, research and editing?

All of these take their toll on our technical and non-technical skills performance. One of the side effects, which will be discussed below, is that as humans get more fatigued, they have a tendency to take greater risks which means they are more likely to encounter an adverse situation which they might not be able to deal with.

Due to the difficulty defining and measuring fatigue, indirect prescriptive methods have been used in high-risk industries to identify and prevent fatigue-related issues. These fatigue management systems attempt to reduce worker fatigue by relating work hours to performance quality. However, it is recognised that they aren't the complete solution. Such systems can produce positive effects because workers' hours, rest and workload are tracked, and shift patterns managed accordingly. However, nothing like this exists in diving for a variety of reasons, not least because the evidence to show there is a large-scale problem is not available, and the risk appears to be managed relatively well in diving given the short periods of exposure when fatigue could be accumulated.

Diving is interesting and this aligns with the common thought that if a task is complex and cognitively challenging it will keep the fatigued subject more awake and alert but if the task is simple, they will be more easily subjected to the effects of fatigue. However, from the research by Griffith and Mahadevan[2], and Durmer and Dinges[3], it appears that the division of tasks is not as straightforward as simple or complex but that some types of both simple and complex tasks are affected by fatigue and that others are not. Monotonous versus motivating and convergent (logic-based tasks) versus divergent (problem-solving and multitasking tasks) may be key variables in whether a task is impacted by fatigue or not.

If fatigue is a known problem in high-risk industries and certain contributory behaviours/activities are 'part of the social fabric of diving' what can we do about it to reduce the impact of its effects on divers? The following paragraphs will address two areas:

Understanding how fatigue occurs by examining human physiology and diver's 'operating' environments.

Highlighting that the problems divers face when fatigued, aren't just related to sleepiness, but that there is a tendency to take greater risks, that their learning efficacy and efficiency is reduced, and finally, reduced vigilance and alertness.

Contributory Factors

Multiple research activities have shown that contributory factors to fatigue include chronic sleep deprivation (including sleep schedules), time of day (circadian effects), task experience, task demands and overall personal workload. In diving, the diversity of tasks and workload means that it is difficult to come up with anything concrete as to how to reduce fatigue, but understanding the circadian process can help identify times when fatigue is going to have a larger impact on performance.

Many human biological and behavioural functions vary regularly and systematically over a period of about 24 hours. These variations are called circadian rhythms and the Eurocontrol's knowledge repository SKYBRARY contains a specific briefing note which looks at these circadian rhythms[4] and the effects they have on human performance. The normal period for this rhythm is approximately 25 hours and while the clock can be reset by about one hour each day, it cannot easily and quickly be reset by the large changes that are needed following significant changes in work/sleep schedule or when undertaking flights which traverse numerous time-zones. The briefing note gives detailed guidance on how to manage the effects to maximise performance, many of which are not applicable to divers. However, at least recognising that we are more likely to make mistakes, take greater risks and learn less is a first step to reducing the impact of fatigue.

Decompression stress, even when external symptoms are not visible, causes fatigue in the body. Anecdotally, it has been stated that diving nitrox reduces post-dive fatigue when compared to diving with air. Research by Harris at al[5] (2003) and Chapman[6] (2006) has discounted this showing that there is no measurable difference between fatigue levels.

Diving which involves thermal stress, e.g. cold waters or cold surface temperatures with inadequate insulation, will contribute to fatigue but the research doesn't provide a measurable amount.

Effects

Increased Risk Taking. In 2011, researchers at Duke University[7] asked participants in a gambling experiment to improve each of several gambles. They could choose to do this by increasing the size of the highest possible gain, decreasing the size of the worst loss, or improving the probability of winning. When participants had been deprived of sleep for just one night, they started to make fewer decisions that avoided loss, and more decisions that maximised potential gain. In other words, sleep deprivation made their gambles riskier and more optimistic. This change in risk taking behaviour was accompanied by changes in activity in brain areas that evaluate negative and positive outcomes. The impact on divers is to increase the impact of the sunk-cost fallacy whereby the more 'x' we have invested (money, time, emotion and resources) the harder it is to say no and therefore take greater risks. If we have flown all the way around the world to Chuk Lagoon, investing nearly $10k in the trip, our rebreather isn't operating how we expected it to in the first couple of dives, and everyone is talking about the awesome wrecks, how easy is it say *"I am going to sit out the dives for the rest of the trip"*?

Reduced Learning. Another area of the brain that suffers dramatically from sleep deprivation is the hippocampus. This part of the brain has been shown to be critical for the storing of new memories. Yoo et al, wrote that *"Evidence indicates that sleep after learning is critical for the subsequent consolidation of human memory. Whether sleep before learning is equally essential for the initial formation of new memories, however, remains an open question."* Their study[8] showed that *"...a single night of sleep deprivation produces a significant deficit in hippocampal activity during episodic memory encoding, resulting in worse subsequent retention."* When memorising a set of pictures, sleep deprived participants showed less activation in the hippocampus compared to rested participants. This reduction hippocampal activity could be caused by sleep deprivation reducing its ability to write in new information. Alternatively, the hippocampus may need sleep to move new information to be stored in other areas of the brain. In this latter case, lack of sleep may cause the storage capacity of hippocampus to fill up, preventing new information from being stored. The relevance to diving is two-fold. Firstly, many divers initially learn to dive when on holiday and may not encode and store critical information due to fatigue which then sets bad habits for future dives. Furthermore, if fatigued divers have a near-miss which will present an opportunity to learn, the encoding process can fail because the memories will not be stored correctly or effectively preventing recall when needed in the future.

Vigilance and Alertness. As already stated, the direct effects of fatigue are difficult to measure but there are many studies which have likened the effects to that of alcohol consumption as way of creating a parallel to understand the issue. Despite fatigue being more prevalent that 'drink driving', there is a better social understanding of the effects of blood alcohol concentration (BAC) on human performance. Griffith and Mahadevan[9] found that *"..performance at 17–24 h of wakefulness can be equated to the same level of performance at BAC% of 0.05 (the legal* limit in many countries); 20–24 h of wakefulness corresponded to a BAC% of 0.08 (the legal limit in the US), and 20–25 h of wakefulness to a BAC% of 0.1." Something to consider when undertaking long-haul travel to a location which involves limited sleep. Would you consider going diving while over the drink-driving limit? It appears from research by Dowse et al[10] that a number of divers would consider this acceptable, even though they wouldn't drive as they considered that unsafe. In the same way that drivers who are over the 'limit' are unaware of their impaired performance, Griffith and Mahadevan showed that people frequently underestimate the magnitude by which their cognitive performance is impaired by partial sleep restriction.

By understanding the contributory factors and likely effects of fatigue, we can better manage our risks more effectively by backing-off from higher-risk activities after a long-haul flight or if the task is absolutely critical, ensuring the fatigue is managed proactively, maybe by arriving early.

Stress

Stress is the body's mental and physical response to perceived threat(s) in the environment. Importantly, it is the *perception* we have about our ability to cope with the threat that raises stress levels. If we do not consider there to be a threat or that we are able to manage it because we have experienced this situation before or have overtrained, these sorts of adverse events become 'normal'. However, if we haven't encountered this before, or we have but weren't happy about the previous outcomes, we are likely to be stressed. Mask clearing is a classic example of a stress-inducing condition. Many divers when they start to dive find this a really difficult skill to master and so get very distressed about not having something over the nose and eyes. And yet once they are used to swimming with their mask off, it doesn't matter. In fact, the only stress is created due to the physiological responses caused by being in really cold water, leading to you wanting to breathe through your nose. A trick I was taught by Clare Pooley to counter this feeling is to breathe through your regulator as if you are breathing through a drinking straw. The reason this works is because you reduce the access to your nose from the back of your throat and you don't suck in any water through your nose.

However, stress in itself is not a bad thing because some stress is normal and healthy. In addition, stress may result in more focused attention, which in some situations could actually be beneficial to performance. This is the eustress mentioned at the start of the chapter. The problem with stress is that it can accumulate and once a certain threshold has passed it leads to reduced performance. Unfortunately, this threshold which is idiosyncratic or unique to each individual and situation.

Stress increases as familiarity with a situation decreases - it is the perceived uncertainty of the situation which leads to distressed behaviours and this is why over-training in difficult situations for technical and cave diving is essential. With a physical or decompression overhead, the ability to immediately surface and get out of the dangerous situation has been removed. This 'no way out' can result in panic, inhibiting the ability to effectively sense, perceive, recall, think or act. Anxiety and fear usually follow when a diver feels unable to respond successfully to the situation being faced. The research shows, and Frank's narrative below where he was lost in a cave on a solo dive demonstrates, once we are severely stressed, memory lapses are common and so we can't remember what we are supposed to do, nor recall what happened afterwards. If anxiety and fear increase, there is a reduction in the ability to think critically or to perform physical acts with accuracy. Unfortunately, because many of the emergency responses for diving are not practiced that often, it is not surprising that, according to media reports, the execution of these skills is not carried out to a high standard. Furthermore, the ability to problem solve a complex problem is reduced. Combining this with nitrogen and carbon dioxide narcosis, cognitive skills are further reduced which can lead to a downward spiralling situation.

Stress also limits the learning during dives. As such, instructors need to find a fine balance between too much stress and reduced learning, and not enough stress to commit items/actions to the long-term memory of the student. The following diagram[11] from a surgical research team's work on Cognitive Load Theory for the Design of Medical Simulations looks at a number of factors which increase or reduce learning and therefore, care needs to be taken in how a learning environment is developed for the individuals present. If we are not aware of the limitations of the working memory, then the likelihood of learning will be reduced.

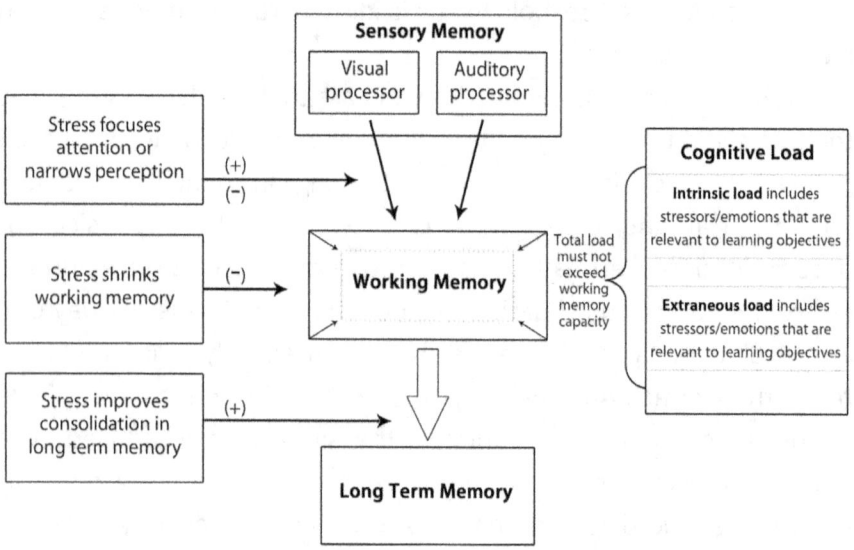

Figure 12. Stress, cognitive load, and memory. (+) indicates potential benefit to learning; (-), a potential impairment to learning.

Panic

At the start of his book, *'Deep Survival: Who Lives, Who Dies, Why,'* Laurence Gonzales describes the stressful event of a US Navy fighter pilot landing his jet on the deck of an aircraft carrier in the dark. He highlights all of the emotions, cognitive and technical skills which have been developed and honed to allow them to catch a wire, a wire they can't actually see, and stop the aircraft in less than the distance of a football field. This activity requires total control of the pilot's emotions. Gonzales goes on to say that, *"Only 10 to 20 percent of people can stay calm and think in the midst of a survival emergency. They are the ones who can perceive their situation clearly; they can plan and take correct action, all of which are key elements of survival. Confronted with a changing environment, they rapidly adapt.*[12]"

In diving, the events where emotions have to be totally calmed down so that panic doesn't take over aren't reported very often. Most of the time dives go to plan, but sometimes they don't and once panic sets in, it is very hard to turn the situation around because the psychological and physiological responses for fight or flight have been hard-wired into us over millennia of development. The signals in the brain which would normally go through the logical part of the brain now route directly to the amygdala which drives the fight/flight response. Panic happens when the perception of what to do next is unclear and the uncertainty is too much to deal with. For example, the logic of keeping the regulator in your mouth, or going to your buddy is overridden by the ingrained survival instinct, that says unconsciously, *"there is air on the surface, I can breathe there, I must get there..."* and bolting upwards. In Frank's narrative below and Steve Boegarts' incident in Chapter 4, we can see that the strong emotions are bubbling below the surface waiting to make an appearance.

Those who survive aren't immune to fear, rather they are able to work out what to do next, and most of the time that is because of overtraining or visualisation techniques. If you look at those undertaking high-risk activities, they are trying to get themselves into 'the zone' before the activity; Tim Clements mentions this in his story in Chapter 3. Those who visualise aren't going through complex problem solving, they are thinking about the simple things, primarily to keep on track so that they don't have to use those learned and developed technical and cognitive skills to problem solve in the moment, and even when they are in a highly stressed situation. Mihaly Csikszentmihalyi described this 'in the moment' response where the person involved has certainty about what to do because they are in 'flow'.

In his book, *'The Rise of Superman: Decoding the science of ultimate human performance'*, Steven Kotler talks about this flow in a number of extreme situations and shows how it allows individuals to solve problems in a slowed-down time akin to the scene in, *The Matrix* where Keanu Reeve's character dodges the bullets. One such example given by Kotler was of a base jumper whose canopy failed to deploy correctly as he jumped into a massive open topped cave system in Mexico and he started to hurtle towards the cave floor. However, the jumper recalls seeing the abseil lines which the cameramen had been using to film the base jumpers' descents, and directed his trajectory towards them, grabbing one of them, and subsequently managing to stop himself from hitting the ground. However, he sustained massive friction burns in the process. Csikszentmihalyi's "flow states" were defined as, *"being so involved in an activity that nothing else seems to matter. The ego falls away. Time flies. Every action, movement and thought follows inevitably from the previous one, like playing jazz. Your whole being is involved, and you're using your skills to the utmost."*[13] (XXXX).

During a recent class I ran in Tulum, Mexico, one of the students, Rob Bartlett, described the situation where he was silted out in a cave with no clear exit and time 'stopped' for him as he tried to find his way out. He had entered a small section of a cave which 'looked ok' without laying a line and all of a sudden the visibility dropped to zero and he couldn't find his way back out for nearly 25 minutes. There were times when he'd look at his dive computer thinking 3-4 minutes had passed but it had been less than 20 seconds. His full account is available on the ProTec website blog[14].

Laura Walton, a PADI instructor and Clinical Psychologist, recently published a paper in the UHMS journal Undersea and Hyperbaric Medicine[15] and develops this in 'diver language' in her blog on the Scubapsyche website[16]. Her articles describe how panic can develop using the analogy of a fire triangle to demonstrate the three elements needed for panic to take hold:

- A stressor. This can be an internal or external event (positive or negative) such as a problematic situation, thought or sensation.
- Hyper- or hypo-emotional arousal which could include anxiety, fear or disassociation which means that emotions are not being

regulated effectively and efficiently.
- A lack of competence, knowledge or equipment to deal with the situation in real time. This lack of resources leads to a feeling of helplessness.

In the same way that a fire can be prevented by removing one of the elements - fuel, oxygen or an ignition source, Walton hypothesises that stress can be prevented by negating one of the elements of the panic triangle.
- By reducing the 'reaction' to a stressor i.e. being proactive or acting rather than reacting. In aviation, the concept of aviate, navigate, communicate can be applied to diving. Stop, breathe, think, do.
- Emotional imbalances can be caused by fear or uncertainty. By facing similar situations through training, continued education and regular debriefs and incident discussions, the level of uncertainty is reduced. It is not possible to provide all of the answers during training, but providing some context to the problem and likely solutions can certainly reduce distress, uncertainty and fear.
- Over-training, deliberate skills development and the correct equipment can all help reduce the anxiety associated with the unknown.

In addition to prevention, it could be hypothesised that in the same way as fire is extinguished by removing one of the elements, panic could be extinguished by removing an element from the panic triangle. However, this would require the diver to be aware that they were in a panicked situation and do something about it. This will be difficult as the brain has taken that shortcut to the limbic system and engaged its 'flight/fight' mode. However, other divers might be able to help by bringing the diver back out if they recognise what needs to be done and understand that 'logic' won't work!

Frank Gutierrez's account below covers every cave diver's worst nightmare - being lost in a cave and not sure which way to go to get to the surface and a finite source of gas which is gradually being consumed. If we refer back to Walton's 'panic triangle' model, we can

see all three elements present.
- Thought/sensation: I am going to drown.
- Emotion: Fear.
- Competence/knowledge/equipment: I don't know the way out. I might not have enough gas.
- In addition, because of the way the brain is wired, it means that when serious threats to survival are considered, the brain shortcuts to the amygdala bypassing all the logical thought processes needed to solve a complicated problem. Consequently, it takes significant mental effort to calm the brain down and revert back to System 2 thinking.

Case Study: Lost in a Cave

I had completed about forty cave dives when I nearly quit diving them altogether. The dive plan was for a long but shallow dive into a pretty complex system which I had not yet visited before in the Yucatan. The cave already had a permanent guideline in place and the dive plan required two jumps off of the main guideline onto secondary lines.

After a pre-dive check, it was time to get on the main guideline which started in open water and was very easy to find as it was tied to the platform. A few minutes into the dive, I found the jumps and installed reels connecting the permanent lines so that my exit was clearly marked and there was a continuous line to the open water.

To this day, I have seen very few caves as beautifully decorated. I was in my own little world, enjoying the amazing view while keeping the line in sight. After an hour or so of penetration, it was time to turn around and go home. I knew it was going to be more than 45 minutes before I saw sunlight but at least the view would be fantastic along the way.

Somewhere near the halfway point of the exit portion I saw something ahead of me that froze every muscle in my body. One of my worst fears was coming true and I was not ready to handle it.

Although we are trained to prevent and overcome getting lost, every cave diver has thought about it at some point or another. I swam up to the unmarked T (intersection) on the guideline and could not believe it was there. A million questions went through my head as I stared at it for what seemed like an eternity. Did someone install it while I was in the cave? Was this the same guideline used during the entry? Did I get turned around somehow? How did I miss this on the way in? Which way is home? Sitting there was absolutely useless and a decision needed to be made since I was chewing through gas pretty quickly. I tried to piece things together by replaying the dive in my head, but my mind was completely blank.

It was probable that the T was there during the entry and I simply did not see it. It did not matter. I had no idea which way would get me out, but it was time to start moving as the clock was ticking. I decided to turn left.

The water was incredible, crystal clear, and that made me very uneasy. I swam along this line for a few minutes when a very powerful feeling came over me that I was going the wrong way, but everything was an uncertainty. Were the jump reels just around the corner or was I just getting further away from the entrance? The water was just too clear. There was no way that I had been there before. If anyone had been diving in that section in the last few hours there would be sediment, percolation, or bubbles on the ceiling.

Gas was getting low and there was no time for another change of heart. It had to be the other line, but even if it was, would there be enough gas in the tanks to get out? It is counter intuitive to slow down when in a time sensitive situation, but it was the only way to conserve the remaining gas which I desperately needed. Managing stress so that things don't worsen is extremely important. Slow, stay calm and breathe slow.

The T came much sooner than I expected but there was no time to stop to analyse it again. In the best case, air was about 25 minutes away and there was barely enough gas to make it out. Compared to having zero awareness on the way into the cave, this was hyper awareness. I noticed everything, and it all looked so unfamiliar. Enormous doubts entered my head about which way was out. I was my own worst enemy, but I knew that turning around was not an option. I would simply drown somewhere near that dreaded T if I turned back. I had to keep swimming. A few minutes later, I saw the second most amazing thing I have seen in my life. A jump spool with my name in big white letters was attached to the guideline. This was my way home. Now that I knew I was going the right way, all I hoped *was to have enough gas to get me out.*

After the dive, analysing my memory of the incident was not helping me understand what happened. The stress I encountered erased some of the details. I knew that I had to repeat the dive for a couple of reasons. First, I would never cave dive again if I didn't. Second, I needed to understand what I did wrong to correct it, so I repeated the dive that evening. On the second dive, I found the T without much effort. It may have not been the easiest intersection to see, but I should have caught it during the initial dive.

Another example of a dive in which a fatality could have been recreated to show that *'the diver wasn't paying attention'* because there isn't a black box to recover and download and yet this wasn't necessarily the case. Therefore, accounts from those who survive are critical to understand what goes through people's minds, especially those who are experienced. Furthermore, the ability to recall information like looking for percolation and sediment is helpful to others who might be in a similar situation, unlike the over-hyped account by Donald Cerone on YouTube who had to blindly find his way out of a cave system near Tulum, Mexico. Unfortunately, this video has so many gaps and inconsistencies as to have false-learning presented. Frank's account above also highlights that there are parts in his memory which he has tried to access to recreate the story, but they are not available so there are still gaps in his and the community's knowledge about what happened.

Summary of Key Points
- Performance shaping factors, as listed in the WITH model, contribute to reduced performance. Prevention is a much better strategy than mitigation, therefore understanding when errors are more likely is critical to high-performance.
- The factors which contribute to stress and fatigue are known. However, the scale, type and context of the factors and their associated effects are unique, varying from person to person, and

situation to situation.
- Internal reflection and external validation from dive team members is essential to help identify precursors and effects, especially as we are often unaware of the impact on our performance.
- Some stress can be good as it focuses the attention, but too much reduces performance to the point of panic. Crucially, instructors need to recognise the impact of stress on learning - if they can't remember the pre-cursors and actions, they won't be able to apply it in the future.
- Effective fatigue risk management requires an understanding of the contributory factors (internal and external) as well as likely outcomes.

Questions to consider
- Looking at the WITH model, what are you going to do to reduce the risk of errors happening?
- Thinking back to the last major trip you did, did you consider changing your dive programme to deal with fatigue?
- What are the signs/symptoms when you personally get stressed? Do your team know this?

Reference Materials
(1) ICAO. Doc 9966, *Manual for the Oversight of Fatigue Management Approaches*, downloaded from https://www.Icao.Int/safety/fatiguemanagement/FRMS%20Tools/9966_cons_en.pdf page xvi
(2) Griffith, C.D., and Mahadevan, S. (2011), Inclusion of fatigue effects in human reliability analysis. Reliability Engineering & System Safety 96(11), 1437-1447.
(3) Durmer, J.S., Dinges, D.F. (2005), Neurocognitive consequences of sleep deprivation. Semin Neurol, 25, 117-29.
(4) SKYBRAY. Circadian Rhythms. (OGHFA-BN). https://www.skybrary.aero/index.php/Circadian_Rhythms_(OGHFA_BN) Retrieved 8 Dec 2018.
(5) Harris RJD, Doolette DJ, Wilkinson DC, Williams DJ. Measurement of fatigue following 18 msw dry chamber dives breathing air or enriched air nitrox. Undersea Hyperb Med. 2003; 30: 285-91.
(6) Chapman, SD, & Plato, PA. (2008). Measurement of Fatigue following 18 msw Open Water Dives Breathing Air or EAN36. American Academy of Underwater Sciences (AAUS).

(7) Vinod Venkatraman, Scott A. Huettel, Lisa Y. M. Chuah, John W. Payne and Michael W. L. Chee. Journal of Neuroscience 9 March 2011, 31 (10) 3712-3718.
(8) Yoo, S.-S., Hu, P. T., Gujar, N., Jolesz, F. A., & Walker, M. P. (2007). A deficit in the ability to form new human memories without sleep. Nature Neuroscience, 10(3), 385–392.
(9) Griffith, C.D., and Mahadevan, S. (2011), "Inclusion of fatigue effects in human reliability analysis." Reliability Engineering & System Safety 96(11), 1437-1447.
(10) Dowse, M., Cridge, C., Shaw, S., & Smerdon, G. (2012). Alcohol and UK recreational divers: consumption and attitudes. Diving Hyperb Med, 42(4), 201–207.
(11) Fraser, K. L., Ayres, P., & Sweller, J. (2015). Cognitive Load Theory for the Design of Medical Simulations. Simulation in Healthcare: The Journal of the Society for Simulation in Healthcare, 10(5), 295–307.
(12) Gonzales, L. *Deep Survival: Who Lives, Who Dies, and Why* (Kindle Locations 268-270). W. W. Norton & Company. Kindle Edition.
(13) Kotler, Steven. *The Rise of Superman: Decoding the Science of Ultimate Human Performance* (Kindle Locations 581-584). Quercus. Kindle Edition.
(14) Bartlett, R. The importance of progressive cave diving experience. http://www.protecblog.com/1423/the-importance-of-progressive-cave-diving-experience/ Retrieved 8 Dec 2018.
(15) Walton, L. The panic triangle: onset of panic in scuba divers. Undersea Hyperb Med. 45:505-509.
(16) Walton, L. How panic starts in SCUBA divers: The panic triangle. Retrieved from https://www.scubapsyche.com/single-post/2018/10/30/how-panic-starts-in-scuba-divers-the-panic-triangle on 8 Dec 2018.

Additional Reading

ICAO. Doc 9966, *Manual for the Oversight of Fatigue Management Approaches*
Gonzales, L. (2017). *Deep Survival: Who lives, who dies, and Why: true stories of miraculous endurance and sudden death.* New York: W.W. Norton & Co.
Csikszentmihalyi, M. (2013). *Flow: The Psychology of Happiness.* London: Ebury Digital,

Chapter 12

Learning from Failure: Improving performance through feedback and reporting

"A lesson is not learned until a positive decision has been made to not change anything, or an action has been completed which will address the failure experienced."
  Unknown Senior Army Officer, Joint Services Command and Staff College, UK.

Case Study: Sometimes the failures we deal with aren't the ones causing the problems

A very experienced technical instructor, rebreather instructor and cave diver gives an account of an incident which happened in a cave system in which he and his team were exploring. This was part of an ongoing project to push the line, a project which had taken place over a number of years.

Myself and my dive buddy were diving in a 50m deep cave, which was the second of two sumps in a system. The water was 6C with visibility in the region of 3-4m. We were both diving CCRs with adequate bailout for both divers. We turned the dive after around 60 minutes, with a penetration distance of approximately 500m. At about 300m from surface, my buddy began to experience gradually rising pO2's which repeated loop flushing and examination of the manual addition valve of the loop did not resolve. They bailed out to their open circuit bailout and closed the oxygen supply to the rebreather to prevent unwanted buoyancy changes. The diluent had also been depleted due to the repeated loop flushes.

We had 6 cylinders of open circuit gas (15/55) available to us for the exit, and then two cylinders of nitrox 50% and two of oxygen for the decompression phase of the dive. This was ample bailout for the dive and would have been sufficient for two open circuit divers.

At 21m, I took the spent cylinders from my buddy and watched the gas switch to nitrox 50%. This was uneventful, but they seemed agitated due to the low volume of diluent available for buoyancy. The buoyancy was resolved by inflating the wing from an alternative source.

My buddy was not comfortable during the decompression phase of the dive from 21m to around 15m, so we elected to accelerate the decompression a little from the planned pragmatic schedule to a more gradient driven approach, as this would reduce the demands on the open circuit gasses. In anticipation that they would be more efficient decompressing once they switched to open circuit oxygen, I elected to switch my set-point to 1.5 bar ppO2 to give myself an ability to keep up with their new schedule and maintain team integrity.

The majority of the remaining decompression was uneventful, but towards the end of the 6m stop, my buddy indicated that they wanted to move to 3m to complete the last 15 minutes there. I followed, but neglected to change my set-point on the rebreather. At around 4m, I began to feel the loop volume increasing and the solenoid was constantly firing. I failed to make the connection that the rebreather was trying to maintain an impossible set-point for the depth. This was due to my focus being switched to my buddy's welfare. I eventually realised the error and switch the set-point to the low setting. By this time, my oxygen cylinder was depleted to approximately 10bar, so I switched to open circuit oxygen to complete the final 5 minutes of the decompression.

Nobody was hurt in this incident, but I feel the lessons that can be learned relate to procedures and distractions. Switching to the higher set-point to attempt to maintain team integrity is not in and of itself a dangerous act; and I would probably do the same thing again. However, it is not a normal procedure. This means that when I needed to shift an amount of my awareness to my buddy's situation, I lost some capacity to remember the fact that I was out of my normal procedures for pO2 set-point for the final phase of the ascent. As soon as I switched my attention back to my own self and equipment, the error was spotted and resolved.

However, the lapse had now placed me into a situation where a bailout was a prudent move.

I'm not sure I would follow a different course of action should the situation arise again, but I might now consider building in a set-point check to be conducted prior to leaving 6m. If this was a routine procedure, it would trap any such set-point switches before the final ascent begins.

This account highlights that even those at the top of their game can have a loss in performance. That isn't to be criticised, because we are all human. We all make mistakes and we also need to recognise that failure shouldn't be shunned. We shouldn't be afraid of talking about mistakes or 'weaknesses'.

Rather we need to congratulate those who talk about failures, mistakes, errors and violations - because they have provided an opportunity for others to learn from their performance. In the US, the Federal Aviation Agency recognises that learning from reported events is a great way to improve safety and performance and as such they provide a level of protection from punitive punishment if a report which facilitates learning is made to the NASA-run Aviation Safety Reporting System (ASRS). That protection doesn't mean that pilots who break the rules won't be punished; but that their reporting will be taken into account when it comes to looking at what happens after the investigation.

Training organisations and dive centres should consider enacting something similar to this to improve learning. I recognise that the legal discovery process and litigation are both major barriers to adopting this. However, it has been shown that changing attitudes towards learning from failure can improve safety. In August 2010, the University of Michigan Health System (UMHS) published a report in Annals of Internal Medicine[1] which showed that after they started fully disclosing and compensating for medical errors, researchers found a decrease in liability claims and lawsuits, lower liability costs, and shorter time to resolution.

Learning from an event requires some sort of feedback loop:

something to say what you were doing was right or wrong; the actions you undertook which gave you the outcome you were looking for; and that you achieved the goals you had set. However, often we focus solely on outcomes and when the outcome was good; we don't look at the journey or process of how we got there. Was there a trail of carnage leading up to the outcome and was it only by luck that the successful outcome appeared? A feedback loop needs to not just look at the immediate, proximate issues, but also the wider cultural, systemic issues if true improvement is to happen. As Duncan MacKillop, a safety specialist colleague of mine says *"The success of any organism is dependent upon the richness of the feedback systems that surround it."*

Failure-free Operations Require Experience with Failure

In diving, we want to have as few as failures as possible, because we want our diving to be safe. However, paradoxically, failure-free operations require experience with failure! To recognise the hazards and deal with the complexity of the real world and, at the same time, remain inside what we consider the tolerable performance/safety boundaries, means that we have to have intimate contact with failure. This can be uncomfortable for many, especially for those at an organisational level who often think that adding more procedures and controls can make an activity safer.

The following concept comes from high-risk industries, but can equally be applied to diving. In systems where operators can discern the "edge of the envelope", then more robust system performance is likely to arise. However, this boundary is where the performance of the system starts to deteriorate, becomes difficult to predict, or cannot be readily recovered. In intrinsically hazardous systems, operators are expected to encounter and appreciate hazards in ways that lead to an overall performance which is desirable. Improved safety depends on providing operators with calibrated views of the hazards. It also depends on providing calibration about how their actions move system performance towards or away from the edge of the envelope. Divers undertake their activity in a hazardous environment; they need have a high-level of technical competence if they are to get close to the "edge of the envelope". If they don't, their responses to abnormal situations e.g. equipment failures, environmental issues, physiological issues is going to be sub-optimal. This links with Cook and Rasmussen's work described briefly in Chapter 4 on Risk in moving towards the edge of failure, and where high-reliability organisations can operate closer to the failure line, because their responses are more predictable and they have a high-level of self-awareness.

A key point made in Cook and Rasmussen's work is that to operate close to a failure line requires you to know how you and your team are performing. That requires feedback. One of the challenges faced in the diving industry is the use of positive reinforcement and that every dive is something to be celebrated as a measure of success. Yes, positive attitudes are needed to encourage and develop students; and at the same time, failures need to be discussed. As Canadian astronaut Chris Hadfield says in 'An Astronaut's Guide to Life'[2] *"Early success is a terrible teacher. You are essentially being rewarded for a lack of preparation, so when you find yourself in a situation where you must prepare, you can't do it. You don't know how."* Framing those failures can be done in a positive way though. Rather than saying, *'What didn't go well on this dive?'* or even something like, *'How do you think that went?'* (because we automatically look for the negative) use something like, *'What do I need to improve on and how am I going to address/fix it?'*

So why doesn't learning from failure happen as often as it should? One of the reasons is the Fundamental Attribution Error, which means that failures are often attributed to personal factors (weaknesses) in others, but to external factors in oneself due to a lack of self-reflection. However, if we look at successes, the flip side is often considered to be true - success is attributed to personal characteristics of the person judging, while success in others is then attributed to external factors. In reality both need to be considered because, as behavioural psychologist Lewin published in 1936[3], behaviour is a function of the person operating within their environment B=f (P, E). Hubris and the Dunning-Kruger effect lead to the supposition that analysis after the event is not necessary, because the person sees the outcome as proof of how good they are in success and what idiots other people are after failure.

The problem with such an attitude is that failures do not get talked about - which means others cannot learn from the event, even if those failures are within the same team. The same goes for successes: we don't talk about them in detail. A key reason why incidents are readily shared in the aviation community is because there is a recognition that the likelihood that all of those same variables aligning for that specific crew are incredibly slim, but they could happen for other crews/operators and so sharing information makes the system as a whole safer. Darwin's theory of evolution could be applied here. It is not the strongest who will survive, but rather those who are the most adaptable. Adaptability and resilience are based on being able to deal with uncertainty. The more uncertainty you can fix, the higher your own performance - because you are moving into skills-based and rules-based performance. In addition, by sharing knowledge of success and failures across teams and communities, it means that lessons can be learned across the system much more quickly without each element (team or organisation) having to fail in the same way. As Eleanor Roosevelt said, *"Learn from the mistakes of others. You can't live long enough to make them all yourself."*

Accelerated Learning Through Debriefs and Reporting

One of the ways in which aviation, and other high-risk domains, has learned to live with failure, and consequently embrace it, is through the application of an effective debrief. The culture in aviation is that a debrief takes place after every mission or simulator exercise. The DEBRIEF format I teach to facilitate this learning is described in Chapter 9 and looks at individual and team successes/failures in a constructive and developmental manner.

However, having a framework or structure isn't enough. The same as deploying checklists isn't enough to actually improve performance and safety. There is a need to change the mindset as to their value, both from the leader/instructor and from the team. The feedback I have had from my human factors face-to-face classes is that deploying the DEBRIEF model is difficult because it is not something they normally do. However, once it becomes the norm, it has allowed failures and successes to be discussed in a non-confrontational manner which increases learning within the team. Importantly, it requires effective role-modelling to create that 'stickiness' within the team.

Incident reporting systems are often put forward as a way of learning from others, and in some cases they are effective. However, divers and organisations need to understand that reporting programmes are part of a wider system and the requirements for an effective reporting system create a dilemma because of the conflicting goals:

- The platform needs to be easy to use, with a simple interface and preferably via a tool which works on a mobile device to allow data to be captured quickly.
- The captured data needs to provide context-rich information within the narrative so that local rationality can be understood.
- There needs to be a feedback loop to acknowledge the receipt of the report as well as showing that change has happened, or if not, an explanation as to why change didn't happen.
- There needs to be confidentiality because of the discovery/litigation issues and those submitting reports might be afraid of the social or professional repercussions if their identity is revealed. Confidentiality trumps anonymity because there is nearly always a requirement to go back to the report to clarify details.
- Captured data can be exposed during 'Discovery' which can identify opportunities for legal cases against organisations or individuals, even though true negligence is not present.

What to Report?

This is a question I often get asked when I give presentations about improving diving safety and developing a Just Culture. Unfortunately, there is no formal definition of what should be reported and this is the topic of a research project I am currently undertaking. However, I would say that if any of the following occur, then they should be reported to an organisation like the Divers Alert Network, the British Sub Aqua Club or your own training organisation:

- Surfacing at the end of a dive with less than 50bar/500psi.
- Unplanned separation which ended in a solo ascent.
- Major Equipment Problem.
- Entanglement or entrapment during a dive.
- Uncontrolled Buoyant Ascent.
- Mild/Severe DCS.[4]
- Physically Out of Gas on a Dive.
- Major Narcosis (nitrogen or carbon dioxide).
- Hypercapnia.
- Hyperoxia.
- Hypoxia.

Some of these might seem trivial e.g. unplanned separation, but the buddy system/team diving is a core aspect of the risk management protocols in diving and so by removing that in an unplanned manner, then the ability to fail safely is reduced. Another controversial topic is surfacing with less than 50bar/500psi because context is important. If you are finishing your dive, or indeed the whole dive takes place on a 5-10m reef, your ability to ascend safely from 5m with less than 50bar/500psi is not going to be compromised. Further, you are not going to catastrophically lose all your gas in a few seconds, so you can ascend while breathing the gas you have. However, on the majority of dives which take place, surfacing with less than minimums compromises your safety and, therefore, such events should be captured and the reasons behind them. Normalisation of deviance is a normal human behaviour that requires positive action to halt its propagation.

What Should be Included in a Report?
When incidents are reported, the following should be considered as part of the narrative.
- The timeline of the event, potentially starting weeks before if it influences the decision-making processes. This is where hindsight bias can be used to an advantage.
- What was the team composition like? What about dive guides/instructors?
- What were the experience levels within the team for the environment / task at hand? Note that having a qualification doesn't mean competent for that dive.
- How were decisions made? What artefacts, skills, mental-shortcuts and experience did they call upon? In effect, how did the sense-making happen?
- Were there any performance shaping factors (See Chapter 11) which drove certain decisions or actions?
- What were the different perspectives of the activity from the rest of the team?
- When looking at lessons learned, note that there is a difference between 'what I'm going to do different next time' and 'what I am going to look for next time', because unless you spot the cues/clues needed for the correct action, you are likely to do the 'wrong thing' again.

I Can't Believe I Ran Out of Gas! I'm a Tech and Cave Diver!
As you read the narratives in this book, you will have seen that they make good incident reports - because they allow learning to take place. They don't just focus on the outcomes. The following narrative from Michael Menduno, the originator of the term 'technical diving', demonstrates the level of detail and candidness needed in order for learning to occur.

It was our second "recreational" dive of the morning. My dive partner, a local open-water instructor, and myself had completed our first dive on the bow of USS Spiegel Grove. It was my first time on the wreck; she had been there many times. The current was brisk at the surface and gradually diminished as we hit the tie-off at 30m on the port side of the 510-foot long wreck, which sits upright in about 42m. We hit a max depth 33m while swimming through the upper compartments during the 26 min dive, and included a 3-min safety stop. We were diving nitrox 32.

The dive boat had moored into the wreck where we prepared for a second dive. In addition to ourselves, there was a four-person tech team on the boat that was planning a single long-open circuit dive, and a rebreather diver. There were also a few recreational divers.

My partner was diving a single aluminium 80s and a dive skin. I was just getting back into tech diving after a long hiatus and I had come from a week-long full cave re-certification course. I had my cave kit rigged for doubles and was wearing my dry suit, despite the 83 F deg. water. The dive shop had provided me with double 80s. Argh. I had been diving over-pumped 108 and 104 doubles all week and was uncertain how much extra weight I would need; I didn't need any for cave diving. I added 4kg for the first dive, and another 2 kg after the dive as the rig felt a little light.

I started the first dive with a 2950 psi (approx. 200 bar) fill and finished my first dive with 1450 psi (100 bar). I was surprised how quickly my gas gauge fell on the 80s. My partner finished with 1000 psi (65 bar) in her 80. No doubt, my doubles and dry suit added additional drag in the current. When it came time to get ready for our second dive, I was concerned that my gas was too low. There was no pumping capacity or an extra stage bottle on the boat.

Should I skip the dive?

My gut said, thumb it! But I had some self-induced peer pressure: it was my first-time diving with my friend and I didn't want to disappoint. "Hey, it's a recreational dive," I thought. "I have roughly the equivalent of Al80. I can just go down to the wreck, swim around a bit then just come back up. Leave the wreck with 500 psi (35 bar), the equivalent of 1000 (70 bar) in a single 80." What about minimum gas you ask? In retrospect, I wasn't thinking correctly.

I decided to take the plunge.

My partner entered the water ahead of me. The divemaster cautioned, "Don't let go of the line. Pull yourself to the mooring buoy and down the mooring line." I held on and jumped. The current was now ripping. My foot popped out of my left fin when I hit the water. Fortunately, the spring strap held around my ankle. I tried to reach back and fix it, to no avail. My fin was flapping like a flag in a gale and all I could do to keep my legs together so it wouldn't slip off. In fact, "flag pole" diving was an apt description. My dive partner, who was 5 feet below me, and I were stretched out like flags on the line. When I turned my head perpendicular to the current, my mask started bouncing on my face.

Just below us the group of tekkies were at their 3m stop crowded around the line. My partner and I literally had to pull ourselves over and around them to grab the line below. There was no letting go. It took nearly six minutes to pull ourselves down to the wreck, where I rebooted my fin. I checked and had about 800-900 psi (55-60 bar) in my doubles.

We had originally discussed using a third of our gas to descend and explore, a third to return to the line, and leave the bottom with a third in reserve. At that point, realising my gas was quite low, I figured I would make a couple of loops on the bow deck, call the dive and then ascend. I didn't inform my partner of my gas situation. I didn't consider what we would do if she had an out-of-gas emergency. We swam towards the super structure with my partner in the lead.

I suddenly realised that she was headed for the first open door. No penetration for me, thank you! I signalled her with my light to get her attention and called out, but to no avail. I later realised we hadn't briefed on light signals. She wasn't using one. She kept on going and disappeared through the doorway.

Should I turn the dive and head back alone or do I go after her?

We had gone through that door on the first dive and I remembered there was a room with an exit just to the right after a short hall way. I decided to go after her. In retrospect, that decision likely saved my life. I caught her at the end of the hallway and called the dive. We started heading back to the line.

The swim was longer than I wanted. As the buoy line came into view, my regulator started pulling hard and not delivering a full breath. What?#@! I felt a sinking feeling in my stomach. A minute later and I hit the line sucked on my reg and got nearly nothing. I pulled out my gauge which read 350-400 psi. Damn, 100 feet down and I can't breathe water. It occurred to me that I could actually, easily, die there. Fortunately, I was calm in an existential sort of way and very focused. Damn!

I grabbed the line, turned around and gave my partner, who was fortunately now within arm's length, the out-of-gas sign. She looked a bit surprised as I reached for her pink octopus, but then gave a reassuring look — "I'm not going to leave you". She grabbed my harness and we began to work our way up the line, face-to-face with the line in between us. I was concerned we wouldn't have enough gas to make it to the surface, and worried what would happen in that event. Would I have enough buoyancy to reach the surface and stay afloat if things came to that?

The current got stronger as we ascended, and it took significant effort to cling to the line. I just wanted to make it to the surface; I was not concerned with a safety stop. Our ascent took 6 minutes. My partner remained cool and collected the whole time. We finally hit the mooring buoy just below the surface and I reached around for the tie-in line and surfaced as the current blew me along the side of the boat. I was not going to let go of that line. "Are you OK," the divemaster asked. I shook my head no.

I felt embarrassed with a big dollop of shame. TECH DIVERS DON'T RUN OUT OF GAS! I made it to the ladder and clung to it to gain my composure. I was grateful when one of the crew jumped in and pulled off my fins.

I was grateful to be alive. I thanked my partner profusely after she came aboard. No doubt the fact we both remained calm was a key factor in the outcome.

I woke up two nights later in a sweat, realising that I was in fact extremely lucky to be alive. Gulp. If any one of a few factors had been different, I would likely have drowned on the Spiegel Grove and been carried away by the current never to be seen again. In retrospect, I am amazed how quickly everything fell apart once I decided to make the dive!

Post analysis: If I would have practiced what I learned in my cave course, *this wouldn't have happened - a class I only completed a week before. Instead, I made grievous errors. I didn't listen to my inner voice and made the dive with too little gas, given the situation. I didn't adequately consider minimum gas or do my maths. I didn't call the dive upon reaching the wreck. I didn't do an adequate job of communicating with my partner pre-dive and while diving. I didn't do a safety stop.*

The good news? I lived and learned critical lessons. I will never make those mistakes again! Despite my embarrassment, when Gareth asked me for a narrative for this book, I decided to write up the incident as a personal penance — call it a learning mnemonic — and to support his drive towards a Just Culture within the diving community. If one other diver might learn from my mistakes and survive, it's worth a bit of discomfort. Don't you think?

As you will have recognised from reading the chapters in this book, and how our performance is a product of the person and the environment we are in, Michael's incident isn't unusual, and it certainly isn't only down to individual behaviour; there were many internal and external factors at play here. In hindsight, it is easy to list the actions that should have been completed, as Michael did in his post-dive analysis, because we now know the significance of each of the elements which contributed to the event that happened. We can also see the performance-shaping factors which contributed to Michael's event.

When Michael sent me his narrative, I was pleased that he had put something so 'obvious' in as a learning experience; that someone so experienced could have made a number of simple mistakes. Furthermore, that he went into the drivers and pressures which were present which led him to follow his team mate into the wreck and then run out of gas on the ascent were extremely welcome. At the same time, I was saddened because of the final paragraph he wrote - the stigma associated with talking about a simple issue, albeit an issue which could have cost him his life. As I have mentioned before, in 2008 Vann and other researchers wrote a paper looking at triggers, disabling agents/injuries and causes of death in 947 diving fatalities. Of the 947 examined in which a trigger could be identified, 41% were categorised as insufficient gas. While it might appear 'obvious' that divers shouldn't run out of gas, it is rarely a simple linear chain of events which causes the outcome, but rather a confluence of, apparently, unrelated and irrelevant issues. Consequently, it is the pre-cursors and drivers we need to be examining in incident reports and research, not just the outcomes.

Michael's narrative reminded me of an article which he published in aquaCORPs in 1993 in which the author, Jennifer Hunt, described the stigma associated with DCS. She showed that unlike other high-risk sports where injuries such as broken limbs are discussed in an open manner, the diving community often hides their accounts of DCS; a copy of which can be found here[5]. I would argue that the same hiding of events like running out of gas or uncontrolled rapid ascents means that the hazards faced by divers on every dive are not given the respect they should be; this is the downside of availability bias. If we don't know the prevalence of a risk, then we won't include it in our decision-making processes. Furthermore, without context-rich narratives like the one from Michael above, and the others in this book, we are unable to determine what the precursors, cues or patterns that the divers were following which led them to make the conscious or unconscious decisions they did. It is only by recognising these elements, and importantly their significance, that we are able to reduce the likelihood of future accidents and incidents from occurring.

Looking in the Mirror

While we can identify external factors and factors in other divers, one of the greatest challenges we face in diving is that of self-reflection and looking at what we did, what we thought or what our motivations were, especially if the dive didn't end up as planned.

Reflection for many is a new skill. A disciplined approach to reflection will return the investment made by improving performance and consequently safety. We all get stuck in the 'doing' at some point. So much so, that we may go around 4-5 times 'doing' the same thing or encountering the same scenario and never really stopping and looking back to see how well we did or how hard we failed. These insights are hiding in plain sight. The 'doing' is only valuable if you can reflect and identify the good, the bad and the ugly from the experience.

While this might sound pretty straightforward, it requires mental energy, and as we've already highlighted earlier in the book, we don't like to expend that energy if we don't see a benefit. Examining your diving and personal progression, how much time have you spent reflecting on your diving, diver training and personal development?

Reflection can be done on a per dive/per trip basis or it can be based around goals you want to achieve over a longer period of time. Paradoxically, the more frequently you attempt reflection, the less time you have to dedicate to it. Reflection should be undertaken as a 'big picture' activity - rather than a dive-specific activity. Per-dive review and reflection should be undertaken using something like the DEBRIEF framework and then the lessons identified/learned feed into the reflection process.

Here are 3 simple pointers to ensure you continually reflect on your achievements, failures and general progress at any point in time to ensure you can learn and develop as a diver, instructor or supervisor.

Timeliness (monthly, quarterly, bi-annual or annually). Be disciplined here! From personal experience, getting into the habit is hard, but once you've done it, you've made the neural pathways [in the brain] to make it easier each time you come to reflect on your actions.

Structure. Ask yourself the same broad questions as a start to each reflective session. What have I done? What did I fail at or would like to do over/ another way if I had the chance? And what did I achieve?

Future thinking. Now position your reflection to point forward and think about the activities you are going to undertake over the next time period. See how on track you are at the follow up to these questions. What do I want to do in the next month, quarter, 6 months...? What enablers do I need to achieve? Where do I want this road to take me? Give yourself some actions!

The above process can be done alone with your favourite pen and note pad, app or computer. Or, if writing isn't your thing, find someone you can trust and then bounce ideas and reflections around. The benefit of having someone else is that they can ask questions that you might not want to ask yourself!

Summary of Key Points
- Failure is normal. Early success is a poor teacher because we think that what we did will work well on all occasions.
- Failure is how we learn. That means we must change attitudes from 'failure is a bad thing' to 'failure is an opportunity to learn'.
- There are many more lessons identified than lessons learned. Own the change needed to learn the lesson rather than just identify it.
- When you fail or others fail, don't look at the outcome. That, to a certain extent, is not very interesting. What is interesting is how it made sense for you or the team to do what they did and end up with a failure. By looking at the context, we have a much better chance of preventing it in the future.

Questions to consider
- When was the last time you spent time digging into a failure to determine why it happened, rather than saying, *"It's just one of those things…"*
- How easy it in your team or organisation to talk about personal failures, especially if you are an instructor?
- If you are an instructor, how often do you speak with your students about the failures you have had which were 'obvious' and 'stupid'?

Reference Materials

(1) Basrai, Z. (2011). Liability Claims and Costs Before and After Implementation of a Medical Error Disclosure Program. Ann Intern Med 2010;153:213–21. The Journal of Emergency Medicine, 40(4), 480–481.
(2) Hadfield, C. (2015). *An Astronaut's Guide to Life on Earth*. New York ; London : Back Bay Books, Little, Brown and Company,
(3) Sansone, C., Morf, C. C., & Panter, A. T. (2004). *The Sage Handbook of Methods in Social Psychology*. Thousand Oaks: Sage Publications.
(4) Mitchell, SJ, Doolette, DJ, Wacholz, CJ, & Vann, RD. (2005). Management of Mild or Marginal Decompression Illness in Remote Locations Workshop Proceedings. Divers Alert Network.
(5) https://www.thehumandiver.com/pages/straightening-out-the-bends-the-stigma-associated-with-being-bent

Additional Reading

Conklin, T. (2016). *Pre-Accident Investigations: Better Questions - An Applied Approach to Operational Learning*. CRC Press.

Dekker, S. (2014). *The Field Guide to Understanding "Human Error"*. Boca Raton, FL: CRC Press.

Hadfield, C. (2015). *An Astronaut's Guide to Life on Earth*.

Chapter 13

Bringing it all Together

Human error cannot be eliminated. However, we can avoid, trap and mitigate errors by ensuring that divers learn, develop and practice non-technical skills. This will allow them to cope with the risks and demands of diving, especially those in higher risk roles, such as instruction, cave, CCR and technical diving.

Gareth Lock

The following narrative from Michael Thomas, an instructor within the UK Cave Diving Group (CDG), highlights that by combining both technical and non-technical skills, we can end up in a situation where going into the flooded cave to solve a problem is the right thing to do, and it doesn't feel that odd!

On the day in question Robert and I had been asked by the show cave to assist in a photo shoot in Wookey Hole. It changes depth many times from three metres to 22 metres and back up to three metres and then back down to 18 metres! It's really not a fantastic dive profile. In fact, it is an aggressive saw tooth profile but at least it's not very deep!

As I was needed to stay stationary underwater close to the surface for some time and not disturb the waters for the photography, I opted to use my Kiss Sidewinder manual CCR (MCCR). After the photo shoot, Robert and I planned to swim up towards chamber 22 as a tourist dive. Between chamber three and 22 are two possible routes, what we call the deep route (max depth 22m) and the shallow route (max depth 16m.). A classic dive is to use the deep route on the way in and shallow route on the way out.

We dived up to chamber 22 using the deep route and returned along the shallow. At a point over half way home the cave passage drops from a depth of five metres back down to 16 metres, you have to go this way to get out. Robert was in front moving along a small bedding plane passage and at the point of going down again he turns and signals that he cannot equalise his left ear. I think, 'This could be fun!' If the ear won't clear, we have either to crash dive and potentially burst his eardrum or return back into the cave to surface in one of the dry chambers. Because I had opted to dive the MCCR on this day, we did actually have a lot of spare gas on us, even though Robert was on his second set of thirds, his outward planned gas. I still had two full cylinders of bailout gas on me. We spent some time moving slowly up and down trying to get the ear to clear but no joy. Considering the consequences of a ruptured ear on any dive, let alone still being in the cave environment, i.e. pain followed by nausea and loss of balance, this was not our best option. We also did not have all day to come up with a solution!

I shouted into the rebreather loop and signalled let's return to chamber 20, this is a little air space that nobody uses anymore. However, it was back into the cave, going the wrong way, but has a surface and safe breathable atmosphere. It also has a dry route through boulders back into a new section of the show cave that was opened up a few years ago. My plan was that, if need be, Robert could climb out of the water and solo cave in his drysuit back to the show cave whilst I would take his diving equipment back underwater to the dive base.

The problem was this was only Robert's fourth dive in the cave and he had never been to Wookey 20. I perceived that making the decision to swim back into the cave to an unknown destination would be mentally difficult for him as he would be using his 'out gas' to go back in to the cave. In fact, doing everything your training tells us not to do!

As we turned to head back into the cave I was now in front and within a few minutes we surfaced in Wookey 20 much to Robert's relief. We discussed the problem on the surface and our options, both by now getting a little chilly in the 10C water. After a check of gas pressures, Robert decided to give diving another go and this time, very slowly, the left ear cleared and allowed us to swim back past the deep point and reach the dive base. On surfacing, Robert had pain in the left ear and deafness that lasted until we got some decongestant from the local pharmacy.

As a cave diver some problems are occupational risks especially when you dive through a cave and surface, or have a cave with depth changes. The knowledge of the cave and all your available options can really help, even if the answer is not the most obvious one in the book. It really does pay you to research your dives or take a good guide.

Robert, the diver with the problem, provides his own perspective of the situation.

After having a great fun dive up to chamber 22, we started our return journey. Getting back to the deep/shallow route split, we started our exit via the shallow route. Just as I started my descent down to the last elbow of the shallow route my left ear blocked. At around five metres, I felt it pressurise. Slowing down and trying to get it to clear had no effect, I eventually had to stop at around seven metres. Staying still for a while I tried to equalise hoping it would clear so I could continue onwards and exit with no major drama. It didn't clear. My initial thoughts were slightly worried and relatively stressed in all honesty. I was already into my outwards third, although gas was not an issue as I was with my father who was on his rebreather and effectively had two full open circuit cylinders available. After signalling that I had a problem, I remember having to force myself to remain calm and think with logic and not the emotions of what could possibly be a tricky situation, clearing my mind and not allowing it to cloud my judgment. Although at no point did I feel close to panic, showing that years of training worked! However, I felt there was a base level of concern present. In this cave system, we had options. However, if it was a system with only one entry/exit and the same problem occurred, all you could do is crash dive and hope for the best, being aware of the side effects of a burst ear drum underwater and in a cave.

Making the decision to swim back into the cave was an odd one, but strangely not difficult to make. Although I knew about chamber 20, I could not exactly remember where it was, so I followed Michael back to the air space. Knowing that the best option was swimming back into the system was actually quite a weird feeling, logic tells you that it's the best thing to do in this situation, but your gut feeling of swimming further away from home when you have a problem isn't nice. Luckily on the way back to 20 I felt the blockage clear. After surfacing and having a chat about what the plan was if my ear blocked again, we gave diving another go and were able to get back to the dive base via the deep route. Now our shortest but deeper way home.

The big lesson for me that I took from this is that having a good knowledge of your dive site is crucial when dealing with these situations. So, if it's a new site make sure you are doing your research; as well as being able to work backwards as the solution will not always be in front of you.

This account to me highlighted that these non-technical skills are present in all dives, it is just how well they are developed that matters. In this case, there was a higher-than-normal level of skills present as they were able to:

- manage stress by having a good understanding of the situation and logically think through the problem,
- develop an understanding of the now and the near future within the context they were operating in, cognisant of biases and emotional pressures that would have been present,
- make effective decisions by gathering information relevant to the task, looking at the options, choosing a way forward and then reviewing their progress as they exited to ensure that they were still on the right track,
- communicate the options, contingencies, concerns and the plan in a timely manner allowing the intent to be understood,
- lead a team in an uncertain situation by using previous experience and knowledge of the cave system and cognisant of the pressures Robert would be under,
- follow in a team and trust the leader, Michael, that he was making the correct decision but also able to challenge him if need be,

- share the story in this book and social media so that others can learn from the event.

You might look at this account and say that it is common sense to do what they did but as we all know, common sense isn't that common and 'obvious', situations are really only obvious after the event when we are able to join the dots of local rationality. There was plenty of scope for this successful dive to go badly wrong and only through the combination of technical and non-technical skills did it end up as a success.

The aim of this final chapter is to further reinforce how you can take the theory from the previous chapters (except systems thinking and human error) and the learning from the case studies and apply it to your own diving.

Ownership

One of the challenges both you and I face is that there is no one-size-fits-all when it comes to diving instruction or equipment configuration because every diver is different and every diving environment is different. As such, divers have to learn to think for themselves and a simple checklist of *'do this, then that and then finally the other'* cannot really exist even though this is where society is going. Unfortunately, there is no simple action plan to describe a plan that you can follow which is personal to you, because you are you, your students are your students, and your team is your team, and I don't know them. Besides, if I said, *"do this"* there would be a portion of the community who would say, *"who are you to tell me what to do!"*

The best I can do is give you a few more practical exercises to reinforce the learning, some more reflection on how you gather information, how you make decisions, how you communicate, how you lead and be part of a team and finally, how stress and fatigue can impact your performance, and hence, safety. Then it is over to you to own this and make a difference to your diving. This isn't primarily about safety, this is about getting out there, diving, exploring, instructing and having fun in the process.

Risk (Uncertainty) Management

How do you take risk and uncertainty management further? Recognise that there is a trade-off between uncertainty and reward and deal with it in a proactive manner. Both the recognition and action required have a lot to do with the culture within the team, group, dive centre or organisation. That doesn't mean by considering these issues it doesn't mean you are risk averse; rather it is about the culture of making conscious and informed decisions around the risks being faced and recognising that failure is at some point inevitable, consequently there is a need to fail safely. Fundamentally, there is always a trade-off between safety, economic viability and workload and only through experience and reflection/debrief are we able to determine if there is a better way of doing something.

A culture can be defined as a common set of beliefs, values and practices and the how and why we do things around here. Consequently, if it is normal to put exploration or the throughput of training students ahead of 'safety', that's the way it's going to be and consequently there's going to be a lot of risk taken. That is perfectly acceptable for some, and indeed massive risks (uncertainties) can be taken safely, but when they are, they should be done in an informed manner which allows the system to fail safely. Care should be taken to ensure that hubris and over-confidence don't get in the way of future risk-based decisions.

When you finish a dive ask yourself or your team, what was the greatest risk we took on that dive and is there a way in which we could do it differently? The same applies to running a training course. What were the greatest risks you took with your students and what will you do to address those risks to reduce them in the future? Remember there is a 100% possibility of an adverse event happening; you are trading off probabilities against resource and time. You cannot reduce the uncertainty to zero, but you can be proactive in terms of reducing its probability and then ensuring you have systems in place, such as rescue training/skills, O2 kits and life assurance to ensure that when failures do happen, you fail safely.

Psychological Safety & Just Culture

Everyone is a leader and trust within the team starts with you as that leader. If you want to increase trust in your team so that the team can learn from successes and failures, then you must lead from the front by showing that you are human too and talk about your fallibilities. Team in this context isn't just 'team diving', but also if you are an instructor with students, you have a team and you are part of it. You have a clear goal which can only be completed if you work together. To build that trust, talk about the slips, lapses, mistakes or violations you made on the last dive or the dive before that. Not something that happened a couple of years ago, but something really recent that your team or students can relate to. It can be minor like positioning to observe a drill; or not being ready for a debrief with all of the details needed to create effective learning; or something as simple as not marking a cylinder that was analysed. Importantly, the failure must identify why the failure happened and what will be put in place to reduce the likelihood of it from happening in the future.

Cultural developments occur top-down and bottom-up. If you are in a leadership or influential position, you can start the development of a Just Culture within the community by recognising that nearly every error or violation provides a learning opportunity - because the diver was doing something which made sense and wasn't aimed at creating personal gain, being grossly negligent or trying to sabotage the system. By recognising this position, learning across the system can be improved by sharing stories of errors and violations. Whenever you read an incident report or social media post about how something went wrong, don't immediately jump to the conclusion that they were an idiot, especially if the mistake was 'obvious'. Put yourself in their shoes (fins!) and ask yourself, what would need to be in place for that situation to make sense. What pressures were they under; what experiences were they likely to have; what cues/clues would they have missed (and why) to prevent it from happening... and, fundamentally, how did it make sense.

When you submit incident reports or social media posts, include as much of the contextual information as possible as this will help others learn from your adverse event (or success). I know this can be hard, especially if you are an instructor or hold an influential position. However, without visible leadership, things will not change.

Decision-making

Decisions, in the majority of situations, are not conscious choices weighing up one option against another in a logical manner. Rather, most of them are based on mental shortcuts, emotions and based on the fear of a loss or overwhelming want of a goal or gain.

To improve your decision-making, you have to be reflective and this is hard if you are not used to it. Whether things go right or wrong, you have to look at the process and context and not just the outcomes if you want to improve. Tools like the DEBRIEF structure in the teamwork section are a great way of looking at how and why it made sense. The 5-whys is often suggested as a way of improving decision-making, but the problem with this is that once you start down a rabbit-hole associated with the first why, it is hard to look at other aspects.

Build better mental models to help with future decision-making by sharing stories within your team or the social media outputs you frequent. Learn from others about how it made sense, not just that doing 'X' was a stupid thing to do. What cues and clues did they use to make those decisions?

Recognise that we are subject to so many biases, most of them lead us to the correct decision. However, when they don't, there will be a reason for this. A good example of this applies to rebreather diving and the use of cells beyond the recommended period of 12 months from manufacture. I often hear, *"These cells are good, I know they will last longer so why do I have to change them?"* You cannot *know* that they will last longer, you don't have a crystal ball to see into the future but you are using a bias to make your decision more quickly.

Situational Awareness

We only see what there is, and we only notice what we think is important and/or relevant. Therefore, we have to do two things to improve our situational awareness. Firstly, free up capacity in our working memories so we are able to focus on what is important and/or relevant in the real-world, and secondly, learn to recognise what is important and/or relevant.

We can do the former by being proficient at our technical skills (buoyancy, propulsion, line-laying, photography...) through deliberate practice. To practice in this manner, requires regular feedback from peers, instructors, preferably with some form of video feedback. That feedback must be focused on improving and developing 'automatic' behaviours, moving from conscious incompetence (know you can't do it) to unconscious competent (doing it automatically without thinking about it). Once we are able to undertake these technical skills 'automatically', then we are able to spend more time perceiving the 'now', processing what it means and then projecting into the future about what might happen. The more experiences we have, the more times our 'prediction engine' will be correct as we match mental models against reality.

To improve our understanding of what is important and/or relevant, we need to look at what we did on the last dive in detail. What did others see? What led them to seeing it if you didn't see it? I go back to my example of scallop hunting when I first started to dive and wondered why I didn't catch any. I was looking for shells on the sandy bottom, I wasn't looking for the little groove in the sand when the mollusc had sucked in water and blown it out. In a similar way, brass objects are easier to find underwater as they have less growth on them as copper, a constituent of brass, is toxic and most living organisms struggle to grow on copper.

Therefore, to improve SA, after each dive, take some time to reflect on what happened, what other divers saw and what led them to see it. If you are an instructor, task your students to remember where they were every 5 mins in the dive, to include depth, time and gas remaining and which way to exit. The first few times it will be really hard for the students because it is a new skill, but over time, instead of remembering 5 or 6 items, they can be clumped together as an 'element' which reduces the mental overhead when it comes to remembering the detail. Ivan Wagner, a GUE instructor, wrote an excellent article in the GUE journal Quest (Vol 17, No 3 - https://www.gue.com/quest/17/3) in which he explains how to improve our memory of events by using three building blocks; PEG (a system used to associate numbers with phonetic sounds), our preferred information channel (e.g. visual, auditory or kinaesthetic) and PAV (paradox, action and vivid). These tools are then used to create stories in which the details of the dive can be remembered more easily. It takes a little time to master, but worth the effort.

Finally, remember that SA cannot be 'lost', it is just pointing in the wrong direction for the task at hand. Consequently, if we want to improve our SA, we need to recognise where it was pointing and why that was the case. Saying 'improve your SA' without understanding this concept will lead to continued failure and frustration.

Communications

We take effective communications for granted because the majority of time it appears to go well, we say something, the other person hears us, and the activity happens. But what about when critical communications are needed? How easy is it to ensure the other party have understood both the content and the intent behind the message so that what you have asked for happens?

In the same way that if we want to improve situational awareness, we need to look at mental capacity to correctly perceive what is import and to know what to look for, in terms of improving communication, we should look at the way things are said (the process), the content of the message (the words and their specific meaning) and the ability to listen to the speaker (or system).

Process: remember that how we say things is often more important than what we say. If the tone, body language and facial expressions are incoherent with what the words are saying, our tendency is to acknowledge the non-verbal communications and ignore the words. If communication did not occur, think about your non-verbal communications and how the message came across.

Content: Improving the content of your message means you must be more conscious of your listener's mental models of the situation. Often we make assumptions to speed up the communications process, but this can lead to missing critical information like turn-time on the bottom, or the minimum amount of gas needed for an air-share ascent, or the specific fish you are looking for and how to find it...and so on. Look for non-verbal cues when talking to others during a brief. They might be slightly confused or disengaged, or they reply really quickly, too quickly, to an asked question. Additionally, when it comes to underwater communications, make sure that the team know any hand signals that might be used. Easy to make an assumption that divers will know what a closed fist held up means. It could mean 'hold there' or it could mean 50 bar. Make sure you talk about any miscommunications on the boat. An error uncorrected but accepted becomes accepted knowledge for the future.

Listening: Telling someone to listen more careful without giving them a strategy to do so means you will have limited success in improving their capabilities. We think we are listening well all the time, until we realise we can't remember what the other person was saying! Communications development and training exercises can appear to be weird, especially if you are in a recreational activity. However, if you are in a team, like that of a dive centre, it is worth taking the time to practice active listening which requires some form of feedback loop to assess how much was heard and then understood.

- One way to improve active listening is via an exercise called slow-motion conversations.
- Pick a topic for pairs of people to discuss.
- Partner A talks. Partner B paraphrases back what they heard Partner A say before they add their own point of view. Partner A paraphrases back what they heard Partner B say before they add their point of view.

- Conversation continues back and forth like that for 5 min.
- Debrief. Ask participants what it was like to listen and be listened to in that way. Ask when this type of listening might be helpful for them.

Teamwork and Teaming

Teamwork is often confused with the buddy system and then they wonder why 'team diving' doesn't work when they dive as buddies! They are totally different. Teams understand each other's strengths and weakness, they have an implicit level of trust, they have a clearly articulated goal which everyone knows and believes in and they operate in a psychological-safe environment.

So how do you create teams in diving? You build relationships. You start to talk with each other. You start to understand what makes each other 'tick'. You understand each other's configuration and how they work, especially when something is going wrong. You realise that you are all interdependent on each other to complete the task at hand – that doesn't mean 'trust me dives' – it means being self-sufficient if you need to in an emergency, but to get the task done you all have to work together towards that common goal. There are numerous case studies in here and elsewhere that show teams perform far better than individuals and if it wasn't for the team, then the outcome would have been much worse.

Teams don't form overnight though. They take time to develop and in the modern world, time is at a premium which makes it hard to do. If you have a group of divers who you'd like to turn into a team, sit down and talk about goals like which trips or expeditions you'd like to go on and why, and what is needed to get there. Discuss your strengths and weakness, and understand what is needed to turn the weaknesses into strengths. Think about training to your weaknesses and then playing to your strengths e.g. if one of the team hates doing the dSMB because they aren't good at it, get them to do it until it isn't an issue and have the team support them in that developmental process. Teams look out for each other and bring others up, they don't dismiss weak performance.

The most powerful tool a team can have is the honest, frank and open debrief. By being able to speak and critique others, and others critique you, then your performance as an individual and a team will improve massively.

Leadership

Leadership in a recreational activity is hard to practice because we are supposed to be having fun and leadership is often portrayed as telling others what to do. But leadership doesn't have to be about telling others, it is also about encouraging, developing, mentoring and coaching others, especially when it is something that the followers might not want to do. In fact, if you can lead effectively in a recreational activity, then you are applying more leadership skills than those in established businesses.

In instructional roles, you are leaders. You set the tone, the mindset, the attitude towards how the learning will happen and how others will behave when they leave your courses. The most effective leaders are those who listen to their students and truly understand their needs, not just ticking boxes and moving on. The most effective leaders are those who will challenge authority when they know something is wrong, like unsafe in-water/exit conditions, or unacceptable equipment states, or breaching standards. The most effective leaders are those who trust their teams to do what they have been asked to do. That means you must have provided your teams with the physical resources, the time and the guidance to follow your intent, and you must have provided them with the opportunity to fail safely. That means you have created a psychologically-safe environment and have developed a Just Culture. That means you must have fostered a learning attitude within your team. That starts with you. Be vulnerable. Talk about your mistakes. Show that you are fallible, even if you are an instructor or expedition leader. Showing your fallibility isn't a sign of weakness, it is a sign of personal strength because it shows you are not perfect and we all know that no-one is perfect. Ask for feedback. Not platitudes. Critical feedback which focuses on specifics. Every dive you make has an opportunity for learning, both as a diver and a leader. Use it.

Performance Shaping Factors

Self-generated stress is one of the biggest issues in diving. Part of that is because we are not used to dealing with uncertainty, ambiguity and complexity. Most of us like things to be ordered and in control and when they are not, we get stressed. The easiest way to deal with stress is to remove the uncertainty and ambiguity. This might sound obvious, but it is what initial and continual training is about. You start with small building blocks and then add more and more issues. The idea isn't so that you can deal with that exact scenario in the future, but rather to build mental capacity so that you can problem solve in real time. Stress takes up some of your mental capacity (those 7 light bulbs you have) and when they are lit, you can't do anything else. By overtraining, you remove the uncertainty about whether you can deal with this.

However, modern diver training programmes are about meeting standards to pass the course and it is only those instructors who are being proactive in their training, who are able to help students manage stressful situations post-class by giving them more tools in their toolbox to solve problems and create a thinking-diver mindset. Those instructors also instil a mindset of continual learning and development within their students. Human nature means that it is easy not to focus on specific skills if I haven't needed them, and if nothing goes wrong, why do I need to practice those skills? Fundamentally, that is what this book is about. Predicting, trapping and then mitigating errors through the application of non-technical skills and therefore reducing the stresses involved, and also creating the mindset that says without the deliberate practice of both technical and non-technical skills, then performance will drop.

If you do end up seriously stressed on a dive and have recovered the situation, use the structured debrief as an opportunity to try and pin-point what the triggers were and what your coping mechanisms were to get out of the situation. If you surface and say, *"I won't do that again"* without actually reviewing the context, you are not helping yourself or others develop.

Chapter 14

Conclusions

"The idea that error is some type of normal or operational failure is hard-wired into our thinking and therefore, error being bad is hard-wired into our investigation and cause determination process."

Todd Conklin

The aim of this book was to expose divers, instructors and training organisations to how human factors, non-technical skills and a Just Culture can be applied to diving thereby improving individual & team performance and diving safety.

The reason? Most diving accidents are not caused by undetectable failures in diving equipment, or unknown (to the community) issues with procedures or health. Rather they are caused by cognitive failures, miscommunication, poor or ineffective teamwork and leadership, and not understanding the impact of stress and fatigue on performance. Often accident and incident reports use general terms like 'human error', 'complacency' or 'loss of situational awareness' but these terms do not help learning. If 'human error' is the conclusion, learning will be extremely limited as we will not know what the error producing conditions or interactions are to avoid, trap or mitigate them in the future. For example, 41% of fatalities in a DAN study had out-of-gas as the trigger event but there isn't the detail to show why the divers ran out of gas – knowing the 'why' is extremely important if we want to improve diving safety.

While errors, violations, and fatalities cannot be eliminated in diving, they can certainly be reduced by applying non-technical skills in combination with technical skills (buoyancy control, population, photography, videography, line-laying...), both of which have been developed through deliberate practice. The irony, as highlighted by Ryan Meyer, co-owner of a diving insurance company and one of my course graduates, is that it is human factors which is preventing divers from learning and applying more about human factors to their diving. Many divers don't see the need to learn about this topic because their cognitive biases are saying to themselves *"What I am doing must be ok because I haven't hurt myself or someone else"* and *"If it was that important, the agencies would be teaching it already."*

Although 'The Human Diver' is my main business, I do work in other domains such as healthcare, oil & gas, construction and power utilities. In these areas, there is increased interest in a field called 'Human and Organisational Performance' (HOP). HOP isn't about safety, it is about developing high-performance teams and individuals by understanding human error and human performance and what can be done to develop, coach and mentor teams and individuals. HOP is not specific to high-risk industries, but the investment argument is easier to make. To facilitate this, there are 5 key principles which are applied in HOP:

- Humans are fallible and even the best people make mistakes.
- Error-likely situations are predictable, manageable and preventable.
- Individual behaviour is influenced by organisational processes and values.
- People achieve high levels of performance based largely on the encouragement and reinforcement received from leaders, peers and subordinates.
- Events can be avoided by understanding the reasons mistakes occur and applying the lessons learned from the past events.

These principles apply in diving too.

If you look to the diving community, diver training organisations and the divers themselves, you can see that in many cases, it is the community and the environment which is shaping behaviours, especially when it comes to adopting best practice. Nitrox, considered a dangerous gas, is now used globally. Trimix, the same. Flat trim and being neutrally buoyant in entry-level classes was considered impossible, and yet there are mainstream agencies who are teaching exactly this in an open-water level class. Those individuals and organisations recognised the benefit and adapted accordingly, and gradually over time, change happened.

It takes time to recognise, adopt and practice these non-technical skills and apply a Just Culture but that doesn't mean we shouldn't try. The aviation community is still learning about how to improve performance through the application of human factors and CRM programmes along with developing a Just Culture, a domain which has legislate that says human factors and CRM must be taught and there must be a Just Culture within organisations!

Diving doesn't have any of this oversight or structure and therefore the adoption of non-technical skills and human factors will take time. I have been working on this topic for more than seven years now, but I can see small changes happening. All because of those who believe that improvement is possible and have started to lead.

When it comes to applying human factors/non-technical skills to diver training and adopting a Just Culture across the global diving community, a wholesale culture change is not going to happen overnight (or at all!). However, even though you cannot change *the* culture, you can change *a* culture, and that is the culture you are directly involved in. Many of those who have completed the online class and all of those who have completed the two-day course have had a change in attitude towards human error, incidents and accidents, their own performance and are now creating a Just Culture in their own communities. They are doing this by recognising that whatever divers do, no matter how stupid, it must have made sense for them to do what they did. If we understand that local rationality, we have a greater chance of reducing incidents and accidents in the future.

To close this book, I go back to Todd Conklin's comment from earlier.

'Safety is not the absence of accidents or incidents, it is the presence of barriers and defences and the ability of the system to fail safely.'

We cannot remove all risk and error from the sport, indeed it would be a boring place if we did, but we should do everything we can to ensure that whenever something happens, we are in a position to fail safely and by applying human factors and non-technical skills, we are in a much better place to achieve that.

Contributors

Not all of the contributors are listed for reasons of confidentiality. Those who are happy to have their details listed are shown below.

Steve Bogaerts. Steve came to the Yucatan Peninsula of Mexico in order to pursue his passion for exploration in the amazing submerged cave systems of the area. During this period, he has been actively exploring many of these unique natural wonders including all 3 of the world's longest underwater cave systems - Ox Bel Ha, Nohoch Nah Chich and Dos Ojos. Steve has been involved in many exploration projects across the globe. Steve holds the highest attainable Instructor ratings in Recreational, Technical and Cave diving. He is an International Fellow of the Explorers Club of New York and is the National Speleological Society Cave Diving Sections Safety Officer for Quintana Roo.

Ryan Booker. Ryan is a software developer, GUE Instructor, and GUE CCR, Tech 2, and Cave 2 diver from Brisbane, Australia. Ryan is an active project diver, and the Project Baseline Tank Cave Project Manager for the Nullarbor Karst Plain Project (NKPP).

Heather Choat Armstrong. Heather has been a technical diver and instructor since 1995. She has extensive experience exploring deep caves, and is also an accomplished wreck diver who has participated in multiple projects and television productions, as well as scientific specimen collection projects. Heather was a founding owner of TheDecostop.com, served as Technical Diving Safety Officer aboard the MV Spree, and is the recipient of numerous awards, including the Abe Davis, Wakulla and Sheck Exley Awards for safe cave diving.

Heather is also a member of several exploration projects, including the Woodville Karst Plain Project; and is a NAUI Lifetime Member, Technical Instructor Evaluator, and Course Director Trainer.

Tim Clements. Tim started diving in 1990 while studying Marine Biology and Oceanography, becoming a BSAC Advanced Diver, followed by MSc and HSE Part IV qualifications. Subsequent diving projects included environmental survey, scientific expeditions, aquarium diving and media projects, harnessing an enthusiasm for communicating marine science. His personal diving includes many countries, wrecks and reefs, but remains focused on temperate seas. Tim began technical diving in 1999, taking part in the 990 Bullring expedition as videographer. He is co-owner of IANTD UK and an active IANTD IT on both OC and CC, writing Self Sufficient, Photogrammetry, and Scientific diving manuals. He is also test diver and factory training manager for the RedBare CCR, with additional ratings on Explorer and MCM100.

Marc Crane. Hailing from the UK, Marc became involved with professional scuba training in 1995 whilst on a gap year. Having worked as an instructor and instructor trainer in East Africa, the Mediterranean, Mexico and the Red Sea, he has been based on Bali Indonesia for the past 5 years where he teaches technical and rebreather diving at diver and instructor level. He is an IT for TDI, SSI and IANTD. When he is not teaching you will probably find him wreck or cave diving. He is still on his gap year.

Garry Dallas. Garry is a cave, technical and recreational instructor trainer, technical advisor, examiner and primary/contributing author in diver training materials for RAID. In his 20-year diving career, he has trained with the major training organisations and has developed as a published photographer, explorer and sidemount skills developer for OC and CCR. Director of Simply Sidemount & Simply Tec, he teaches throughout the year and across the globe, sending passion through vibes on media channels. A keen conservationist and member of 'Arctic on the Edge', an organisation which promotes the protection of marine life and ecology through media and by presenting at schools and international/national dive show events.

Andy Davis. Andy is a RAID technical instructor and trimix wreck diver living in the Philippines. Over 25 years actively diving, he has earned instructor ratings with BSAC, PADI TecRec, ANDI and SSI. He is known as a pioneer of sidemount diving in SE Asia and as a writer for varied diving magazines and his popular blog; scubatechphilippines.com. Andy has been involved in designing technical diving courses for several scuba training agencies. He retired from the Royal Air Force as an officer in 2007 and has been a full-time technical diving professional ever since.

Astrid de Jager. Astrid has been a full-time sport and technical diving coach on sunny Bonaire since 2009. She's the dive safety officer for the Institute for Sustainable Technology, and owner of Technical Diving Services, through which she provides open and closed circuit sport and technical dive training, and coaching. She also provides training and mentoring programs for dive masters and instructors and for scientific divers.

Matt Duke. Matt started his diving career in 1986. In 1999, he trained to use helium in order to enjoy the deeper wrecks off the UK coast. In 2002, he moved to Norway, teaching for the Norwegian Diving Federation (CMAS) and in 2006 he took his first GUE course, which led to him being trained to GUE Cave 2 in the following years. Matt considers himself as a conservative *'boring'* diver, happy to spend over three hours cave diving, but not really one to push any boundaries or limits. He owns a leading Scandinavian dive information portal, www.dykkepedia.com, with information on over one thousand dive sites in Norway. He lives in Bergen, Norway with his wife and two children, a location just 30 minutes from world class diving.

Jill Heinerth. Jill is a veteran of over thirty years of filming, photography and exploration on projects in submerged caves around the world with National Geographic, NOAA, various educational institutions and television networks worldwide. She is the inaugural Explorer in Residence for the Royal Canadian Geographical Society, recipient of Canada's prestigious Polar Medal and the diving world's highest award from the Academy of Underwater Arts and Sciences, the NOGI. As a motivational speaker, Jill Heinerth educates and inspires people about our fascinating underwater world. Partnering with Penguin Random House in Canada and Harper Collins in the US, Jill will soon be releasing four new major-market, non-fiction and children's books.

Gene Hobbs. Gene is a technical diver and founding board member of the non-profit Rubicon Foundation. Gene has served as a medical officer for the Woodville Karst Plain Project since 2004 and was named the 2010 Divers Alert Network/ Rolex Diver of the year. Gene was a hyperbaric technologist and simulation coordinator at Duke Medical Center before taking a position as the Director of Simulation for the University of North Carolina School of Medicine and Clinical Instructor in the Department of Pediatrics. As of 2018, he is the business manager for the UNC Health Care Department of Neurosurgery.

Dr Dawn Kernagis PhD. Dawn is a Research Scientist in the area of human performance optimisation and risk mitigation for operators in extreme environments, such as those working undersea, at altitude and in space. She completed her PhD and Postdoctoral training at Duke University as an Office of Naval Research and American Heart Association Research Fellow. Dawn has also been a diver with numerous cave and wreck projects since 1993, and was a crew member of NASA's undersea NEEMO 21 mission.

Jon Kieren. Based out of High Springs, Florida and Playa del Carmen, Mexico, Jon has been working full-time in the dive industry for over 10 years. He is an active GUE Instructor, NSS-CDS Cave/CCR Cave

Instructor, IANTD Cave and Technical Instructor Trainer, and TDI Instructor Trainer Evaluator. Jon spent several years as the Training Director for TDI conducting accident analysis and quality assurance investigations, as well as developing new training programs and managing the standards and procedures for training technical, cave and CCR divers and instructors. Outside of dive training, Jon is an active project diver for Karst Underwater Research as well as an avid skydiver.

Steve Lewis. Steve is a writer, pilgrim, and adventurer. He's also an enthusiastic cave, mine and deep wreck diver, with instructor-trainer/evaluator ratings in these activities from leading technical diving agencies. In life and teaching, he puts strong emphasis on the role of mindfulness and focused meditation on risk management. Author of several books including the best-sellers, *The Six Skills, Staying Alive*, and *Death in Number Two Shaft*, he is a Fellow of the Royal Canadian Geographical Society, was elected to the Explorers Club in 2005 and has won several honours including the Sheck Exley International Safety Award.

Richard Lundgren. Richard Lundgren has worked as a diver professionally around the world for more than 20 years. He has been fortunate to participate in many sensational exploration projects including the HMHS Britannic (sister ship of the RMS Titanic) and the discovery of the mighty admiral ship, Mars the Magnificent, sunk during the Nordic seven-year war in 1564. Richard pioneered Technical and Cave diving, exploration diving in Scandinavia in the early 1990s. He is a founding member of the exploration organization, GUE, Global Underwater Explorers, serves on their board of directors and is also a fellow member of The Explorers Club.

Michael Menduno. Michael is an award-winning reporter and technologist who has written about diving and diving technology for 30 years. He coined the term "technical diving." His magazine "aquaCORPS: The Journal for Technical Diving" (1990-1996) helped usher tech diving into mainstream sports diving. He also produced the first Tek, EUROTek and ASIATek conferences, and organised Rebreather Forums 1.0 and 2.0. Michael received the OZTEK Media Excellence Award in 2011, the EUROTek Lifetime Achievement Award in 2012 and the TEKDive USA Media Award in 2018.

Jamie Obern. Jamie is a former investment banker who left London to set up a life-style diving business in rural New Zealand. He has been diving since 1988 and holds multiple instructor ratings, including GUE Tech 2 and Instructor Trainer. When not teaching, Jamie conducts safety audits across the adventure tourism industry in NZ, primarily focussed on diving and caving operators.

Clare Pooley. Clare is a retired technical instructor for GUE and IANTD and keen cave and wreck diver who dived with exploration groups in the UK and the US. She now serves on the BSAC Council taking responsibility for Governing Body matters to try to promote and protect Diving as a sport in the UK.

Reneé Power. Reneé has served on the Cambrian Foundation dive team since 1999 and has been involved with cave exploration and research diving in Mexico, Bermuda and Florida serving at times as the Expedition Dive Safety Officer. She is a PADI Master Instructor and IDC Staff Instructor, and holds various recreational, cave and technical instructor ratings with PADI, NAUI, NSS-CDS and TDI. Reneé is the owner and founder of Dive By Design, mentoring divers to develop skills in a safe and positive learning environment that facilitates growth during performance based progression. Her full-time role is in Computerized Tomography at a local hospital in Florida, having over 30 years of career experience.

Anton van Rosmalen. Anton is a self-employed civil engineer specialised in risk management for large infrastructure projects from The Netherlands. He has been diving since 1989 and took up technical diving around 2006. As a project diver he has since been involved in many cave and wreck exploration projects including EKPP, MCEP, MARS the Magnificent, the Oliero Exploration Project, project Morpheus and the Project Baseline Mediterranean Expedition. He is the founder of the Event de la Coudoulière Exploration Project (ECEP) focussing on the survey and exploration of a major cave system in the Hérault province in Southern France. He is also an avid trainer and public speaker combining his expertise on technical diving and risk management in his consulting practice.

Cameron Russo: Cameron began diving in 2003, and has lived, dived and worked in Australia, New Zealand and Mexico. He is passionate about cave diving, exploring and mapping, which has led to Cameron becoming a member of the Cave Divers Association of Australia, Mexico Cave Exploration Project, the Mexico Cave Survey Team, the Hoyo Negro Project, and several GUE Project Baseline teams across the globe. An Aussie living in Auckland New Zealand, Cameron can often be found holding his breath, posing for photos taken by Alison Perkins of www.InspiredToDive.com

Joel Silverstein. Joel has been at the forefront of technical diving for three decades. His companies Scuba Training and Technology Inc. and Tech Diving Limited, distribute technical diving equipment and high-level training to consumers worldwide. His other company Sea Wonders LLC, is a communications consulting firm exclusively for the development and authoring of papers, publications, education training programs and market development. Since 1990 Joel has been training divers to all levels of expertise in both recreational and technical diving practices. As a speaker and educator, he is known for asking the hard questions and collaborating to develop viable solutions to complex problems.

Michael Thomas. Michael started his underground journey as a young child with his father caving across the UK, started diving in 1987 and in 1992 started cave diving with the cave diving group in UK. He is now the Training officer for the Somerset section of the CDG. He started teaching with TDI in 1996 whilst working on the Drager Atlantis SCR project. In 2015, after a fatal incident of a diver in a flooded mine in North Wales, he was asked to start teaching cave diving, adding some of the hard-won skills from experience to the standards of modern-day cave diver training. He uses the same skill- and knowledge- base on all technical diver training - planning to fail well.

Lanny Vogel. Lanny is a full-time Cave, Tech and CCR Instructor and the owner of Underworld Tulum, a purpose built dive centre with accommodation next to 8 of the 10 biggest underwater cave systems on the planet. He is the founder of Cave Camp, an annual event bringing together divers from all over the world for courses, presentations, socials and great cave diving. He has been diving for over 20 years and teaching people to dive since 2003. Previously a Commander in the Royal Navy, he retired in 2014 to prevent work getting in the way of cave diving.

Dr Laura Walton CPsychol AfBPsS. Laura is a Clinical Psychologist and PADI IDC Staff Instructor who took her first breaths underwater on the Great Barrier Reef in 2006 and was instantly captivated by the underwater world. As Laura was a Psychologist before she became a diver, she could never help but view her diving experiences through that lens and now shares information about how psychology can help us to understand what we do as divers through her website 'scubapsyche'. After becoming a scuba diving professional in Scotland, she has taught and guided in cold water since 2013, and from 2015 – 2017 was the Training Secretary for Deep Blue Scuba, Edinburgh.

Roger Williams. Roger is basically a complete slacker who is always somewhat confused to find himself surrounded by the luminaries of technical diving. For over a decade he's been working as an instructor at the recreational and technical levels as well as a long stint as the Dive Safety Officer at the New York Aquarium. Topics of conversation that do not include diving, dive training, or dive safety bore him to tears. Most recently he has opened XOC-Ha, a bed and breakfast catering to cave divers in Mexico's Riviera Maya. None of this tempers his surprise at being included here.

www.ingramcontent.com/pod-product-compliance
Lightning Source LLC
Chambersburg PA
CBHW070047080526
44586CB00013B/945